Death Is A Good Solution

The Convict Experience in Early Australia

A.W. Baker

University of Queensland Press

First published 1984 by University of Queensland Press
Box 42, St Lucia, Queensland, Australia

© A.W. Baker 1984

This book is copyright. Apart from any fair dealing for the
purposes of private study, research, criticism or review, as
permitted under the Copyright Act, no part may be reproduced
by any process without written permission. Enquiries should
be made to the publisher.

Typeset by University of Queensland Press
Printed in Hong Kong by Silex Enterprise & Printing Co.

Distributed in the UK, Europe, the Middle East, Africa, and the
Caribbean by Prentice Hall International, International Book
Distributors Ltd, 66 Wood Lane End, Hemel Hempstead, Herts.,
England

Distributed in the USA and Canada by Technical Impex
Corporation, 5 South Union Street, Lawrence, Mass. 01843 USA

Cataloguing in Publication Data

National Library of Australia

Baker, A.W. (Anthony William), 1936–
   Death is a good solution.

   Bibliography.
   Includes index.

1. Australian literature — History and criticism.
2. Convicts in literature. I. Title (Series:
University of Queensland Press scholars' library).

A820.9'3520692

Library of Congress

Baker, A.W. (Anthony William), 1936–
   Death is a good solution.

   (The University of Queensland Press scholars' library)
   Bibliography: p.
   Includes index.
     1. Australian literature — History and criticism.
2. Prisoners in literature. 3. Penal colonies in
literature. 4. Australia — History — 1788–1900.
I. Title. II. Series.
PR9605.6.P75B3   1984   820'.9'994   83-23556

ISBN 0 7022 1685 2

Il est utile que je m'en aille; la mort est un bon arrangement.
                                    Victor Hugo, *Les Misérables*

Contents

Publisher's Note   *ix*
Preface   *xi*
Acknowledgments   *xv*
Abbreviations   *xvii*

1 The Background   *1*
2 1788–1829: The Beginnings of Convict Literature in Australia   *31*
3 1830–68: The End of Transportation; The Beginning of Fiction   *78*
4 After 1868: Transportation in Retrospect   *124*

Appendixes
I   Factual British Criminal Biographies   *148*
II   Fictional British Criminal Biographies   *150*
III Factual Convict Accounts and Biographies (1792–1830)   *152*
IV   Factual Convict Accounts and Biographies (1830–68)   *156*
V   Fictional Convict Accounts and Biographies (1830 to the Present)   *160*

Notes   *164*
Bibliography   *183*
Index   *215*

Publisher's Note

This book is in a series designed by the University of Queensland Press to make available reference and specialist works. Titles in the series normally will not be stocked by booksellers and may be obtained by writing directly to the publisher.

Preface

"Truth of fact", Virginia Woolf is said to have written, "and truth of fiction are incompatible."

This work examines aspects of a body of literature where there does appear to be a variation between the truth of fact and the truth of fiction, for the book deals with "convict literature": writings by or about the convicts of the transportation era in Australia.

For a considerable period of our short history, convicts were the focus of life here. Their concerns and the concerns of those set over them formed the substance of what was written. In the nation's formative years the ambit of life and the ambit of writing were virtually identical.

Faithful records were kept of the truth of facts: durations of tours of duties; lengths of sentences; pounds of flour; heads of sheep. Other details were also set down: the conduct of the convicts; the nature of the native-born; convict reformation. These latter "facts" were obviously less amenable to objectivity.

Objectivity was even more at risk because an accepted code was being used to describe phenomena incompatible with it. The official frame of reference, with components like industry and reformation, did not match the reality of the convicts' outlook and activities. Official versions of convict life formed a species of fiction.

There was another level of fiction of which the convicts were conscious, and this was the long-standing popular method of describing a criminal's life. This provided a formula the convicts could use to describe their life before transportation. It also provided a tone and perspective which would eventually impose a pattern on popular accounts of the life of a convict in the colonies. Frequently, the resulting tale was more fiction than fact.

It is not surprising that witnesses of transportation disagreed about the nature of the reality they perceived. In the 1830s, for example, Archbishop Richard Whately believed that transportation was, in effect, a free passage "to a country whose climate is delightful".[1] Father (later, Bishop) William Ullathorne bemoaned the pouring of "scum upon scum, dregs upon dregs . . . building up with them a nation of crime".[2] Lieutenant-Governor George Arthur, on the other hand, having presided over Van Diemen's Land, was content to believe that transportation relieved "England of the depraved individual and, in a majority of cases [it would] effect a reformation of his character". Captain Alexander Maconochie, penal reformer and one-time commandant of Norfolk Island, admitted that the administration of convicts was "able" but believed that the principle of the system was "vicious".

It is not surprising, either, that attempts to represent transportation in literature caused disagreements. Henry Parkes, who spent much energy over a long period in debates about transportation, objected to William Astley (Price Warung) that a "healthy spirit would scarcely seek enjoyment" in Astley's stories. The latter explained that

> the Convict System was an historical episode and if it is to be dealt with in the guise of fiction, the spirit of that episode must be presented with *vraisemblance* . . . I did not make my subject. All I sought to do was interpret it.[3]

In life, many surviving convicts became an embarrassment, best eliminated by death. As late as 1939, Miles Franklin and Dymphna Cusack in their *Pioneers on Parade* found a subject for satire in some people's efforts to hide their convict "connections". Indeed today, while many Australians would agree with R.D. FitzGerald when he wrote of convict Maurice FitzGerald "could I announce that Maurice was my kin I say aloud/I'd take his irons for heraldry and be proud",[4] others would be moved to litigation were such ancestry to be imputed to them.

This work, then, seeks to make a contribution to an understanding of interpretations of our origins. In general, it seeks to trace the sources of these interpretations, and their mutations. Appendixes at the end of the book set out summaries of tales about criminals at various stages of this development. While the study concentrates on the period 1788–1868 (the years during which convicts were transported to Australia), the bibliography contains a representative range of texts from the beginnings of transportation until 1970.

In the body of the text there is an attempt to convey the substance of the convict experience. Some accounts of it are summarized. The summaries should be used in conjunction with the appendixes.

In seeking to describe the substance of the convicts' lives, I have drawn heavily upon the work of historians, much of whose work is "convict literature". I gratefully acknowledge my debt to the historians. I hope that I have not trespassed upon their domain; I trust that they do not begrudge this view through the lattices.

Australians have formulated an experience for themselves in a variety of ways, so that the truth of fact does not always coincide with the truth of interpretation or fiction. Perhaps this is how all nations account for their beginnings.

Many people have helped me during the writing of this book. I trust that I have sufficiently thanked them all. I am particularly grateful to my family, who have endured a form of captivity with the convicts for so long.

Notes

1. Richard Whately, "Transportation" in *Select Documents in Australian History*

1788-1850, ed. C.H.M. Clark (Sydney: Angus and Robertson, 1958), p. 157.
2. William Ullathorne, *The Catholic Mission in Australia* (Liverpool: Rockliffe and Duckworth, 1837), p. 12.
3. William Astley to Sir Henry Parkes, 2 November 1892, in Parkes Papers ML.
4. R. D. FitzGerald and Alexandra Hasluck, *Unwilling Emigrants: A Study of the Convict Period in Western Australia* (Melbourne: Oxford University Press, 1960), p. 43.

Acknowledgments

The author gratefully acknowledges the helpfulness of the following authors, owners of copyrights, and publishers who have given permission for quotations to appear in this book: Australian National University Press for quotations from *Hobart Town* by Peter Bolger; Cat and Fiddle Press for a quotation from *The Tasmanian Gallows* by Richard P. Davis; Curtis Brown (Aust.) Pty Ltd, Penguin Books, Eyre & Spottiswoode and Jonathon Cape for quotations from *Voss* and from *A Fringe of Leaves* by Patrick White; Faber and Faber Ltd for quotations from *Convicts and the Colonies* by A.G.L. Shaw; The Grolier Society for a quotation from "Convicts and Transportation" by A.G.L. Shaw in the *Australian Encyclopedia*; Melbourne University Press for a quotation from *The Convict Settlers of Australia* by Dr Lloyd Robson, and for a quotation from *Quest for Authority in Eastern Australia* by Dr Michael Roe; Oxford University Press, Australia for quotations from *Australian Painting 1788–1960* by Bernard Smith; Reed Books Pty Ltd and the estate of Charles Bateson for quotations from *The Convict Ships* by Charles Bateson; Review Publications Pty Ltd for quotations from *Notes d'un Condamné Politique* by François-Xavier Prieur, translated by George Mackaness; Sydney University Press for quotations from *Pressmen and Governors* by E. Morris Miller.

Abbreviations

ADB	*Australian Dictionary of Biography*
ALS	*Australian Literary Studies*
BMC	*British Museum Catalogue of Printed Books to 1955*
DNB	*Dictionary of National Biography*
HRA	*Historical Records of Australia*
HRN.S.W.	*Historical Records of New South Wales*
JRAHS	*Journal and Proceedings of the Royal Australian Historical Society*
ML	Mitchell Library, Sydney
n. ed.	new edition
PTHRA	*Proceedings of the Tasmanian Historical Research Association*
TA	Tasmanian State Archives, Hobart

1
The Background

> My grandfather was a shorter, and my father was a smasher; the one was scragg'd and the other lagg'd.
>
> *The Romany Rye*

The findings of anthropologists continue to push the beginnings of human habitation of the Great South Land further back into the past. The events of these countless generations have been handed down and interpreted in the myths of the Dreamtime. The very timelessness and enigmas of these myths display the accommodation of the Aborigines' spirit to that of their homeland.

The findings of archaeologists indicate a long history of European and Asian contacts with Australia. Wrecks and artefacts pose mysteries that will doubtless be resolved with scientific exactitude.

There is no puzzle about the date of the beginning of European habitation of Australia (though *why* it began may never be resolved). The foundation and early years of Australia have been more extensively documented than those of many other nations. Unlike their Aboriginal compatriots, white Australians lack a dreamtime.

The effect of this lacuna is yet to be determined, though Mircea Eliade's generalization about western societies appears relevant.

> Through culture a desacralized religious universe and a demythicized mythology formed and nourished western civilization — that is, the only civilization that has succeeded in becoming exemplary. There is

> more here than a triumph over mythos. The victory is that of the *book* over oral tradition, of the document — especially of the written document — over a living experience whose only means of expression were preliterary.[1]

The thousand or so founding fathers (convict or free) of this nation would not have given a fig for Eliade's observations. Theirs was a "land of d____d realities" as Charles Lamb noted. It was a land where the here and now inhibited reflection on the hereafter, on the why or the wherefore.

This was because survival was difficult, and because for many years the majority of European settlers were professional criminals transported as a punishment for their misdeeds. Between 1788 and 1868 some 160,000 persons were thus transported. Known variously as government men, lags, exiles, convicts and felons, they played a part in the foundation of every Australian state, with the exception of South Australia.

The typical convict, we are told,

> was an urban thief, single, aged twenty-five, previously convicted at least once and transported for seven years for larceny. He was well treated according to the standards of the day on the voyage to Australia and when he arrived he was assigned to a settler. He probably had a number of masters and suffered punishment five times, mainly for such offences as being absent without leave or drunk. If he were a rebellious spirit and his master turned nasty, his transportation could become a very severe punishment, which it was meant to be. He might be flogged; but no more than approximately fifteen per cent of prisoners were ever sent to a penal settlement, and most convicts were not flogged. Usually men secured a ticket of leave within three years and this enabled them to work for themselves provided they reported regularly to the police. Upon fair behaviour (not necessarily exemplary behaviour) the prisoner would be granted a conditional pardon before full sentence was completed.[2]

Apart from its valuable insights into the background of the convict, Dr Robson's description is noteworthy for two other reasons.

In the first instance, it is obvious that the description is at variance with the popular conception of the convict's life as it was portrayed in works like Marcus Clarke's *For the*

Term of His Natural Life: "However, when all is said, the horrors depicted by Marcus Clarke in *For the Term of His Natural Life* are not in the least typical of Australian conditions. Considerably fewer than ten per cent of the prisoners transported ever saw the inside of a penal settlement and many who did so were there only for brief periods".[3]

Nevertheless, when Marcus Clarke set off for Tasmania to gather material for his book, he informed his publisher that he was going to "write up the convict documents". William Hay, whose bent was far less sensational, believed that this procedure was inevitable for any writer of an Australian historical novel.[4] Most other writers about the convict days also claimed familiarity with the records.

It is clear that those who wrote (and indeed, write) about the convict days tended to portray a reality that did not correspond at all points with historical facts.

It appears reasonable to infer that there is a received mode of writing about the convicts. That is, despite the wealth of documentation, writers and readers have hit upon an interpretative code which is acceptable as an account of our beginnings. According to one's perspective this code may be designated as a myth or fable or legend; one may believe with Mark Twain that it reads like "the most beautiful lies".[5]

Dr Robson's description, cast as it is as an approximation of a biography, is a reminder that most of the early writings about convicts were biographical in form. Individual convict records were tersely biographical and generally speaking, factual. It was when these biographies were published without official sanction or control that they exhibited the perspective, content and tone that have become accepted. These attributes became evident within decades of the date of first settlement.

The traditional criminal biography

"It is natural to suppose that, during the early years of its foundation, a dependent colony will draw to a considerable extent upon the literary as well as the general resources of the mother country."[6] The early emergence of a formula to describe the convict's life implies the adoption of an existing model. In fact, when the first convicts came to Australia, and throughout the transportation era, there was in England a long-standing mode of discussing crime and punishment. This tradition was embodied in criminal biographies, which were widely disseminated.

Convicts transported to Australia used this traditional form when they came to write about their experiences. They also tended to use the form orally when they told their stories to observers.

The biographical form was modified to suit Australian conditions, first by the selection of a vocabulary, and second by the adoption of an increasingly stylized formula. This formula, in turn, underwent modifications as experiences in Australia became more diversified.

There was a concomitant oral tradition. Largely anecdotal, this tradition contained stories of celebrated incidents and personalities. The oral tradition was encountered by succeeding waves of transportees in prisons, hulks and convict ships. In Australia, convict tales were rehearsed around camp-fires, in bark huts and drawing-rooms. Towards the end of the nineteenth century these tales became the property of the convict residuum on the one hand and variants of them became the property of pioneering families on the other. Ultimately, parts of both oral traditions found their way into written accounts.

Thus, when works of fiction came to be written, the criminal biography and the oral traditions provided their structure. When writers had recourse to the documents, this structure was reinforced, since the documents were primarily biographies, the stages of which corresponded to those of the traditional English formula.

This formula contained recurrent components: "early life"; "introduction to crime"; "progress in crime";

"capture"; "trial"; "execution" or "transportation". Interwoven with the foregoing were "hardships"; "sufferings" and "reformation". Obviously, the formula provided no precedents for describing life in the antipodes. Moreover, as will be seen, the experiences of convicts transported to America provided minimal guidance.

The modifications of the formula and its amplification to include components describing life in the colonies represented one of the first achievements of Australian literature. In the eighteenth century English literature was rich in resources. It was the nature of the early — and unwilling — colonists that determined that one of the first borrowings would be the treatment of crime and punishment and its usual focus: the criminal biography.

While foreign observers believed that enthusiasm for this kind of account was peculiar to eighteenth-century Englishmen, the English had long displayed an interest in such matters.

With the advent of printing, and the progressive secularization that has characterized the history of English literature since that time, old tales of transgressions against the law, such as those contained in the *Disciplina Clericalis*, were often translated without their edifying codas. Even where sin was described to convert the sinner, there was always the problem that the sin might be more fascinating than conversion. Thus in a collection of stories like *C. Merry Tales* (1526), despite the author's concluding that "By this ye may see ... ", the reader was led to admire the cleverness of the Welshman who stole the Englishman's cock, rather than to despise theft. The tension between reformatory zeal and the insidious charms of vice is found throughout the literature to be discussed here.

As writers outgrew random collections of tales, they were confronted with the problem of unifying the anecdotes they presented. One method they employed was to allow the reader to witness a procession of rogues, or to take him on a tour of infamous haunts. Such literary devices were adopted by John Skelton in "The Tunnyng of Elynour Rummyng" (1517); by Robert Copland in *Hyeway to the Spytel House* (1535), and *Howleglas* (1510); and by John Awdeley in *Fraternitye of Vacabones* (1565). While these accounts were at times lurid, a more sober note characterized William Baldwin's collection, *A Myrrovre for Magistrates* (1559). This set of poems, written by "dyvers learned men whose many gifts nede fewe praises", contained many of the biographical components that will be dealt with in these pages.

Thomas Dekker claimed to be innovating when he wrote *English Villainies Discovered by Lantern and Candlelight* (1608): "And the honest intelligencer that first opened the den of these monsters was the Bellman of London".[7] Dekker's exposé purported to be a tour of dens of iniquity by Pamersiel, who had been sent from Hell to make fresh converts for the Devil. In rapid succession the reader learned of the depredations of "gull-gropers", card-sharps, horse-stealers, prostitutes, and so on. Pamersiel's visit to a prison was a model for many subsequent accounts.

Meanwhile, denunciations of specific crimes had emerged in pamphlets such as Gilbert Walker's *A Magnificent Detection of the Most Vile and Detestable Use of Diceplay* (1552) and in Robert Greene's *The Third and Last part of Cony-Catching with the New Devised Knavish Art of Fool-Taking, the Like Cozenages and Villainies Never Before Discovered* (1592).

This pamphlet, claiming to be based on notes provided by a justice of the peace, contains anecdotes about rogues. For example, the reader is told of the cutpurse who has a cutler fashion a knife. The cutler knows the criminal purposes for which the knife is being made, but he cheerfully puts the fee in his purse, which becomes the thief's first prize. In this anecdote there is the exuberance of criminal ingenuity that characterizes many of the English criminal biographies. The same vigour is to be found in James Hardy Vaux's *Memoirs* and James Tucker's *Ralph Rashleigh*. However, it dies out in the Australian biographies, to be replaced by a notable sourness and sullenness.

Throughout the seventeenth century similar accounts of criminal behaviour and prison life were produced. For example, Geoffrey Mynshul (who had been in prison with Dekker) wrote *Certain Characters and Essays of Prison and Prisoners* in 1618.

A more sensational note soon began to creep into the titles of pamphlets: John Reynold's *The Triumphs of God's Revenge Against the Crying and Execrable Sin of Murther in Thirty Severall Tragicall Histories* (1621) went through several editions, being augmented in 1679 by ten stories showing "God's Revenge against the Abominable Sin of Adultery". Titles of similar tenor appeared, including *A true Relation of the Lives and Deaths of the two most famous English Pyrats, Purser and Clynton* (1639) and *The Penitent Murderer* (1657).

The development so far outlined progressed from a survey of crime, to specific crimes, to stories of perpetrators of crimes; that is, biographies. Richard Head's *Meriton Latroon* (1655) is an early example of the biography of a criminal. An important precursor of similar eighteenth-century works, it will be dealt with subsequently.

In this brief outline it has been possible to do no more than sketch in some of the kinds of literary works inspired by crime and punishment. It was a subject which interested many writers.[8]

Side by side with the collection and surveys that have been noted were the ballads. If we may generalize from the case of William Ainsworth, who had some claim to knowledge of this literature, the ballads do not appear to have been known outside the haunts in which they were sung.[9]

Visits to haunts of crime, denunciations of crime, the production of criminal biography, and the importation of a sensational tone, continued to be popular during the eighteenth century.

A successor to Dekker's *Bellman,* Ned Ward's *The London*

Spy (1698-1700) appeared in eighteen monthly parts. In this work Ward took an ironical view of the seamier side of London life, as did Tom Brown in his *Amusements Serious and Comical Calculated for the Meridian of London* (1700) and in his *Cheats of London* (1704).

The eighteenth century also saw a more scientific and dispassionate note introduced into the discussion of crime and punishment: it became important to examine why so much crime existed. At the beginning of the century, Jonathan Swift saw a connection between crime and poverty. He believed that much poverty (and resultant crime) was self-inflicted:

> Perhaps there is not a word more abused than that of the poor, or wherein the world is more generally mistaken. Among the number of those who beg in our streets, or are half starved at home, or languish in prison for debt, there is hardly one in a hundred who doth not owe his misfortunes to his own laziness or drunkenness, or worse vices.[10]

Daniel Defoe, however, believed that necessity drove people to crime. This sentiment is to be found throughout his works, but most clearly in the *Review* (1711):

> Men rob for bread, women whore for bread. Necessity is the parent of crime; Ask the worst High-Way Man in the Nation, ask the lewdest strumpet in the town, If they would not willingly leave off the Trade if they could live handsomely without it — And I dare say not one will but acknowledge it.[11]

In his *Enquiry* (1751) Henry Fielding asserted that it is the "lower orders'" love for entertainment that leads to crime. He believed that they should learn to curb their appetites, while "the great" must "answer for the employment of their time to themselves or their spiritual governors". At the end of the century Patrick Colquhoun shared these sentiments,[12] while William Godwin declared that the "criminal is propelled to act by necessary causes and irresistible motives".[13]

There were other, and very important, discussions of crime written by lawyers and philosophers: Beccaria's *Treatise of*

Crimes and Punishments was translated into English in 1765; in the same year Blackstone wrote his *Commentaries*. Howard's *State of the Prisons* appeared in 1777; in 1780 Bentham's *Introduction to the Principles of Morals and Legislation* appeared. Romilly completed his *Rights and Duties of Juries* in 1785 and his *Thoughts on Executive Justice* in 1786. Colquhoun's *Police of the Metropolis* was published in 1795, two years after Godwin's *Enquiry Concerning Political Justice*. Interested readers could also have delved into the relevant treatises of Voltaire, Rousseau and Kant. The foregoing works were written for the serious reader. Popular tastes were well catered for in other ways.

To put these "other ways" in perspective it must be remembered that the publications were chiefly biographical and that for the most part they stemmed from public executions. At the scaffold it was usual for the criminal to be accompanied by a clergyman (for example, the ordinary of Newgate). Above the tumult, the ordinary would strive for the soul of the condemned person, while the latter would deliver his "last dying speech and confession".

The custom of making such a speech appears to be of ancient origin. In England, for example, both Henry VIII and Thomas More knew that the latter would be expected to speak at the scaffold. Fearing More's eloquence, Henry ordained that More speak briefly. More complied. While the text has not survived, its general thrust and various aphorisms have been preserved.

To add to their income the ordinaries began the custom of publishing these speeches. The *British Museum Catalogue* records such a speech as early as 1684;[14] however, it was Paul Lorrain (ordinary of Newgate, 1698–1719) who in 1712 began the custom of regularly printing them, copies being available at eight o'clock on the morning following the execution.[15] It is probable that the ordinaries, having to write in such haste, fell back on the model offered by the familiar printed funeral panegyric, with the obvious substitution of the criminal's misdemeanours for the hero's or saint's virtues.

In fact, the ordinary's account became so perfunctory and so little attuned to the sentiments of the crowd that it came to be held in almost universal contempt. In a letter to Pope, for example, Bolingbroke referred disdainfully to "that great Historiographer, Paul Lorrain".[16] Again, in John Gay's *The Beggar's Opera* (1728), Mrs Peachum gives the following directive to Filch: "But now, since you have nothing better to do, even go to your book and learn your catechism: for really, a man makes but an ill figure in the ordinary's paper who cannot give a satisfactory answer to his questions."[17]

Fielding was one of the many who expressed similar sentiments: "The ordinary's account where all the apologies of the lives of the rogues and whores which have been published within these twenty years have been inserted".[18]

The ordinary's account may not have been very efficacious, but it was profitable, and the ordinaries did all they could to maintain proprietorship of it. Nevertheless, last dying speeches were also printed as broadsheets and disseminated widely. In the nineteenth century, as many as 2,500,000 broadsheet copies were made of the last speech of a notorious murderer.[19] The broadsheets were often decorated with crude drawings and embellished with ballads and edifying verses. Ballad singers were among the principal purveyors of these sheets. In their hands the broadsheets became even a greater travesty of their avowed intent, since the ballad singers often worked hand-in-glove with pickpockets, as John Gay pointed out (1716):

> Let not the ballad singer's thrilling strain
> Amid the swarm thy list'ning ear detain
> Guard well they pocket, for these Syrens stand
> To aid the labours of the diving hand:
> Confed'rate in the cheat they draw the throng;
> And cambrick handkerchiefs reward the song.[20]

This complicity is depicted in Rowlandson's engraving, *Last Dying Speech and Confession*.

It is pertinent here to outline some nineteenth-century developments of the broadsheet, as it continued to be a possible element of the "education" of transported convicts.

The heyday of the broadsheet coincided with that of the presses in the Seven Dials, particularly the Catnach Press (founded 1813). Other centres of the trade were Birmingham, Lincoln and Preston. Henry Mayhew was told by one of the Seven Dials writers that:

> Many ballads are written expressly for the Seven Dials press, especially the Newgate and political ones. . . . There are five known authors of the Dials press, and they are street ballad-singers. I am one of them myself. My little knowledge I picked up bit by bit so that I hardly know how I came by it. I certainly knew my letters before I left home, and I got the rest off the dead walls and out of the ballads and papers I have been selling. I write most of the ballads now for the printers in the Dials. I get a shilling for a "copy of verses written by the wretched culprit the night previous to his execution".[21]

Whatever truth remained in the written word tended to be dissipated by the enthusiastic patter of the vendor:

> Now my friends, here you have, just printed and published, a full, true and pertickler account of the life, trial, character, confession, behaviour, condemnation and hexecution of that unfortunate malefactor. Yes, my customers to which is added a copy of the serene and beautiful verses, pious and immoral, as wot he wrote with his own blood and skewer.[22]

Thus, those who did not witness the execution, and those who could not read, could still be regaled with the salient details of the crime and punishment.

The broadsheets were printed on cheap paper. More durable bound collections of chronicles of crime and punishment were also available. For example, that indefatigable biographer, Captain Alexander Smith, published in 1713 his *History of the Lives and Robberies of the Most Noted Highway-Men, Foot-Pads, House-Breakers, Shop Lifts and Cheats of Both Sexes in and about London and Westminster*. This two-volume compendium was followed by a third volume in 1720. Between the production of these two parts Smith found time to publish (1716) *The School of Venus*, or *Cupid Restor'd to Sight: Being a History of Cuckolds and Cuckoldmakers.*

In 1728 the first edition of *The Newgate Calendar* appeared; there was another in 1773, and a third in 1809; there have been at least eight others produced since then. A work of similar scope but of more obvious reformatory purpose had been published as early as 1690.[23] The *Annual Register* first appeared in 1758; ten years later the *Tyburn Chronicle* was printed.

In the nineteenth century this genre continued to be popular. The two volumes of the *Terrific Register* became available in 1825; it was followed by George Borrow's *Celebrated Trials* in the same year, and "Camden Pelham's" *Chronicles of Crime* (1841). In the preface to his six-volume collection, Borrow denounced the *Newgate Calendars* as "chronicles of roguery and vulgar depravity in their various forms, [which] have usually been compiled in language which sympathized and accorded with their subjects".[24] As his work was for "respectable and popular circulation", Borrow excluded cases which involved "details contrary to decency". He mentioned that he drew upon the *Causes Célèbres* and "many curious documents" but that he "adopted no existing model".

"Camden Pelham's" accounts of early crime were " ... derived from sources of information peculiarly within the reach of the editor while those of a later period are compiled from known authorities as accurate as they are complete".[25]

The bound chronicles noted above were usually biographical in form and reformatory in purpose. Borrow's charge that the *Newgate Calendar* "sympathized" with its subjects was often made by other writers; yet a dispassionate reading of the *Calendars* (and Borrow's own *Chronicles*) reveals little of a provocative tendency.

Between the broadsheets and the chronicles and calendars were the chap-books. These crude publications contained lurid accounts of the crime and punishment of criminals like

Judas Iscariot and M. Bamfylde Moore Carew. Other chapbooks dealt with *The Horrors of Jealousie or the Fatal Mistake* or *The Unfortunate Family*. These publications contain a bizarre combination of fact, superstitution and exhortation to virtue. They are frequently illustrated with woodcuts and often include verses.[26]

Yet another eighteenth-century method of treating crime and punishment was the engraving. Horace Walpole complained in 1750: "You cannot conceive the ridiculous rage there is of going to Newgate, the prints that are published of the malefactors and the memory of their lives set forth with as much panache as Marshal Turenne's".[27]

Henry Fielding, on the other hand, discerned great merit in Hogarth's work: "I almost dare affirm that those two works of his which he calls the Rake's Progress and the Harlot's Progress are calculated more to serve the cause of Virtue and the Preservation of Mankind than all the Folios of Morality that have been written".[28]

Hogarth produced his *Harlot's Progress* (1732) and *The Rake's Progress* (1735) for a wealthy clientèle, but for his series *Industry and Idleness* (1747) he drastically lowered the purchase price so that it "would be within reach of those for whom [it was] chiefly intended". Contrary to his usual practice, he embellished the series with symbolic motifs and descriptive verse.

The criminal biography in works of fiction

This outline of eighteenth-century ways of treating crime and punishment has so far dealt with accounts which were supposedly factual. Even without analysis, it will be obvious from some titles cited that there was a good deal of exaggeration, even of fantasy, in some works. In other words, there was a perceptible drift from reportage to fiction.

It is customary to view the early and middle eighteenth century as witnessing the birth of the novel. Whatever may have been the first novel, whoever may have been the father of the genre, the fictional works of the eighteenth century were primarily imitations of biography. The life of a fictitious individual became the force that lent cohesion to his picaresque ramblings.

At the end of the century, James Boswell belived that he had devised the best mode of biography: "I am absolutely certain that my mode of biography, which gives not only a *history* of Johnson's *visible* progress through the world and of his publications, but a *view* of his mind in his letters and conversations, is the most perfect that can be conceived and will be *more* of a life than has ever yet appeared".[29]

Yet, however revolutionary Boswell's strategy may have been, in recording Samuel Johnson's judgments so exactly he helped to perpetuate Johnson's own methods of recording and evaluating the lives of others. In other words, biography was encouraged to remain – as it has been in hagiography and in the "pleasant history" of the seventeenth century – a matter of considering a man's acts and sentiments as emanating from discrete faculties and of measuring these acts and sentiments against absolute standards of good and evil.

Howard Miles sums up this outlook and procedure:

> Johnson uses certain plain terms that for him stand adequately for distinct and definable qualities – *openness, confidence, affection, brave, benevolent, honest.* Similarly, the feelings or passions are distinct and nameable. . . . Elsewhere Johnson sees the mind as constituted of various distinct faculties – *genius, judgment, knowledge.*[30]

It is to be expected, therefore, that Johnson would stress the normative aspect of fiction. Having described contemporary fiction as that which "exhibits life in its true state – and influenced by passions and qualities which are readily to be found in conversing with mankind", he proceeded to specify the proper end of fiction:

> In narratives where historical veracity has no place I cannot discover why there should not be exhibited the most perfect idea of virtue, of virtue not angelical nor above probability, for what we cannot we shall never imitate, but the highest and purest that humanity can

reach, which exercised in such trials as the various revolutions of things shall bring upon it, m͏͏ ͏͏ɤ, by conquering some calamities, and enduring others, teach us what we may hope for and what we may perform.

Those of Johnson's contemporaries who strove to create works of fiction based on crime and punishment, indeed many of the other earlier novelists, professed to share his moral concern: if they did not exhort to "the most perfect idea of virtue", at least they displayed the consequences of vice, and presumably, thereby encouraged virtue. Daniel Defoe realized that the "gust and palate of the reader" will determine the degree of edification got from a book: "But as this work (*Moll Flanders*) is chiefly recommended to those who know how to read it and how to make the good uses of it which the story all along recommends to them, so it is to be hoped that such readers will be more pleased with the moral than the fable".[31]

In the same year he prefaced similar sentiments to *Colonel Jacque*: in reading about the Colonel (Defoe maintained) one can perceive " . . . Virtue and the ways of wisdom every where applauded; Vice and all kinds of Wickedness attended with Misery [and] many Kinds of Infelicities".

Some dramatists evinced the same moral purpose. Thus, however ironical his intent, Gay's Beggar declared in *The Beggar's Opera*: "Through the whole of the piece you may observe . . . a similitude of manners in high and low life. Had the play remained as I first intended, it would have carried a most excellent moral. 'Twould have shown that the lower sort of people have their vices in a degree as well as the rich: and that they are punished for them."

Three years later (1731) George Lillo wrote in the Dedication of *The London Merchant*: " . . . the end of tragedy [is] the exciting of passions in order to the correcting such of them as are criminal either in their nature or through their excess".[32]

It will have become obvious that the realities of criminal life were not readily amenable to being viewed with a moral squint. In the underworld there was a solidarity that made nonsense of attempts to describe crime solely in terms of sin and virtue. The tension that this contradiction caused lay at the heart of the criminal biography, finding expression in literature as sanctimoniousness, cynicism, irony or naiveté. In penal administration it bred idealistic schemes doomed to failure, or a pragmatism that most often expressed itself as brutality; cruelty seemed to produce results.

The nature of the underworld and a narrowly reformatory vision merit closer attention.

In his *Fraternitye of Vacabones* Awdeley had described an organized criminal class. The leader of the gangs he portrayed was known as the "upright man" who took the lion's share of booty for himself. The gangs had their argot or cant which served as a bond of solidarity and as a means of concealing the thieves' plans from outsiders. The use of an argot for such a purpose no doubt goes back to the beginnings of civilization; certainly thieves' guilds and argot existed in ancient Greece and Rome. However, Dekker later believed that English thieves' cant was of relatively recent origin: "By none but the soldiers of these tattered bands is it [cant] familiarly or usually spoken yet within less than fourscore years now past not a word of this language was known. The first inventor of it was hanged, yet left he apt scholars behind him who had reduced that into their method which he on his death bed (which was a pair of gallows) could not so absolutely perfect as he desired."

In the lives of Meriton Latroon and Bamfylde Moore Carew and in Vaux's *Memoirs* we find primitive cant dictionaries. In subsequent sections it will be seen that many observers noted the use of cant among the Australian convicts.[33]

Dekker provided more information about these gangs: "There is no lusty rogue but hath many sworn brothers and the morts his sworn sisters vow themselves body and soul to the Devil to perform these ten articles ... " He provides us with the criminals' *curriculum vitae*: "But the Devil is their tutor, Hell their school, thieves' roguery and whoredom the arts they study. Before Doctor Storey they dispute and at the gallows are made graduates of Newgate and other gaols, the hangman's colleges."[34]

Because he showed such promise as a thief, Head's Meriton Latroon was invited to join a society of thieves: "If I would swear to be secret and faithful, and become a Brother of the Society he would not only tell me how all this (afore recited) might be performed, but would likewise introduce me into the place where these jolly blades used to congregate."

Over a century later, Fielding exclaimed: "What indeed may not the public apprehend when they are informed as an unqestionable fact that there are at this time a great gang of rogues, whose number falls little short of a hundred, who are incorporated in a body, have officers and a treasury and have reduced theft and robbery into a regular system".[35]

In *Moll Flanders, Colonel Jacque, Jonathan Wild* and *The Beggar's Opera* we are given further insights into these societies. *Jonathan Wild* (1743) contains an extensive description of one of them. Possibly because Jonathan Wild's career as a receiver offered a glimpse into the workings of the underworld, he was a figure who appealed to the popular imagination. In the year he was executed (1725), he was the subject of eight full-scale biographies.

If it was not Wild, it was some other receiver who was usually depicted as playing a vital part in the workings of a criminal society. Receivers were often pawnbrokers, and Colquhoun complained that: "Any person, even the most notorious rogue or vagabond who can raise ten pounds to pay for a licence, may at present set up trade as a pawn-broker; and it is even said that some have got licences, who have actually been on board the hulks. This class of swindling pawn-brokers are uniformly receivers of stolen goods".[36]

Rightly or wrongly, Colquhoun believed that Jews were prominent among the receivers. His judgment may have been correct; he may have been alarmed at the revival of the widely misunderstood Cabbala or he may have been guilty of what Chesney Kellow was to describe later as "the prejudice of the Victorians".

A number of ironic attempts were made to present a rationale for criminal societies and behaviour. For example, in 1714 Bernard Mandeville claimed that: "If all people were strictly honest, and nobody would meddle or pry into anything but his own, half the smiths of the nation would want employment; and abundance of workmanship is to be seen everywhere both in town and country that would have never been thought of, but to secure us against the attempt of pilferers and robbers".[37]

In a similar vein, John Gay has Mat and Mint say in *The Beggar's Opera*:

> We retrench the superfluities of mankind. The world is avaricious and I hate avarice. A covetous fellow, like a Jackdaw, steals what he was never made to enjoy, for the sake of hiding it. These are the robbers of mankind; for money was made for the free-hearted and generous: and where is the injury of taking from another what he hath not the heart to make use of?

Whatever the real sentiments of the denizens of the thieves' kitchens were we do not know, but it is obvious that these criminals were organized and that they had a secret language. At the heart of these societies lay a tension between loyalty on the one hand and the individual's self-interest on the other. Out of this tension sprang both defiance of legal authority and treacherous capitulation to that authority: some criminals "died game", while others betrayed their companions. A similar solidarity and treachery will be found in accounts about transported thieves and other criminals.

The equation of crime with sin was expressed succinctly by Henry Mayhew as late as 1862: "To thieve, however, is to offend, at once socially, morally, and religiously; for not only does the social but the moral and religious law, one and all, enjoin that we should respect the property of others".[38]

Criminal acts were usually described in terms of "dissipation", "profligacy", "idleness", "irregularity", "riot", "debauchery", and "licentiousness". Thus, when he wanted to demonstrate the virtues of Dr Johnson, Boswell asserted that: "In a man whom religious education has secured from licentious indulgence, the passion of love, when once it has seized upon him, is exceeding strong; being unimpaired by dissipation and totally concentrated in one object".

This frame of reference was to be often employed by observers describing Australian convicts. John Dunmore Lang, for example, believed that "The concentration of an emancipated convict population, as Governor Macquarie's experiment sufficiently proves, will infallibly be a concentration of vice and villainy, profligacy and misery, dissipation and ruin."

We have seen crime attributed to necessity, compulsion and poverty; other observers believed that evil-doing had its basic cause in the depravity of the human heart. "Failure and defects [are] inseparable from humanity", wrote Johnson. Edward Gibbon, who could not be reckoned overly religious, perceived it as one of the historian's tasks "to discover the inevitable mixture of error and corruption which she [religion] contracted in a long residence upon earth among a weak and degenerate race of beings".[39]

William Wilberforce (1759-1833) put the matter more bleakly: "From it [Christianity] we learn that man is an apostate creature, fallen from his high original, degraded in his nature and depraved in his faculties: indisposed to good and disposed to evil; prone to vice, it is natural and easy to him; disinclined to virtue, it is difficult and laborious; that he is tainted with sin, not slightly or superficially, but radically, and to the very core".[40]

If crime had these sinful overtones, then turning away from crime was frequently described in terms of religious reformation. Daniel Defoe defined the scope of reformation with some precision:

> "But hark ye William", says I, "the nature of repentance, as you hinted once to me, included reformation, and we can never reform; how then can we repent?"
> "Why can we never reform?" says William.

"Because", says I, "we cannot restore what we have taken away by spoil."[41]

More frequently reformation meant a general sorrow for one's sinfulness. To effect this change of heart in the criminal, authorities looked to the Bible and to the Church. However, the Latitudinarian church of the eighteenth century seemed to have little to offer: "Never was there a time when religion in England was at a lower ebb, or when vice was coarser or more shameless."[42]

While Boswell admired the fervour of Mr Moore at the execution of Gibson and Payne[43] and John Wesley was impressed by Mr Vilette,[44] the ordinaries of Newgate were usually seen as defective tools of the law:

> The ordinary of Newgate came to me and talked a little in his way, but all his divinity ran upon confessing my crime, as he called it (though he knew not what I was in for), making a full discovery, and the like, without which he told me God would never forgive me; and he said so little to the purpose that I had no manner of consolation from him; and then to observe the poor creature preaching confession and repentance to me in the morning and find him drunk with brandy by noon — this had something in it so shocking that I began to nauseate the man and his works too by degrees for the sake of the man; so that I desired him to trouble me no more.[45]

More fervent clergymen may have met with some success, but Johnson probably expressed the general level of the clergy's attainment when he said: "'Sir, one of our regular clergy will probably not impress their [criminals'] minds sufficiently: they should be attended by a Methodist preacher; or a Popish priest.'"[46]

When subordinates perceive a considerable gap between a professed ideal and what is actually accomplished they are often provoked into hostility or cynicism. These attitudes towards religion were adopted by many of the English and Australian convicts. Satire was employed frequently by eighteenth-century writers and in the disparity between the power of organized crime and the helplessness of the law and religion they found scope for their talents.

Components of the criminal biography

Not all writers were satirical, of course. No doubt there were many who believed simply and sincerely that in writing cautionary tales they were fostering the spiritual welfare of their readers. Whether satire or edification were their motives, many writers used the components of the criminal biography to achieve their aim. The first of these components was "birth and parentage".

Gibbon believed that this component occurred so frequently in biography that "it must depend on the influence of some common principle in the minds of men".[47] He may have been right, but a sufficient explanation is to be found — at least for western readers — in hagiography, which no doubt was based originally on the biblical precedents, where the Old Testament begins with the origin of Adam and the New Testament with the genealogy of Christ. So frequently does the Old Testament give the antecedents of its personages that the Church Fathers often commented on Melchisedech, whose forbears are not named. The Roman Breviary and the various lives of the saints perpetuated the biblical custom,[48] and it was natural for writers of secular biography to use this time-honoured model. The addition of details about education may possibly be attributed to Calvinistic and Scottish influences.[49]

Despite "good parents" the criminal embarked on a life of crime. Most biographies record the central character's introduction to crime, which was frequently ascribed to weaknesses of character like idleness or vanity or Pope's "ruling passion strong in death". Sometimes the beginning of a life of crime was seen as the result of swearing, sabbath-breaking or gambling. Often criminals blamed "bad companions" for their fall.

Considerable space was given to describing how the character became increasingly wicked. A progress in vice or virtue had been common in popular thought since the late medieval period, when the metaphors of the ladder to heaven or hell became fused with the concept of the stages of the life of man. Hogarth's *Idle Prentice* series is an excellent illustration of the downward path trodden by the eighteenth-century criminal. It should be noted that progress in crime was most frequently represented by the criminal's increasing addiction to alcohol and whoring, or by his adoption by a gang of thieves; thereafter his moral deterioration was conveyed by the frequency and audacity of his criminal acts.

However celebrated the criminal's career, the genre demanded that he be captured. In numerous biographies the criminal is captured many times, sometimes by fate, or through the more obvious agency of the Bow Street Runners, into whose hands he may have been betrayed by his own folly or the treachery of his accomplices. Considerable stress is frequently placed upon the capture which preceded the criminal's execution or transportation.

John Howard (1726–90) observed that the builders of Old Newgate "seem to have regarded in their plan, nothing but the single article of keeping prisoners in safe custody".[50] He discovered many deficiencies in the English prisons, but the indiscriminate bundling together of prisoners was one of the chief defects criticized by many observers. After the loss of freedom, the prisoner's chief source of torment seems to have been his fellow-prisoners.

Gaols had long been demoralizing places. Dekker, for example, concluded that he could

> call a prison an enchanted castle by reason of the rare transformation therein wrought, for it maketh a wise man lose his wits, a fool to know himself. It turns a rich man into a beggar, and leaves a poor man desperate. He whom neither snows nor alps can vanquish but hath a heart as constant as Hannibal's — him can the misery of a prison deject. And how brave an outside soever his mind carries, open his bosom and you see nothing but wounds. Wouldst thou dive into the secret villanies of man? Lie in prison.[51]

"Hell" was a metaphor frequently used to describe prisons. For example, when Tobias Smollett (1762) depicts Sir Lancelot Greaves in prison, the chapter is entitled "In which

our Hero descends into the Mansions of the Damned".⁵²
"The children of wretchedness" seem to have delighted in
confirming each other in perdition: "In some gaols you see
(and who can see it without sorrow) boys of twelve or fourteen eagerly listening to the stories told by practised
criminals of their adventures, successes, stratagems and
escapes".⁵³

This perverse educative function had been noted by Pepys
in 1667: "He [Sir Richard Ford] says also [it] hath been
made appear to them [the court of aldermen] that the
keeper of Newgate, at This Day, hath made his house the
only nursery of rogues and whores and pickpockets in the
world; where they were lived and entertained and the whole
society met."⁵⁴

Despite Howard's efforts, the prisons remained schools of
crime at the end of the eighteenth century: "Convicts discharged from prison and the hulks after suffering the
sentence of the law: [are] too often instructed in all the arts
and devices which attach to the most extreme degree of
human depravity and in the perfect means of perpetrating
crimes and eluding justice."⁵⁵

Well into the nineteenth century prisons still retained the
image of the *alma mater* for criminals as they picked their
way through the *Newgate Calendar*.⁵⁶

Scarcely less intolerable than the shifts of fellow prisoners
were the vagaries of justice when the prisoner was finally
brought before the court. Some accounts satirized the greed
and corruption of lawyers and witnesses. Great stress was
frequently laid upon the ceremonial of pronouncing the
death sentence. After the imposition of this sentence
prisoners often urged their friends to petition for mercy.
If mercy was exercised, the sentence was commuted to transportation. If mercy was refused, the criminal underwent the
grim ritual of the final service in the chapel and then faced
his execution.

Fielding described Wild's execution as his "apotheosis".
Earlier, Swift had ironically advised his footman to

> Mount the Cart with Courage. Fall on your knees. Lift up your eyes: Hold a Book in your Hands although you cannot read a word; Deny the fact at the Gallows; Kiss and forgive the hangman and so Farewell: You shall be buried in Pomp at the charge of the Fraternity: The Surgeon shall not touch a limb of you, and your fame shall continue until a successor of equal renown succeeds in your place.[57]

Despite the riotous behaviour around the gallows and the frequent obduracy of the condemned criminal, Shaftesbury believed that the "mere Vulgar of mankind often stand in need of such a rectifying Object as *the Gallows* before their eyes", and Dr Johnson regretted the abolition of the procession to the scaffold (1783) because "the publick was gratified by a procession; the criminal supported by it". Thirty years earlier, Fielding with a magistrate's eye viewed the matter differently:

> His [the convicted felon's] procession to Tyburn and his last moment there, all are triumphant; attended with the compassion of the meek and tender hearted and with the applause, admiration and envy of all the bold and hardened. His behaviour in his present condition, not the crimes how atrocious soever which brought him to it is the subject of contemplation. And if he hath any degree of decency, his death is spoken of by many with honour, by most with pity and by all with approbation.[58]

The irony of the public execution is nowhere better portrayed than in Hogarth's engraving *The Idle 'Prentice Executed at Tyburn* (1747). We see the ordinary ensconced in a carriage while in the tumbril a dissenting minister labours to move the condemned man; the vast throng is in a holiday mood; the dominant foreground figure is that of the ballad singer hawking the last dying speech.

Some criminals escaped execution only to find themselves sentenced to transportation. Although criminals were banished to the American colonies as early as 1607, large-scale transportation did not begin until 1717. Between then and the cessation of transportation in 1767, some 30,000 English and Scots and about 10,000 Irish criminals were transported. It was the custom for gaolers to hand over convicts to contractors who sold their interest in their "cargo" to American planters for the terms of their prisoners' sentences. This phase of penal history appears to have made little impact on the popular imagination either in America or in England:

> The convict element in the composition of early American society long since dropped out of sight, so much so, indeed that it is difficult now [1889] to find even an allusion to it in the literature of the present century. The explanation is not difficult. The convicts scattered over the immense territory of the plantations were so rapidly absorbed in the general population that all traces of their identity were soon lost in the crowd, a result largely owing to the means of reformation afforded them by free grants of land and assistance in the work of cultivation.[59]

Among the first of the few biographies which include transportation is Richard Head's *Meriton Latroon* (1665–71).[60] In the first section of this biography Latroon's life follows the conventional pattern: he is born of prosperous parents and receives a sound education. Having diligently entered upon his indentures, he is led astray by an evil companion and he begins to drink and whore. His progress in crime leads him to associate with gypsies (from whom he learns thieves' cant) and with a gang of thieves. He is caught and finds prison to be "a temporary Hell", and "a place that will learn a young man more villainy if he be apt to take it in six months than at twenty gaming ordinaries, bowling alleys or bawdy houses and an old man more policy than if he had been a pupil to Machiavel". He is released, and after many other adventures is returned at the end of the first part of the book to Newgate, where he exhorts his reader to avoid such a terrible fate and asks forgiveness if any parts of his story have offended against modesty. In the second part we find him and some companions condemned to transportation. In transit they are captured by Turks and experience adventures in Ceylon, Siam, Mauritius and Bantam. Thus, in this biography, transportation plays only a token part.

Fifty years later (1722) Daniel Defoe treated transportation more fully. Moll Flanders is told that "many a Newgate bird becomes a great man" in America, and she certainly prospers there.

Although he is trepanned and not transported, Defoe's Colonel Jacque finds his lot cast with that of transported convicts. The Colonel mentions numerous convicts who prospered on the termination of their sentences. He himself becomes a compassionate overseer and ultimately a well-to-do planter. During his twenty-year sojourn in America he witnesses numerous scenes and encounters many problems that were to recur in Australia. For instance, as an overseer he must decide his attitude to corporal punishment. He resolves to be humane and he is applauded by his master, who abhors flogging as "a Violence upon Nature in every way [and as] the most disagreeable thing in the world to a generous mind". Other problems considered are the cause of crime, remorse, recidivism and the need for penal reform. These issues were to be faced in Australia, but the texture of Defoe's novel differs from its Australian counterparts because *Colonel Jacque* is a picture of a different society. This difference appears very clearly in the steps that were taken to set up the well-conducted American expirees on their own plantations. In the early days, Australian expirees received land grants, but many of these persons frittered their opportunities away and, generally speaking, they did not enjoy the esteem bestowed upon their American counterparts.

Latroon, Moll Flanders and Colonel Jacque were fictional characters; Bampfylde Moore Carew was an historical personage whose life was first written in 1745 and reworked "a couple of dozen"[61] times thereafter. Of "no ordinary and mean Parentage" he early took an "immoderate Delight in several Sports and Exercises" and associated with bad companions and gypsies. He, too, learned cant from these persons and included a cant "dictionary" in his *Life*. After many adventures he was transported for seven years. He was perplexed "Whether at that Period of Time, Mankind was more profligate than usual; or whether there was a more than ordinary Demand for Men in his Majesty's Colonies".

This ironic tone is maintained throughout his account, which includes a brief sketch of his eleven-week voyage to Maryland and a lengthy description of that settlement. Upon landing and being asked his occupation he replied that he was a "Rat-Catcher, Mumper and Dog-Merchant". His prospective masters were nonplussed by this reply and placed him in custody. He absconded, was caught, flogged and loaded with an iron collar. He absconded a second time, and fell in with Indians whose king, Lillycraft, befriended him. After much imposture he contrived to return to England only to be trepanned: "dragg'd to Slavery by the lawless Hand of Power, without the mandate of sovereign Justice". On his second voyage the convicts were racked by a "violent fever". On arrival Carew again managed to escape. Although this expedient was highly dangerous he incurred the risk because he "though Death preferable to Slavery".

It will become obvious that some of the components and vocabulary of Carew's story are included in Australian convict narratives. It is impossible to determine the extent to which *The King of the Beggars* influenced them but it is quite probable that at least James Hardy Vaux and James Tucker had read Carew's book. Carew's *Life* also appeared in chap-book form which is likely to have been widely disseminated, and thus known to many of the Australian convicts.

Among other eighteenth-century writers who wrote about transportation, Fielding opposed the principle of commuting sentences to transportation: he believed that it was "the sixth encouragement of felons". His disapproval of transportation in itself was indicated by his inclusion of a spurious period of transportation in the life of Jonathan Wild, who was represented as spending his sentence in a "continued scene of whoring, drinking and removing from one place to the other". Later in the century Bentham,[62] Godwin[63] and Coleridge,[64] also opposed transportation.

In the nineteenth century Macaulay recalled the story of 841 Puritans whom Judge Jeffreys (1648-89) sentenced to transportation to the West Indies. More than one fifth of the convicts were "flung to the sharks"; crowding, illness and scanty provisions on board the transport made the survivors so feeble that they had to be fattened before they could be sold. Macaulay found this story in a manuscript, so that in all probability the account was not widely known before he related it.[65]

In all, there would appear to be little evidence that the first convicts transported to Australia knew much about transportation. It is true that Lord George Gordon (1751-93) transmitted to Pitt and the keepers at Newgate "a petition from the prisoners at Newgate to Lord George Gordon praying him to prevent them from being sent to Botany Bay", but the petition appears to have been a function of Gordon's dementia rather than an expression of the general will of Newgate. Watkin Tench reported that the first convicts felt apprehension at leaving their homeland but he did not say that they feared the horrors of transportation.[66] The accounts of the first convicts were so confused and fragmentary that it is obvious that they had no models to fall back upon when they described their Australian experience. Head, Carew and Defoe may have influenced later writers like Vaux and Tucker, but a sufficient explanation of similarities may be found in experiences and sentiments which convicts transported to America and Australia had in common.

In appendix I and appendix II (pages 148 and 150) schematic presentations summarize the ways in which the components discussed in this chapter were used in treatments of the criminal biography until transportation to Australia began.

* * *

William Godwin had come to maturity by the time the First Fleet set out for Australia in 1787. By that year he had abandoned religious belief; he had also become a republican. (In many ways, his shifts in intellectual position and his varying fortunes make his career similar to that of the more prominent convicts sent to Australia.) In the 1790s he published three books which set out his political theories.

One of these books, *The Adventures of Caleb Williams or Things as They Are,* was a novel, written as "a general review of the modes of domestic and unrecorded despotism by which a man becomes the destroyer of man".[67]

To his usual research in religion and politics Godwin added, as a preparation for this book, the reading of works like "God's Revenge against Murder" and he became "tremendously conversant with the *Newgate Calendar* and the *Lives of the Pirates*". He was therefore familiar with a range of literary treatments of crime and the criminal.

In Godwin's novel, Caleb Williams, of poor and humble stock, receives a sound but rudimentary education before becoming secretary to the wealthy Falkland. A precursor of the Byronic hero, Falkland is led by "the persecution of malignant destiny" to murder a "tyrannical" squire, Tyrrel. Falkland suffers paroxysms of guilt, both for the murder and for allowing others to be convicted for it. He purges his guilt by admitting it to a sympathetic court. Then he dies.

Falkland has other grounds for remorse: through his imprudent curiosity Williams discovers his master's secret. Falkland falsely accuses him of theft and Williams embarks upon a flight which leads him among a gang of thieves. He is arrested and cast into prison where he suffers from the caprice of gaolers and the villainy of his fellow captives. He is eventually exonerated but remains miserable knowing that he was in some sense responsible for Falkland's exposure and death.

Godwin's debt to the popular tradition is obvious. He was also indebted to the gothic novels for the portrait of Falkland. Like the convicts and officials who had recently settled in Australia, Godwin was heir to centuries of tradition. At the end of the eighteenth century the beaten track can be seen to split into two paths. Godwin took one path. He would be followed by Dickens, Ainsworth, Bulwer Lytton and many others. The convicts and their observers stumbled along the other path. They had no difficulty in describing their journey to the parting of the ways, but for what lay ahead there was no precedent. The mapping of the new path would produce a new literature.

2
1788-1829:
The Beginnings of Convict Literature in Australia

> The most murderous, monstrous, debased, burglarious, brutified, larcenous, felonious and pickpocketous set of scoundrels that ever trod the earth.
>
> *British Monthly*
>
> Methought I smelt the bones and heard the groans of dying patriots.
>
> John Grant (a convict)
>
> A thief's most vulnerable part is his belly.
>
> John Macarthur

Centuries of tradition taught the convicts how to describe their careers before their arrival in Australia, but they had few guidelines for their response to experience in the "Thief-Colony". The comments quoted above reflect the mixture of moral appraisal, idealism and pragmatism that came to be found in accounts of life here.

A convict society

Between the convicts and the officials placed over them there was from the outset a cleavage that was ironically bridged in the "Prologue" erroneously ascribed to George Barrington:

> Grant us your favour, put us to the test,
> To gain your smiles we'll do our very best;
> And, without dread of future turnkey Lockets,
> Thus, in an honest way, still pick your pockets.[1]

Unfortunately the two classes were not in fact so easily reconciled. All shared the hardships of the early days, but the convicts and their superiors viewed their sufferings differently. Their initial confusion over, the former adopted a defiant tone that was to degenerate into sullen acquiescence in their fate. The latter, realizing with John Macarthur (1767-1834) that there was a connection between their own prosperity and the efficient management of the convicts, came to tolerate and draw profit from their degenerate charges. *Sic fortis Etruria crevit.*

The first convict literature — writing by or about convicts — was reportage, to be found in journals, letters, documents, memoirs, and newspapers. Some of these accounts were exaggerated, imaginative, even fanciful, but they purported to be factual. Around 1830 avowedly fictional writings began to appear but from 1788 to 1830 eyewitnesses strove to describe the Australian environment, and conditions in the new society. It seems almost miraculous that this small group, scattered over a tiny portion of the eastern seaboard of a vast unexplored island, ever survived. Few societies can have had such a bleak beginning.

About one-third of the total number of convicts eventually transported to Australia arrived between 1788 and 1830. By that year there were some 72,000 Europeans living here. In New South Wales there were 46,276 white people, of whom forty per cent were convicts. In Tasmania the white population of 24,504 included 10,195 (forty-two per cent) convicts. Estimates of the extent of convict connection in these settlements vary from seventy to ninety per cent. In Western Australia there were about 1,500 persons, none of whom were supposed to be convicts. Some idea of the distribution of the sexes in the eastern colonies can be gauged from the fact that in New South Wales in 1828 there were 16,422 male, and only 1,544 female, convicts. Marriage among convicts was therefore of necessity uncommon and even among the women "marriage rates were not as high as might confidently have been expected in a population so numerically dominated by males".[2] We often hear of homosexuality, but its full extent remains unknown.[3]

In such an oddly-composed society it was to be expected that there would be a general spirit of lawlessness. Convicts and emancipists were numerically prominent among lawbreakers, but the relative number of convictions recorded in Australia declined over the years.

By 1830 settlements extended from Fort Wellington in the north to Hobart in the south; from Norfolk Island in the east to Perth in the west. As a result of exploration, some persons in New South Wales were living hundreds of kilometres from Sydney.

In addition to embryonic cities and the farming settlements there were "Cities of Repentance" at Norfolk Island (founded 1788); Coal River, or Newcastle (1801); Macquarie Harbour (1821); Moreton Bay (1822); Port Macquarie (1821); Maria Island (1825) and Port Arthur (1830).

At first the settlers and convicts were subject to a very simple mode of government: when Ralph Clark heard Governor Arthur Phillip's commission read he believed that no man had ever had such sweeping powers. The governor of New South Wales was also responsible for Van Diemen's Land from its foundation until 1825, when government, for all intents and purposes, passed into the hands of its lieutenant governor. The gradual attrition of the governor's powers and their transfer to legislative councils occasioned much bitterness and controversy in both colonies. Acrimony also surrounded the composition and powers of the law courts, which were to some extent liberalized by a Charter of Justice authorized in 1823, and by further reforms in 1828.

Governor Phillip had been instructed to prevent "every sort of intercourse" with foreign ports but it was necessary for the survival of the colony to trade with centres closer than London. For lack of a merchant class, trade was at first carried on by the marines and the members of the New South Wales Corps. By 1800 Robert Campbell was challenging this monopoly; he was followed by many other ex-convicts like Simeon Lord, Mary Reibey, James Larra, and Andrew Thompson who gained wealth, if not respectability, through commerce.

In September 1788 Phillip had urged his supporters to send out free settlers, if only to supervise the convicts. The first free settlers arrived in 1793. By 1820 the *Times* was encouraging emigration to Australia, and emigrants' manuals were being written. In 1830 the annual rate of emigration to both colonies reached 772.

Life in the colony was hazardous for all. To natural calamities like death, flood, fire and drought were added such human difficulties as economic slumps, labour shortages, a clash of interest among agriculturalists, pastoralists and traders, and a shaky monetary system.

These vicissitudes were reported by the colonial press. The *Sydney Gazette and New South Wales Advertiser* was founded in 1803 by George Howe, who had arrived as a convict in 1800. He declared that he opened "no channel to Political Discussion or Personal Animadversion: — information is our only purpose".[4] He had little choice in the matter, since his paper was subject to such a degree of censorship that John Dunmore Lang (1799-1878) believed "it was conducted as if its editor's function had been that of mastiff to his excellency".[5] Later, Wentworth's and Wardell's *Australian* (1824) and Edward Smith Hall's *Monitor* (1826) took a more independent tack. In Van Diemen's Land, the *Van Diemen's Land Gazette and General Advertiser* had a brief existence in 1814. In 1816 Andrew Bent founded the *Hobart Town Gazette and Southern Reporter*. As personal and political feuds developed in Van Diemen's Land other journals like the *Colonist* (1824), the *Austral-Asiatic Review* (1828) and the *Colonial Advocate* became involved in a complex interaction. The vigour of the press nettled

Governor Ralph Darling in New South Wales and Lieutenant-Governor George Arthur in Van Diemen's Land; when these governors attempted to impose restrictions on the press, uproar and vituperation ensued. Dr Morris Miller believed this bitterness passed into convict fiction: "Altogether his [Robert Lathrop Murray's] outpourings of venom and wrath against penal discipline in Van Diemen's Land . . . prepared the way for Marcus Clarke and succeeding novelists."[6]

Penal discipline gradually fell into a pattern. The assignment of convicts began in 1789; twelve years later Governor Philip Gidley King instituted the ticket of leave. As early as 1790 Governor Phillip had been empowered "to remit either absolutely or conditionally whole or any part of a prisoner's sentence of transportation"; the first convict to enjoy this remission was John Irving, in February 1790. Like many later emancipists, Irving elected to take the grant of land offered him. The system of assignment, ticket of leave and pardon was administered according to the whim or convictions of governors as different in personality as Lachlan Macquarie and George Arthur. Further variations in the system marched with the vagaries of magistrates, overseers and masters, so that James Tucker was one of many to lament "the execrable system of tyranny and intolerable oppression perpetrated by the convict overseers, constables, watchmen and others 'dressed in a little brief authority'".[7]

Those convicts who were not pardoned (or further sentenced to places like Macquarie Harbour) eventually came to the end of their sentence. Some expirees returned to England.[8] Those who remained in the Colony joined the emancipists in irritating their "betters" by their "profligacy of manners" and, perhaps more disconcertingly, by their commercial or professional success. The prosperity and ability of many emancipists led them to expect a social advancement that was often begrudged them. The community became so divided over the emancipist question that Lord Bathurst saw little prospect of Commissioner John Bigge's (1780-1843) being able to effect a reconciliation.

The colony experienced upheavals like the Irish Rebellion of 1804 and the deposition of Governor William Bligh in 1808. There were spectacular events like the escape of the Bryants in 1791 and the depredations of the bushranger Michael Howe (1787-1818). There was also the less striking but more tragic deterioration of relationships between the Europeans and the Aborigines.

The society which produced the early convict literature was querulous, divided and raw.

The outlook and idiom of early convict literature

At first glance it would seem that the documents[9] relating to the foundation of the new settlement revealed little either about official attitudes to the convicts or about how they were to be controlled. If the general tenor of the documents was mundane, their passage through the British Parliament was witnessed by influential men who were inspired by a great idealism. Among these were William Smith, Edward Eliot, Henry Thornton and William Wilberforce; these men were later to join with others in what came to be known as the Clapham Sect.

After a "good deal of debate" with himself, Wilberforce had gone in 1784 to ask for spiritual advice from Rev. John Newton, a leader in the evangelical revival. Under Newton's guidance Wilberforce began his struggle for the emancipation of the slaves, and for the general betterment of mankind.

Reviewing the loss of the American colonies, the *Evangelical Magazine* believed that England needed "some ... *distant region of the earth* to which we might transport the outcasts of society who had endangered the peace of their fellow citizens by their crimes, and where, secured from escape, they might, *by a life of labour,* be rendered useful to the nation they had injured and dishonoured and thus again be restored to society, *corrected and amended*".[10]

The phrases emphasized in the above quotation will be

dealt with subsequently. It is first appropriate to consider the action taken by the evangelicals to secure their objectives.

John Newton was also a foundation member of the Eclectic Society, which "was instituted early in the year 1783 by a few of the London clergy, for mutual religious intercourse and improvement and for the investigation of religious truth."[11] "The very first plan" of the Society was that of "sending a chaplain to Botany Bay". Rev. Richard Johnson (1753-1827) was selected for this post with the approval of the Archbishop of Canterbury, Sir Charles Middleton and many others. It was Wilberforce who secured Johnson's appointment, as William Pitt (1759-1806) acknowledged: "the colony of Botany Bay will be much indebted for your assistance in providing a chaplain".[12]

Wilberforce also supported the appointment of Marsden, who in turn was "allowed . . . to chuse associates in the ministry and schoolmasters of his own mind and principles".

One of Newton's close colleagues indicated that Johnson's mission was not merely to minister to the convicts:

> I trust that he [Johnson] will prove a blessing to these lost creatures! Those that stole will there steal no more; for having no receivers of stolen goods, no ale-houses etc., they will be under no temptation to steal. With what pleasure may we consider this plan of peopling that far distant region and opening other connexions with the Heathen, as a foundation for the Gospel of our God and Saviour to be preached unto them.[13]

Newton shared this aspiration: "I please myself with the hope that Port Jackson maybe the spot whence the Gospel light may hereafter spread in all directions and multitudes may rejoice in it".[14]

When in one of his sermons Samuel Marsden (1764-1838) contemplated "a new heaven and a new earth", he was thus picturing the ideal of Venn and Newton. They may have been stimulated by Emanuel Swedenborg who, in 1757, had declared that a "new age opened in the heavens and a new church began on earth that was to be the Crown of all Churches".[15] Swedenborg used the term "church" loosely, but five ex-Wesleyan preachers established the Swedenborgian New Jerusalem Church just a week before the First Fleet sailed[16] — bearing copies of Swedenborg's works.[17]

If the official documents did not express this vision, they nevertheless envisaged that there would be decorous, religious behaviour and wholesome toil in the new and remote outpost. Phillip was enjoined to use "all proper methods [to] enforce a due observance of religion and good order among the inhabitants of the new settlement, and . . . to take such steps for the due celebration of publick worship as circumstances will permit".[18] He was also to

> proceed to the cultivation of the land, distributing the convicts in such manner, and under such inspectors or overseers as may appear to you to be necessary. The assortment of tools and utensils which have been provided for the use of the convicts and other persons who are to compose the intended settlement are to be distributed according to your discretion, and according to the employment assigned to the several persons.[19]

Earlier, Lord Sydney (1733-1800) had drawn up his Heads of a Plan

> for effectually disposing of convicts, and rendering their transportation reciprocally beneficial both to themselves and to the state, by the establishment of a colony in *New South Wales a country which, by the fertility and salubrity of the climate, connected with the remoteness of its situation* (from whence it is hardly possible for persons to return without permission), seems peculiarly adapted to answer the views of Government with respect to the providing a remedy for the evils likely to result from the late alarming and numerous increase of felons in this country, and more particularly in the metropolis.[20]

In the Judaeo-Christian tradition the wilderness was invested with saving power. It was there that Hosea hoped to reform his unfaithful spouse, and it was to the deserts that the anchorites and hermits went seeking purification. The theme was, of course, often taken up in secular literature. Jean-Jacques Rousseau for example, believed that "men are devoured by our towns. In a few generations the race dies out or becomes degenerate; it needs renewal and it is always renewed from the country." Again, Fielding's formerly-dissipated Mr Wilson related that "We soon put our small fortune . . . into money, with part of which we purchased this place, whither we retired . . . from a world full of bustle, noise, hatred, envy and ingratitude to ease, quiet and love".[21]

It was in this vein that Erasmus Darwin (1731-1802) wrote his "Visit of Hope to Sydney-Cove near Botany Bay", where "JOY'S loud voice was heard from shore to shore − / Her graceful steps descending press'd the plain / And Peace and Art and Labour joined her train".[22] A similar picture was incorporated in the Great Seal of the Colony: " . . . on the reverse, a representation of convicts landing at Botany Bay, received by Industry, who, surrounded by her attributes, a bale of merchandise, a beehive, a pick axe, and a shovel, is releasing them from their fetters, and pointing to oxen ploughing, and a tower rising on the summit of a hill".[23]

The evangelicals' idealism obviously found expression in the documents and the Great Seal, but the Heads of a Plan reveals a pragmatism that became increasingly more obvious as the practicalities intruded themselves.

Captain Arthur Phillip had had first-hand experience in dealing with convicts: during his secondment to the Portugese navy (1774-78) he was given command of a ship carrying convicts to Brazil. A serious illness laid low the crew; Phillip called upon the convicts to help sail the ship, promising (and obtaining) pardons and land grants for them at the end of the voyage. His plans for regulating the new Colony are set out in a "Memo" written "soon after he received his appointment".[24]

He hoped to arrive in New South Wales some months before the transports so that he could see to the temporal welfare of the convicts, of whom he had few hopes: "The sooner the crimes and behaviour of these people are known the better, as they may be divided, and the greatest villains guarded against in one transport. The women in general, I should suppose, possess neither virtue nor honesty."

He had his own view of the destiny of the new colony:

"As I would not wish convicts to lay the foundations of an empire, I think they should remain separated from the garrison and other settlers. . . . " To this he added: "There can be no slavery in a free land, consequently no slaves."

Various reports of his first address to the convicts have come down to us. In the compilation of his *Account,* he is said to have reminded the convicts that in being transported they had received mercy and should expect no more; removed almost entirely from temptation, "they were now so placed that, by *industry* and *good behaviour* they might in time regain the advantages and estimation in society of which they had deprived themselves".

The other governors appeared to adopt the same doctrine. Lachlan Macquarie, for example, defended his administration by recalling that he " . . . used every means both by precept and example . . . to inspire a religious feeling among all classes of the community; to incite sentiments of morality and to inculcate temperance and industry". In Tasmania Lieutenant-Governor William Sorell encouraged the free settlers to "check the customary depraved habits of the convicts, and promote industry and virtue"; Arthur's efforts earned him descriptions like "a little Jesuit" and "sanctimonious poseur".

The governors were not always rewarded with the enthusiastic support of their officials. Even the co-operative Watkin Tench found supervising the convicts "peculiarly disgusting and troublesome". Phillip had hoped "that officers would, when they saw the convicts diligent say a few words of encouragement to them; and that when they saw them idle, or met them struggling in the woods they would threaten them with punishment", but he grieved to find that "they absolutely declined to interfere with the convicts in any way". The lieutenant-governor, Robert Ross, headed a faction that opposed Phillip. When, for instance, the latter reported that "there is not an individual from the Governor to the private soldier whose situation is not more eligible at this time than he had any reason to expect it could be in the course of the three years' station", Ross had earlier written that "there is not a man in this place but wishes to return home". Ross was imprudent enough to air his grievances before the convicts, and Phillip had to remind him that "those people draw their conclusions from what they hear, and perhaps very different from what the words are intended to convey". Every governor in Australia from 1788 to 1830 complained of similar opposition: John Hunter, for example, believed that he was surrounded by a group of malicious people who would not have hesitated to re-crucify Jesus Christ had he ventured among them.

In view of this dissension it is not surprising that hopes for religion and industry were somewhat thwarted in the antipodean wilderness.

An idea of the tenor of the religious principles inculcated by the evangelical clergy can be gained by an examination of Richard Johnson's *Address*[25] to the growing population of New South Wales. The *Address* is divided into two sections. In the first, Johnson noted that comparatively few persons had been converted in the Colony, despite the fact that death awaited all, when the unrepentant would be damned. He reiterated his doctrinal position: scripture contains the totality of revelation, which teaches that man is a fallen being (the Colony, he remarked, provided concrete evidence of this truth). Jesus Christ offers hope to fallen men and conversion to Him can be attained only through the Spirit.

The second part (which appears to lean heavily on the Catechism) dealt with practical applications of religion: man's obligation to show forth faith and works, among which Johnson enumerated reading the Bible, observing the sabbath, and prayer. All should avoid swearing, adultery, theft, villainy and idleness. Everyone should be diligent and industrious in his lawful calling, and submissive to superiors. The *Address* ended with a fervent plea to readers to reform their ways.

Phillip appears to have been indifferent to Johnson; Francis Grose denounced him as "a very troublesome discontented character", yet many convicts recorded their gratitude to him. Johnson became depressed and Newton had to encourage him with the thought that "now like Lot, you are grieved with the madness and wickedness of the ungodly".

Two other early clergymen, Henry Fulton (1761-1840) and William Cowper (1778-1858), the former a convict, appear to have been generally esteemed, but their confrères, Marsden, Knopwood and Bedford, had, at best, an ambiguous reputation. Marsden, "The Flogging Parson", a sheep-breeder, a magistrate and a zealous missionary, remains a puzzle. Rev. Robert Knopwood was undoubtedly amiable, but a fellow clergyman noted that "of his [Knopwoods's] success in their [convicts'] reformation nothing is recorded". William Bedford had been an ordinary of Newgate. He was hated by the convicts and the free settlers, one of the latter denouncing him as "a pompous ass, with well-cased ribs — fasting not being one of the virtues on which he laid stress — and speaking with a slight lisp as if his mouth were full of hot pudding". It is only fair to remark that the Anglican clergy battled against tremendous odds: many officials were indifferent; most convicts were hostile; there was little to show for their work and since in 1830 there were only fifteen Anglican priests on the whole continent, their difficulties must have appeared insuperable to them.

The first Roman Catholic clergymen to come to the colony arrived as convicts. Macquarie was later to attribute the early Irish disturbances to "the machinations of a couple of unprincipied Catholic Priests". Phillip Conolly and Joseph Therry, who arrived in 1820, were the first Catholic priests to exercise an uninterrupted ministry.

The Presbyterian minister, John Dunmore Lang, arrived in 1822. He believed that "it seemed as if some spirit of darkness had obtained the patent of Colonial Adviser-General in the first settlement of convicts, and had, in order to prevent if possible, the reformation of its depraved inhabitants, cast poison into every spring, for in order to neutralize the moral and religious influence of the colonial chaplain, he was generally made a magistrate".[26]

If the achievements of the clergy within the colony are open to some dispute, it is equally difficult to determine how much success attended attempts to evangelize the Pacific, but one missioner remarked that "the very name of missionary stunk at Sydney".[27]

If perfection could not always be discerned in the convicts' masters spiritual, their masters temporal appear to have fallen even shorter of the mark. King (on Norfolk Island), Collins and Davey (in Van Diemen's Land) lived openly with mistresses. Their loneliness and anxiety may make this "irregularity" understandable to us now; possibly some of the convicts were prepared to overlook it. But the habitual ruthlessness and greed of many officials no doubt taught the convicts to despise religious ideals and good conduct. Joseph Holt could not excuse the weaknesses of his superiors: "But what morals, or good conduct, can be expected from the lower orders, when their Governor sets them an example of profligacy?"[28]

Far from being the intended centre of Christianity in the Pacific, the Colony was frequently denounced as a hotbed of vice: "Immorality and vice of every kind, yea, all manner of sin and abominations prevailed in this colony — fornication and adultery — the two latter of which so prevail and is [sic] practised to such a degree at present as not be equalled, I think in any country whatever".[29]

The other objectives envisaged (wholesome toil and reformation to be achieved in the wilderness) also proved difficult to realize. Industry became something of a shibboleth. In the absence of a clergyman, one overseer fell into biblical cadences in his weekly "homily" to the convicts:

> Now my men listen to me. I want you all to get on. I was once a poor man like you, but I used to work perseveringly, and do things diligently and as such got taken notice of until I became a captain of the 46th. Now, I want you to work perseveringly; do things diligently, and that will make you comfortable, and I will assist you,

that you may have houses for yourselves and rise up to be equal to me.[30]

Many convicts described their progress in terms of industry. James Lacey wrote that "the convicts . . . who chuse to apply themselves to Industry are much better off than the labouring people in England".[31]

Bartholomew Reardon suffered from floods and "Bandityes" but he was "determing it shall not dwo away with my industerry".[32] The term could also be used to explain recidivism: "Ye labourer not being able to live by industry he resorts to his former type of life and plunders the honest settler".[33]

It will be recalled that Lord Sydney had hoped that transportation would benefit both the state and the convicts. Men bent on profit like John Macarthur soon perceived that convict labour speeded the acquisition of wealth. Possibly (it is hoped) with tongue in cheek he observed that "When men are engaged in rural occupation their days are chiefly spent in solitude — they have more time for reflection and self-examination — they are less tempted to the perpetration of crimes, than when herded together in towns amidst a mass of disorders and vices".[34]

Colonel Arthur believed that it was not the wealthy owner of a large estate who would reform the convicts: "the most likely masters to succeed [are] such as having few [convict servants] are daily over them and witnesses of every part of their conduct and . . . keep them in their proper place".[35]

The marriage between the convicts' labour and their masters' acquisition of wealth was officially blessed by the Select Committee on Transportation (1812): "They [the Committee] feel that its [the Colony's] improvement in wealth and the means of properly employing and reforming the convicts are essential to the progress of each other".[36]

Labour was also seen as a punitive measure: the convicts at Macquarie Harbour were to engage in "constant, active, unremitting employment — in very hard labour: even if only "opening cavities and filling them up again".³⁷ Darling was even more explicit:

> 1. As an aversion to honest Industry and Labour has been the Chief Cause of most of the Convicts incurring the penalty of the Law, they shall be employed at some species of Labour of a uniform kind which they cannot evade, and by which they will have an opportunity of becoming habituated to regular employment.
>
> 2. . . . The use of the Hoe and the Spade shall be as much as possible adopted, and when the Number of Men who can be employed in Agriculture is sufficient to raise Food for the Settlement with these Implements, the use of the Plough shall be given up and no Working Cattle are to be employed in operations which can be effected by Men and Hand Carts.³⁸

The pragmatism that tempered the idealism surrounding the foundation of the colony can be seen to have become more and more pronounced. The irony and tragedy inherent in these blighted dreams did not escape the convicts. The first writings about the colonies, however, did not come from their pen, but from those who wrote despatches and journals.

Early writings about the convicts

The great English diarists, John Evelyn (1670-1706) and Samuel Pepys (1633-1703), died long before the establishment of New South Wales. As their diaries were not published until the second decade of the nineteenth century, it is highly unlikely that their existence was known to the early journal writers. They may have been acquainted with the *Memoirs* (1734) of Sir John Reresby and the *Turkish Letters* (1763); they would certainly have known of the journals of men like Behrens, Bougainville and Hawkesworth, which were popular and profitable: "Naval men . . . were well aware that specimens and drawings of 'non-descript' products of natural history sent back home to scientists and collectors with influence in the official circles often led to preferment and advancement".³⁹ Prominent among these patrons was Sir Joseph Banks, with whom the early governors and some officers corresponded. Precedent and such patronage determined the subject-matter of the early Australian journals: natural history, indigenous peoples and nautical observations.

Eighteenth-century interest in indigenous peoples can be gauged by the popularity of John O'Keefe's pantomime, *Omai: Or a Trip Round the World* which was repeatedly performed between 1785 and 1788. The European career of Omai, a native of Huahine, provoked a great deal of discussion about the concept of the "noble savage". The Australian Aborigine was at first invested with this status; but the early art of the colony shows that he was soon strippped of this glory.

The early Australian journals[40] tend to concentrate on common points of interest. For example, there are descriptions of the ports entered on the way to Australia, of the attempted mutinies on the *Scarborough* and the *Alexander* and La Perouse's sudden appearance shortly after the First Fleet arrived. These similarities can be explained partly because "the transactions . . . were penned as they occurred"[41] and also because, once arrived, the officers became part of a very isolated community where memories could be endlessly rehearsed and "even a litter of pigs was a subject of conversation and enquiry".[42]

The journals contain for the most part descriptions of the natural phenomena of the new colony and of the appearance, habits and vocabulary of the Aborigines. The acts of the governor and the early privations were, of course, also described. Individual convicts did not receive extensive treatment. Like later officials such as Therry and Fyans, the journal writers carefully avoided recounting the lives of the convicts in the traditional formula; instead they focused on the crime committed, providing only an outline of the criminal's background. For example, Collins, Tench, Hunter, Bradley and White all record James Daley's fraudulent claim to have found a deposit of gold, and Collins, Tench, White and Easty describe the execution of John Bennett — "young as he was . . . an old offender".[43]

More frequently we find the convicts as a group described in bleak terms. For example, Surgeon Arthur Bowes tells us that on the night the first female convicts landed "the scene of debauchery and riot that ensued . . . may be better conceived than expressed".

David Collins (1756-1810) complained that it had often been his task "to show the predilection for immorality, perseverance in dissipation and inveterate propensity to vice which prevailed" among the convicts. He shought in vain for some general explanation of this predilection, attributing it sometimes to alcohol and at other times to gambling.

Fortunately, there were some favourable accounts of the convicts. Tench displayed compassion and tolerance for them: "For the last time I repeat that the behaviour of all classes of these people since our arrival in the settlement has been better than could, I think, have been expected from them".

If James Tuckey (1776–1876) in his account of the abortive settlement at Port Phillip could not record the same happy observations, he nevertheless showed some of Tench's compassion.[44] Rev. Robert Knopwood's diaries provide an artless and, at times, eccentric background to the early days on the Derwent.[45]

The journals were generally well received in England; Collins's *Account* was pronounced the best[46] and Tench's *Narrative* was seen to atone for the "vague and trifling accounts in the newspapers".[47]

The first news from Australia arrived in England on 25 March 1789, and the official despatches were published in the newspapers. When the scandal of the Second Fleet became known, all the relevant despatches were again published. The newspapers also carried some private letters that had been sent from the colony. For example, an officer on board the *Scarborough* wrote that a convict had been drowned, noted that seamen were implicated in the attempted mutinies and that "the more rational part" of the convicts were convinced "that on their arrival at Botany Bay by industry and attention they [would] enjoy all the requisites reasonable beings [could] desire". Some convicts were said to have been removed from "wicked companions" and the "seducing opportunities in London". On the other hand Daniel Southwell's (1764?-1797) letters reveal the progressive disenchantment felt by those with whom he aligned himself: "Men of estimable and weighty judgment fail not to say that the scheme seems to hold out no other than prospects of long continued heavy expense to the m'r country . . . indeed this is here so generally the opinion that it may be called a universal one".[48]

Meanwhile, events like the French Revolution and wars in Europe occupied the newspapers, and a condition of "apathy as to the state of the colony descended on English public opinion, which was only partially lifted by the news of the deposition of Governor Bligh in 1808, and prevailed until the 1812 Committee recalled England once more to a realization of her responsibilities".[49]

* * *

While the English press may have been preoccupied with affairs on the Continent, news from the Colony continued to arrive and to evoke responses from sections of the populace.

There is no way of knowing what news of the colony was brought back by seamen. Some of the officers painted a very gloomy picture: Major Grose found it necessary to silence John White and Ralph Clark who were "infamously" representing the Colony, and David Collins lamented that his countrymen had "a disposition too prevalent for regarding it [the Colony] with odium and disgust".

In official circles the Colony was periodically assessed. A Select Committee on Finance and Police and Convict Establishments (1798) was gratified that criminals had been removed, but wondered whether, with increasing prosperity in the Colony, the terrors of transportation were not being attenuated. It has already been seen that the Select Committee of 1812 declared that a prosperous Colony afforded the best "means of employing and reforming convicts". In 1819 a Select Committee on the State of the Gaols and a Select Committee on Criminal Laws provided some indirect guidance for Commissioner John Bigge, who was about to begin his investigations in the Colony. The Select Committee on Criminal Laws (1819) recommended that the number of capital felonies be lessened and that the laws relating to forgery be simplified.

As for transportation, the Committee found that "by enforcing discipline, labour, abstinence, solitude, restraint and decorum, the system could answer every purpose of terror and reformation".[50]

News from the colony inspired Jeremy Bentham to write his *Pantopicon versus New South Wales* (1802) and *A Plea for Constitution* (1803). Writers of more imaginative works were also aroused. It was the fate of "the illustrious triumvirate", Thomas Muir (1769-99), Thomas Fysshe Palmer (1747-1802) and Maurice Margarot (1745-1815), which drew Coleridge's attention to the penal settlement:

> Men cannot starve: they must either pick their countrymen's pockets — or cut the throats of their fellow creatures because they are Jacobins . . . if the former they are hung [sic] or transported to Botany Bay. And here we cannot but admire the deep and comprehensive Views of Ministries, who, having starved the wretch into Vice, send him to the barren shores of New Holland to be starved back again into virtue.
>
> It must surely charm the eye of humanity to behold Men reclaimed from stealing by being banished to a Coast, where there is nothing to steal, and helpless Women, who had been
> "Bold from despair and prostitutes for Bread",
> find motives to Reformation in the source of their Depravity, refined by Ignorance and famine-bitten into Chastity.[51]

Despite the indignation expressed in this passage, Coleridge (1772-1834) at this time supported Pantisocracy. "The leading Idea of Pantisocracy", he wrote, "is to make men necessarily virtuous by removing all Motives to Evil – all possible Temptations." The saving power of the wilderness, where temptations would be removed, is expressed in "The Dungeon":

> With other ministrations thou, O Nature!
> Healest thy wandering and distempered child:
> Thou pourest on him they soft influences
> Thy sunny hues, fair forms, and breathings sweet,
> Thy melodies of wood, and winds and water,
> Till he relent; and can no more endure
> To be a jarring and dissonant thing,
> Amid the general dance and minstrelsy;
> But, bursting into tears, wins back his way,
> His angry spirit heal'd and harmoniz'd
> By the benignant touch of Love and Beauty.[52]

Coleridge's close collaborator of this period, Robert Southey (1774-1843), explored the same theme in his "Botany Bay Eclogues" (1795).[53] The first of the four sections of this poem is "Elinor". Elinor had spurned the counsels of her father's "virtuous bosom" to become "the slave of Vice and Infamy". She was therefore transported to

> The drear scene
> The marshy plain, the brier entangled wood
> ... where for lowing herds
> And for the music of the bleating flocks
> Alone is heard the kangaroos [sic] sad note
> Deepening in the distance.

Nevertheless, she finds comfort that

> On these wild shores the saving hand of Grace
> Will probe my secret soul, and cleanse its wound,
> And fit the fateful penitent for heaven.

In the second part, Humphrey and William exchange the stories of their misfortunes. Humphrey's domestic bliss had been shattered when he shot some of his master's animals which were feeding on Humphrey's crops; William's decline was caused by boon companions acquired during service in the army; he tells how they

> Kissed me, coax'd me, robb'd me and betray'd me
> Tried and condemned me.

And now,

> His Majesty transports me,
> And here, in peace, I thank him, he supports me.

In the third part, John, formerly a sailor, and Richard, formerly a soldier, tell their stories to Samuel, who is to decide which of the narratives has the greater merit. The honours appear to be evenly divided, but it is John who has the last word:

> But all's for the best . . . on the world's wide
> sea cast,
> I am haven'd at peace in this corner at last.

The hero of the fourth part, Frederick, is not immediately so acquiescent. We find him lost in the woods and brooding:

> the world
> Had wrong'd me first: I had endured the ills
> of hard injustice . . .
> Blasted were all my morning hopes of youth
> Dark disappointment followed on my way.

However, he hears a shot fired to guide him home; his spirits revive:

> O strengthen me
> Eternal One, in this serener state!
> Cleanse thou mine heart so Penitence and Faith
> Shall heal my soul, and my last days be peace.

The "Eclogues" are ponderous but they are nevertheless significant. The stories of the various convicts conform to the traditional formula — that was to be expected — but Southey anticipated some elements that were to recur in Australian convict literature. Elinor, for example, becomes the prototype in convict literature of the wronged woman who fights against her fate.[54] Frederick shows some of that fire which was to figure so prominently in the early convict reminiscences. If the setting of the poem is artificial, Southey is no more to blame than the eyewitnesses who also found it difficult to capture their new environment.[55] Again, he cannot be called to account for investing the wilderness with a fatuous regenerative power: as we have seen, many others entertained the same hopes.

There are numerous passing references to the colony to be found in the works of other writers. Hazlitt (1788-1830), for example, alluded disparagingly to "Botany Bay theatricals". Later in life Sir Walter Scott (1771-1832), having helped a friend to emigrate to Australia, was embarrassed and perplexed when he received in return the gift of "a couple of Emusses"; however when he reflected on the penal system in 1788, all that occurred to him was imprisonment in England or execution.[56]

Charles Lamb's (1775-1834) correspondence with Barron Field (1786-1846), judge in the Supreme Court of New South Wales, gave rise to the former's essay "Distant Corresponents":

> I cannot imagine to myself wherabout you are . . . Sometimes you seem to be in the *Hades of thieves* . . . What must you be willing at this time to give for the sight of an honest man! You must almost have forgotten how *we* look. And tell me, what is it your Sydneyites do? Are they thxxx all day long? We hear the most improbable tales at this distance . . . Is there much difference to see between the son of a thxxf and the grandson? or where does the taint stop?[57]

The banter (some might say smugness) of Lamb's essay does not accord with the realities of the life of the Sydneyites.

The outlook of the convicts

To read through documents like the "Alphabetical Record Books of Convicts arriving in Australia" is a depressing experience. There is something very disturbing in reading an entry, the writer and its subject being dead for more than 150 years, which describes how a convict, shortly after his arrival in Tasmania, was found attempting to have intercourse with a sow: he was given 100 lashes across the breech and shipped off to Macqarie Harbour. There is pathos in the crude rebellion of the convict who hid her mistress's laundry rather than wash it, and in that of the convict who threw stones at the church door during Divine Service. One is reminded that if hundreds of thousands of people endure hardships, the sufferings of one man or woman are sufficient material for tragedy.

It is necessary continually to call to mind that the average convict experience was not, objectively speaking, horrific.

About eighty per cent of the Australian convicts were sentenced for some kind of larceny; between half and two-thirds of convicts transported to the eastern states had been previously convicted. The largest single group of convicts was that comprising urban thieves, and much of the rural crime was committed by "migrant depredators".[58]

There was also a small group of dissident spirits: the Scottish Martyrs (1794); Naval Mutineers (1797); the Agricultural Rioters (1830); the Tolpuddle Martyrs (1834); the Canadian Rebels (1839) and the Chartists (1842). In all, there were few more than 1000 in this category.

The Irish provided convicts in both of the above classes and in another: that of the "village hampdens". In 1792 the first Irish convicts were transported in the wake of political troubles.[59] They came to be described as "fond of Riot, Drunkenness and Cabals" and as a "deluded and infatuated people". It seems to be generally agreed, however, that Irish convict ships "contained a higher proportion of people not dependent on crime for a living than did similar ships from England and Scotland".[60] Nevertheless, even if "more Irish male convicts conformed to the 'Village Hampden' theory than did prisoners of other nationalities"[61] there is every reason to believe that they were not more readily submissive to their English (and Protestant) supervisors in Australia, than were the professional criminals.

Bearing in mind the composition of the convict population, it becomes immediately obvious that few concepts could have appealed less to the majority of them than religion, good behaviour and industry in the primitive antipodes. A British report puts the matter succinctly: predatory crime proceeds "from a disposition to acquire property with a less degree of labour than ordinary industry".[62]

It is not that the convicts were inactive: they were seen to be very busy, but after their own fashion. Tench found that one convict, Frazer, "had passed through innumerable scenes in life; he had turned thief in fifty different shapes; was a receiver of stolen goods; a soldier, and a traveller".[63]

Collins observed feverish activity among the convicts in general: "It required something more than common application to adapt remedies to the various irregularities which from time to time grew up in the settlement, and something more than common ingenuity to counteract the artifices of those whose meditations were hourly directed to schemes of evasion and depredation."

Various convicts expressed an awareness of some power which seemed to compel them. Major J. G. Semple spoke of his "usual busy fate" and George Barrington complained: "With the best of hearts and dispositions there is, God knows, an overbearing fate that counteracts our best designs and makes us act (that is pickpockets) in spite of ourselves".[64]

James Hardy Vaux (b. 1782) several times adverted to the same compulsion: "Surely there must, let moralists argue as they will, be something like a fatality which governs the fortunes of some, if not all men; and which impels them headlong to their ruin, against the voice of reason and conscience and the dictates of common sense".[65]

In 1826 George Farquharson, on being condemned to death, is reported to have repined that "by some means a cloud had long hung over him which to his sorrow he could never extricate himself from".[66]

Australian convicts were not singular in believing that criminals were driven by some compulsion. William Baldwin had made Jack Cade say:

> There is no trust in rebelles raskall knaves,
> In Fortune Lesse, which wurketh as the waves:

> From whose assautes who lyst to stand at large
> Must foloue skyll and flye all worldly charge.

And Meriton Latroon had admitted that he "could never indure Idleness, I was ever in action; either writing or contriving, or putting in execution my contrivances". In 1818 Scott wrote that the hapless Captain Porteous was thought to be fey: "a Scottish expression, meaning the state of those who are driven on to their impending fate by the strong impulse of some irresistible necessity".[67]

While most convicts were probably unable to formulate exactly what presided over their fortunes, there was sufficient unanimity among them to prompt Dr James Ross, one of Arthur's associates, to say: "It can scarcely be doubted that the main body of convicts are under mental delirium – they see and appreciate everything through a false medium".[68]

We find an anlysis of this "medium" in the works of Edward Gibbon Wakefield (1796-1862) who was imprisoned in Newgate from 1826 to 1829. He spoke with the prisoners and read widely about Australia. He expressed his reflections on his researches in two works: *A Letter from Sydney*, first published in eleven parts in the *Morning Chronicle* in 1829 and *The Punishment of Death in the Metropolis*.[69]

In the latter, after asserting that "a thief is hardly ever – I am tempted to say never – reformed", Wakefield explained:

> Thieves generally, almost without exception, believe everything to depend on calculations of chance. In the thieves' language, the word most frequently used is "chance". Every thief utters the word many times every day. Next to the active business of robbery, and before enjoying its fruits, the most important concern of their lives is the calculation of probabilities; and in this pursuit they show such a degree of acuteness and arrive at such just conclusions, as would be surprising, if one did not consider the excitement of their minds, and their deep interest in avoiding mistakes. They are practical philosophers, convinced, though they might be at a loss to explain their view of the subject, that every event has a cause, and that a sufficient knowledge of particular causes, and of the general operation of causes would enable men to foretell events. Now the calculation of the chances of impunity just mentioned, is strongly impressed on the

mind of every thief — the more sanguine, indeed somewhat enlarging the period, whilst others make the average a little shorter.

Taking the shortest period of perfect immunity to be two years, or the general impression among thieves to be, that it is two years, and bearing in mind the enticement of a thief's life, it will appear that in London the trade of thieving may be properly compared to a game of hazard, in which, as said before, *the player always wins until he loses all.*

One might be inclined to dismiss Wakefield's thesis, were there not evidence to corroborate it. Wordsworth's observation of criminal activities in France led him to conclude that the malefactor, "having indulged a habit, dangerous in a man who has fallen, of dallying with moral calculation, becomes an empiric and a daring and unfeeling empiric. He disguises from himself his own malignity by assuming the character of a speculator in morals, and one who has the hardihood to realize his speculations".[70]

In Australia, Surgeon-Superintendent Peter Cunningham's (1789-1864) association with the convicts led him to the same conclusion:

> The life of a thief is indeed *calculated,* like the success of a new play, and such a one is said to have a *good* or a *bad run,* according to the length of time he has been able to evade the penalties of transportation or the gallows. You will often hear old acquaintances when they meet during fresh debarkments from England, on inquiring how Bill or Tom such-a-one fares, and hearing that he is still "a-going at it" exclaim in surprise "What a lucky dog! what a *good run* he has had!"[71]

Ten years later Major Thomas Wright (Commandant of Norfolk Island, 1827-1828) testified: "The rule among them [convicts] is never to throw a chance away; that is the prisoners' creed; he considers a man a fool and a flat who throws a chance away".[72]

Wakefield believed that the prisoners in Newgate found their philosophy validated not only by their own exploits but also by the gamble of sentence and commutation and the uncertainty surrounding these operations of the law.

In Australia, the convicts' fate was frequently described as a "lottery", in which the capricious nature of assignment and the whims of magistrates, masters and overseers multiplied the odds. When the *good run* finished, some convicts showed the true gambler's equanimity in losing: "Seeing the die is cast with them, and it is only by adhering to those who have power they can hope to improve their condition, they adopt at last the hackneyed motto 'Honesty is the best policy'."[73]

It is obvious that the professional criminals' view of their situation had very little in common with any of the official intentions for convict management. Moreover, ignorance and superstition were added to the empirical philosophy just outlined. Tench remarked upon the convicts' "love of the marvellous" and found them "particularly happy in fertility of invention and exaggerated descriptions". Collins frequently records examples of uninformed rumour-mongering and superstitious credulity.

It would be wrong to represent all convicts as "empirics" or as superstitious dupes, but despite the many acts of treachery they perpetrated against each other, they were seen to possess a uniform character and solidarity. Collins tells us that the "First Fleeters" remained a separate entity and he relates that a special order had to be given forbidding convicts assembling in numbers "under any pretence of making complaint". Common sufferings and privations would thus have been one source of solidarity.

There can be no doubt that some convicts at least were also bound together in the compact of the criminal societies outlined in chapter 1. Tench asserted that "indulgence in . . . infatuating cant is more deeply associated with depravity and continuance in vice, than is generally supposed" and from time to time we read of ceremonials and oaths.[74]

In convicts' accounts of their experiences, little of the outlook discussed appears. There are two explanations for this. First, letters were supposed to be subject to inspection[75] and second, as we have seen, the whole tradition of writing about crime demanded that it be overtly edifying. Moreover, many convicts were illiterate, so that they relied upon an amanuensis who could be playful,[76] but more usually he seems to have adhered to the expected edifying norm. Thus, when a party of convicts absconded in 1798, they sent a note to the Governor "pretending to have their eyes opened to the danger with which attempts at desertion from the colony must ever be attended, and promising to convince the minds of their ignorant countrymen that every such attempt must be followed by inevitable ruin".[77]

The journalist David Collins observes that "the language of this letter was far above the capacity of any of the party".

The few extant convict letters of the early days of the colony follow no pattern. A female convict lamented her fate in her "solitary waste of creation" where the huts were miserable, "the savages do all the injury they can", and where there was "much dissatisfaction among the officers". She reported that the women were distressed "beyond description" by the deprivation of tea and "other things they [had been] indulged in by the seamen".[78] A male convict had more pleasant news: through "rendering [himself] useful to the Captain" he had been given a good character; he was working as a "Master Taylor", his clientele including the Governor and "all the Gentlemen". He reported that other convicts were not so fortunate: they were "obliged to work from sunrise to sunset, excepting the interval of rest from eleven o'clock till two in the afternoon". Goods of every description were scarce and prices were high. This convict had no doubt that he would return to England.[79]

Besides those who expressed similar reactions, there was in the First Fleet a group of mutineers from the American transports the *Mercury* and the *Swift*. In fact, the immediate cause of the despatch of quite a large number of the first fleeters lay in their participation in this mutiny.[80] To this rebelliousness was added, towards the end of 1791, a "spirit of resistance and villainy lately imported by the new comers from England and Ireland".[81]

Whether a more thorough-going assessment of the convicts' situation is attributable to these men we cannot say; the fact is that in the 1790s there appeared a viewpoint and a vocabulary that were to characterize many convicts' accounts throughout the transportation period. One of the first examples of this response is provided by Private John Easty who at the time of writing the following passage had been associating with convicts on Norfolk Island, which he described as a

> Pore Mersable Place and all maners of Creuelties an *opresion* uesed by the Governor *flogging* and beeting the people to Death that it is better for the pore unhappy Creatures to be hang'd. Allmost then to come under the Command of such Tyrant and the Govner behavs more like a mad man then a man *in trusted with the Gorvment of an Iland . . Belonging to Great Britain.*[82]

"Opresion", "flogging" and "Tyrant", and the irony of sufferings inflicted by officials of Great Britain are recurring parts of the early convict frame of reference. The artist Thomas Watling (b. 1762) complained that *"Oppression and mean souled despotism* are so glaring and frequent as to banish every hope of generosity and urbanity from such as I am — for unless we can flatter and cajole the vices and follies of superiors with the most abominable servility nothing is to be expected".[83]

George Thompson, a gunner of the *Royal Admiral,* distinguished himself on the passage to Australia by his "unremitt'd attention to the health and comfort of the unhappy men under his care". He spent three months in Sydney, associating freely with one of the Scottish Martyrs, Thomas Fysshe Palmer. Thompson found the colony to be a "land of slavery" where the convicts suffered from "the Heat of the Sun, the short allowance of provision and the ill treatment they receive from a set of merciless wretches (most of them of their description) who are their superintendents, [so that] their lives are rendered truly miserable".[84] Another witness, Robert Murray, recorded that "Of the State of the Colony at this [1794] I need only repeat what I have before said, with the addition that I now thought . . . that Tyranny Oppression and Fraud had arrived at their Meridian in Port

Jackson under the auspices of the Officers of the New South Wales Corps".[85]

The provenance of this outlook may have been prison gossip and the political catchcries of the day. John Howard, for example, was possibly reflecting prison talk when he described "loading prisoners with heavy irons" as "tyranny",[86] and Watling compared the "wanton cruelty practised on board the English hulks, on poor wretches without the least colour of justice" to sufferings in the "*French Bastille*". Thomas Paine (1737-1809) saw the storming of the Bastille as a matter of "freedom or slavery", oaths as "the remains of tyranny on one part, and slavery on the other", and asserted that his mission was "to extirpate the horrid practice of war, and break the chains of slavery and oppression".[87]

The French *Declaration of the Rights of Man and of the Citizen* (1789) and the American *Bill of Rights* (1791)[88] gave constitutional form to the aspirations of Paine and many other idealists. Article 13 of the Bill of Rights proclaims "Neither slavery nor involuntary servitude, except as a punishment for crime whereof the party shall have been duly convicted shall exist within the United States, or any place subject to their jurisdiction". The Scottish Martyrs, Muir, Palmer, Skirving, Margarot and Gerrald (sentenced 1793-94) were among those who were certain that they had not been duly convicted. These Scots also form part of an intelligent and articulate group of convicts who were active in the colony between 1795 and 1810. This class included, among others, Sir Henry Browne Hayes (sentenced 1801), Michael Massey Robinson (1796) and John Grant (1803). The extent to which they formulated the convicts' wrongs cannot be fully determined, but there is abundant evidence that they were regarded as subversive elements. For example, King complained of "the Seditious Language [Hayes] and his coadjutors have lately attempted to disseminate among the convicts"[89] and a group of officials empanelled by the Governor found that "the three Persons [Robinson, Hayes and Margarot] their conduct having on various occasions been highly reprehensible it would conduce to the peace and happiness of this part of the colony to send them to such different parts of the colony as His Excellency may direct".[90]

Robinson (1744-1826) made his public contribution to Australian literature by writing a series of pedestrian birthday odes; privately, he wrote some of those pipes (short poems) which satirized and threatened the leadership of the early colony.[91]

An idea of the way the educated convicts expressed their lot can be gained from the writings of John Grant.[92] Born in 1776, he was sentenced in 1803 to transportation for life for shooting a solicitor who thwarted his love affair. Grant was at first disturbed by the "abandoned sett" that surrounded him; he came to be even more upset by the state of the colony, which he found to be "a devilish Country for Parties". Major George Johnston (1764-1823), one of the numerous powerful officials to whom Grant had an introduction, warned him to "talk little and be extremely careful and shy of forming acquaintances in a place where so few merit an honest man's confidence". Grant saw himself as the "wretched Sport of a Capricious Fate", and his acquaintance with Sir Henry Browne Hayes (1762-1832) and Maurice Margarot was certainly fateful. Grant was to deny that he was led by them, but it is only after this friendship began that we find him adopting the terms and viewpoints already discussed: "The idea of Emancipation itself is an atrocious bug-bear, because men arriv'd at their destination when banished are under the influence of the Grand Magna Carta of England . . . this Noble Charter is here violated. Men are sent forcibly to the Hoe under pain of dreadful flagellation and made slaves of." In this letter we find some additional terms: "banishment" which with "exile" came to be a euphemism to denote transportation; and the "hoe" to which Darling ascribed such salutary qualities, and which Grant continued to denounce. This implement also became the subject of a ballad:

> Despised, rejected and oppressed in tattered rags I'm clad.
> What anguish fills my aching breast and almost drives me mad,
> When I hear the settler's threatening voice say, "Arise, to labour go,
> Take scourging, convicts, for your choice or work the labouring hoe."

Grant became embroiled in the misfortunes of many of the convicts. He spurned his chances of advancement as he sought to redress his own and others' injustices by abusive letters and conduct; he went so far as to accost the Governor at a levee, and later, when imprisoned, Grant denounced an act of injustice from the prison walls. He was transported to Norfolk Island, flogged, and then set apart on Isle Phillip where he continued to write his journal — and for some time on banana leaves.

At times Grant echoes the sentiments of those around him. At others, he was highly individual in his response: writing to King, he informed him that when he reflected on "the massacre of prisoners in March 1804", "Methought I smelt the bones and heard the groans of dying patriots and at your [King's] door lies all the blood spilt in struggles of half-starved men for personal liberty in this country". In tears for the afflictions of Hayes and Margarot, he framed his "Bond of Union": "*Whereas* a system of government predominates in New South Wales and its Dependencies, having Slavery for its basis, Tyranny for its actions. . . . " However, his was virtually a lone voice; his "friends" were too discreet to act so openly. Grant's health collapsed; he was returned to the mainland where he acted from some time as unordained chaplain at Newcastle. He was granted an absolute pardon and left for England in 1811.

Grant's papers were lost for almost one hundred and fifty years, so that it cannot be claimed that he had an influence on the direction of convict literature. His chief value lies in the evidence he provides of the type of sentiments entertained by some of the convicts in the second decade of the Colony's existence. He also provides us with some evidence that gives an idea of the texture of early life: he records the recapture of Charles Boyle, who takes up the story:

> They ordered me to go before them, pointing their Bayonets at me, but when we came to the Brickfields . . . I tried to run away: they follow-d me — I turn'd round upon them, I seized and wrested the Musquet from one, and tripp'd up the other's heels, and shd have got away with their Arms, but the Man on the ground got my little finger in his Teeth, and with his hands squeezed my private parts so hard, that others coming to assist him, they took me.

In addition Grant has left some birthday odes and other poems:

> I plead this rising Nation's prayer:
> Let Juries here establish'd be,
> And Equal Rights that all feel free:
> To extinguish Dissention's fire
> Great Prince, within each breast inspire
> Just Principles, in Bond of Union tye
> With Collins — Paterson, Foveaux, with Johnston — Bligh.

In her paper, "Mine is a Sad yet true Story: Convict Narratives 1818-1850",[95] Anne Conlon suggests that similarities in the accounts of three convicts who never met can be explained by their common use of a fourth text. The similarity may also be attributable to the work of a literary hack, but there was another common source: the oral tradition:

> It is the old resident, he who still calls Sydney with its population of twelve thousand bustling inhabitants *the camp,* that can appreciate [improvements]; he who still recollects the few earth-huts and solitary tents scattered through the forest brush surrounding Sydney Cove . . .
> You may hear people even now, in gossiping over old adventures, relate their tales of shooting parrots to make pies of . . . or of losing themselves in the thick brush . . . while the *veteran convict* will point out to the *rogue of yesterday* the tree, still green and flourishing near the house of the naval officer, dedicated in older times to the office of a triangle, under whose boughs many thousands of lashes have been inflicted on well-deserving backs.
> Or if the newcomer peevishly whimpers about the blusterings of *Humpy Dick,* or the bullyings of *Terrible Billy,* the other will console him by relating the pranks of *Dandy* ——, who would walk out behind the hoers in his morning-gown and morocco slippers, with a *Penang Lawyer* hugged close under his right arm, or borne

like a royal sceptre before him ... drumming such a tatoo upon the shoulders of the woeful wight whose ground was not completely chopped and grass fairly uprooted, as made the whole brush dance with fire-flies before him.[94]

The oral tradition also contained stories of celebrated incidents:

> The prisoners, who wage war with society, regarded [the capture of the *Cyprus* in 1829] with exultation; and long after a song, composed by a sympathising poet, was propagated by oral tradition, and sung in chorus around the fires in the interior. This version of the story made the capture a triumph of the oppressed over their oppressors. The stanzas set forth the sufferings of the prisoners from the cruelty of the masters they vainly attempted to please. It related their flight from torture to the woods, and drew but a dreary picture of the life of an outlaw. It passed through the details of conviction and embarkation, and then described the dashing seamanship of the pirates in managing the brig, once destined to carry them to that place of suffering; but which bore "bold Captain Swallow" to the wide ocean and liberty. Such was the song; but the facts were different.[95]

As we have seen, rumours also figured in the tradition. Tench relates that some of the convicts absconded because "they were made to believe [they knew not how]" that they would reach China. Again, there is much evidence that the convicts' conversation was frequently about crime.[96]

Variants of all these stories were carried back to England by absconders and expirees, some of whom fell into their former ways and became active instigators of crime.[97] Some of these were caught again, and propagated their stories in prison, where convicts awaiting transportation learned what might await them.[98]

Ultimately, the tradition came to contain a number of components that exerted a grisly fascination:

> "Pebbles" — a rank which implies something of chivalry and something of devoteeism in the thoroughgoing felon-character, inasmuch as they only attain it who have evinced the boldness to brave every restraint and the endurance to bear every penalty which the law can inflict on persons in their position. To incur in succession the long list of punishments known in that peculiar code termed "convict

law" argues no inconsiderable amount of ingenuity and daring in that youthful felon who ultimately attains his object.[99]

It can be perceived that the oral tradition and much of the early written tradition afford a very bleak picture of the early convict experience, and it will be seen in subsequent sections that this picture continued to be represented.

However, life for the convicts was not uniformly bad: there were among the transported some at least who fared well, and came to be grateful for their sentence.

James Grove was one of these more fortunate convicts. He was transported for life in 1802 for forgery. In the two following years he wrote forty-five letters that were eventually published.[100] This correspondence reveals that he underwent a conversion in prison. However we also learn that some gaolers had "hearts callous to every feeling of humanity", while clergymen, too, could cause endless trouble to an unco-operative prisoner. While awaiting transportation, Grove formed an acquaintance with "a prisoner that came here about ten days ago for stealing a bed quilt and who has been to the Bay [who also] furnished me with every particular about the country". Grove heard conflicting reports about the "Bay": "In a greater sense, a greater good could not have befallen me — speaking according to probability"; however, later he heard that "the Bay is a most wicked abandoned place". When he finally sailed (after reading as much as he could about the colony) Grove was transported with the small party that was to settle first at Port Phillip and later, on the Derwent. He was allowed to take his wife and child with him, and he quickly earned the esteem of Knopwood and Collins, the latter believing Grove to be a "very ingenious, useful and well behaved man".[101]

Grove was "astonished to see what a set of poor, cowardly, mean-spirited wretches [there was] on board", but he appears to have had little to do with them. Indeed, he experienced a rapid advancement once he arrived in the new colony, and he was grateful: "Yet my good, my merciful, my gracious God has made this thorny bed a bed of roses — this bitter cup the sweetest draught I ever took in my life." He provides us with an insight into the exaggeration that crept into the oral tradition: "The Irish croppies [in 1804] demanded their liberty, and about three hundred were killed in resisting lawful authority." Grove died shortly after David Collins in 1810.

Another example of a more fortunate convict experience is to be found in a set of papers in the Lancashire Records Office. The set comprises the correspondence of Thomas Holden or Holding (1812-16) and that of two step-brothers, Richard Taylor and Simon Brown (1840-59).[102]

The Holden correspondence contains letters from Holden to his relatives and their replies. Holden must have been unable to write, for his letters are written in a variety of scripts and idiom:

> I Cannot say that I go of in good Spirrits on account of Leaving my Native Country on this false Charge that as been Laid against me.
> [8 June 1812]

> I take this opportunity by the ship *Alexander* with pleasure to inform you that Mr Allan as procured a promise from the Governor of Emancipation for me . . . which renders me a free man of this Colony . . . and do expect to leave Mr Allan in hopes of getting into some more lucrative employment. [30 May 1815]

Holden's letters are simple: they reflect his confusion on being sentenced and confined in prison and the hulks. Apparently he was robbed twice, so that he frequently assured his relatives that he was avoiding association with his fellow prisoners.

His relatives' letters refer to some of Holden's correspondence that has been lost. They were amazed at his tale of a snake, and alarmed that he had written about absconding: "Dear son make yourself Content in your situation as well as you can and behave yourself." Holden apparently heeded their advice.

The step-brothers Richard Taylor and Simon Brown were quickly separated, the former being sent to Sydney and the latter to Hobart. Taylor died without meeting or corresponding with his brother, though Brown tried to seek him out, and he corresponded with Taylor's widow. Both sons wrote home regularly for several years, then a lengthy break ensued. Their father was obliged to lodge an official inquiry about their whereabouts, and this apparently spurred them to begin writing again.

The letters are full of sentiments of reformation:

> Dear farther i wish i had taken your Advice I Should not have been placed in this unhapy Situation but i hope god as done it for the best if i had kept from bad Company i should not been placed in this unhappy Situation. [14 April 1840]

> I must live for a better world for my part I his Determined to Leed a godley Life and you must Let my Father Brothers and Sisters and all my Relation to shun bad Company. [22 April 1840]

Taylor became a cook at Sydney Hospital and waxed fat. He gave a generally glowing account of the colony, and was pleased to report:

> It is expected that very shortly something very handsome will be done for the unfortunate prisoners, next year the Colony will have a House of Assembly of its own & then it will be impossible to keep Englishmen in slavery. [12 September 1841]

In 1845 he assured his parents that through sobriety and diligence he would do everything in his power to return home, for he could never be happy away from them. In 1850 he wrote his first letter for five years, informing them that he would not return, that he had been married six years, and that he now had three children: "this is the land of plenty and perpetual summer". Five years later he was dead, leaving his widow in difficult circumstances.

Simon Brown was moved to quote verse on his departure:

> The distant shores of England striked from sight
> and all shores seems sad that once was pure and Bright
> But now a convict dooms me for a time
> to suffer hardships in a forien clime
> farewell a long farewell to the my own my Native Land
> and would to god that i was free upon they strugling strand.
> [31 May 1841]

This mournful tone immediately disappeared once he reached Van Diemen's Land, for thereafter he has nothing to report but his prosperity, though he writes:

> Before I was married I was just as wild as I was used to be at home. I had a good deal of money but I wasted it all follishly but now it is the reverse for I am Saving all I can to Get a place of my own and it will not be long first for my wife is very Steady industrial woman.
> [2 February 1846]

It was possible, therefore, as the correspondence shows, to depict convict life without including details of suffering and degradation. Nevertheless, even in these more optimistic accounts it will have been obvious that overtones of the more lurid tales make themselves heard. The more successful convicts tended to adopt the official idiom,[103] but they were clearly aware of the more usual frame of reference that has been outlined in this subsection.

This frame of reference was expressed in a formula which contained recurring components.

There were some experiences which virtually all convicts underwent. With the exception of some of the Irish who may have been transported without trial, all convicts were charged, tried and either received the sentence of transportation or the death sentence, which was later commuted.[104]

Like their predecessors, convicts bound for Australia usually found prison a "hell"; for the wealthier prisoners, however, detention could be reasonably agreeable. Some prisoners, like Barrington, complained of their peremptory removal from the prison to the hulks, where life was generally described as miserable. Conditions on the voyage to Australia varied. The horrors of the Second Fleet were denounced for the scandal they were, but White and numerous other witnesses marvelled that their own passage had been so smooth and healthy. Conditions on the convict ships showed a continuing improvement.

Mention has already been made of the abortive mutinies on the *Scarborough* and the *Alexander*. Throughout the transportation era mutinies, or rumours of mutinies, continued to be reported: "perhaps no vessel ever crossed the line without some plot rumoured or real".[105] Mutiny thus became part of the oral tradition.

Conduct on the female ships was frequently "irregular". John Nicol relates that "when we were fairly out at sea, every man on board took a wife from among the convicts, they nothing loath".[106]

This selection of helpmeets was not without its touch of romance: "I had fixed my fancy upon her [Sarah Whitelam] from the moment I knocked the rivet out of her irons upon my anvil".

The well-to-do, or well-connected convicts could enjoy a pleasant passage, but most convicts and officials were pleased when their journey was over.

Upon arrival the prisoners were inspected, their details were recorded, and they were invited to voice any complaints. Their conduct was noted and the governor usually addressed them. Then, depending on the period, the convict might be assigned or reserved for government labour. The hazards of assignment have already been noted. The amount of labour expected of a convict depended on the prevailing conditions and the Governor's regulations.

Those convicts who were industrious and submissive could look forward to a ticket of leave, which entitled them to seek their own employment in a restricted district, and thereafter, a conditional pardon, which conferred freedom in the Colony, or an absolute pardon which allowed them to return home. Most convicts were pardoned before their sentence elapsed.

The refractory convict exposed himself to a range of punishments. Uppermost among these in the popular imagination was flogging. Brutality cannot be condoned, but it is well to remember that corporal punishment was liberally applied in the armed services at the time transportation began, and that whipping was very common in the schools; indeed as late as 1842, we hear of children being beaten in factories.

We are told that Ralph Clark had women flogged until they fainted, that Lieutenant-Colonel Joseph Foveaux laughed when men under the lash screamed for mercy, and that magistrates at Parramatta ordered successive floggings to obtain confessions. Corporal punishment was not legally administered without a magistrate's sentence, but these sentences were not hard to arrange when the plaintiff was the magistrate's friend, or even the magistrate himself. A perusal of the records shows that severe flogging was not universal but that at the same time it was not rare.

If the lash failed, there were always the penal settlements where "the worst class of Convicts are to be sent . . . [there] the legitimate terrors which originally attached to a state of transportation cannot fail to revive and to resume their powers of checking inroads of crime".[107]

In the period 1788–1830 these settlements were Norfolk Island, Moreton Bay, Maria Island and Macquarie Harbour, which West "associated exclusively with the remembrance of inexpressible depravity, degradation and woe". Some of the commandants of these outposts have passed into history as monsters.

Other punishments included the shaving of women's heads, the pillory and the spreadeagle, and of course, gaol, where on one occasion there was "a Prisoner perfectly mad, chained to a Wall" and where, some prisoners were sentenced to a year in solitary confinement on bread and water.

Some convicts died on the gallows, where the scene could be exactly as it had been in England:

> One of the unhappy men [Lynch] seemed sensibly afflicted at his situation; and with a fervor suited to his circumstances attended to the exhortation of the Minister [Marsden] and acknowledged himself guilty of the offence he was about to expiate.
>
> Tracey on the contrary assumed an air of sullen hardihood, denied his being accessory to the fact of which he was convicted, and reproached the penitent whose deportment was contrasted with his own.
>
> [Lynch] hoped his melancholy fate would operate on the minds of others as a caution against falling into similar vices . . . He was

interrupted by his unrelenting companion who harshly desired him not to satisfy the spectators.[108]

George Howe knew how to employ the language of the calendars and the broadsheets: "[Charles Crump] having recently entangled himself with infamous company, lost sight of his duty, and ultimately fell a victim to the gratification of licentious appetites".

Even the most jaded of the Seven Dials hacks could not have failed to be impressed by the cannibal, Alexander Pearce's last dying speech, which Rev. Mr Connolly had to deliver "to prevent any embarrassment".

Many convicts were innocent of this reticence: West tells us that they were "anxious to commit to writing their own last confession of guilt to secure a posthumous interest in the terror or pity of mankind". In exasperation one convict dismissed a clergyman who refused to write down the last dying speech.

Two further components remain to be dealt with: relations with the Aborigines and absconding. The convicts were usually at loggerheads with the Aborigines, possibly because the natives were believed by the convicts to be even lower than themselves.[109] Some Aborigines like Musquito and Black Jack became the unfortunate accomplices of the absconder.

William Buckley, John Graham and David Bracefell[110] were three convicts who lived for lengthy periods with their "sable companions", who, it is said, at times believed the white men to be reincarnations of deceased relatives.

The tendency to abscond was displayed as soon as the first convicts arrived. As we have seen, the tradition quickly sprang up that they could get to China or to some other civilized area. At times a sea escape was made, the most famous being that of the Bryants in 1792.[111]

Some absconders became outlaws. Bushranging was known, if not by name, as early as 1791. Its origin was attributed at times to the Irish, since "gang disorder was too regular a feature of Irish life"[112] and at other times to the degree of freedom allowed the convicts in the early days of the colonies. Bushranging was also no doubt a protest against the sufferings which many endured. Many bushrangers received widespread support; some were not without "those equivocal virtues which are compatible with a life of violence and guilt",[113] and others displayed a grim sense of humour. Nevertheless it should not be forgotten that they *did* rob, murder and rape and that they could be as brutal as their former overseers: "they [bushrangers] half hang them [Aborigines], cut their heads with Clubs in a Shocking Manner, or flog them unmercifully with cats made of Kangaroo Sinews."[114] The periphery of the convict experience was marked out with grim boundary stones, which came to be described much more frequently than the less obtrusive and more average phenomena within the confines.

The traditional English formula suggested this dreary focus, and this influence was strengthened by the hardships inseparable from founding a new penal colony. The formula also supplied a model for the description of the convict's career before transportation; in addition, it furnished the precedent that the criminal should express regret for his misdemeanours and hope that others would take warning from his plight.

The Australian convict narrative was thus a blend of the English formula, the convict's frame of reference, and lip service to the official intention of reformation. The convict — or the hack — was at first surest in the description of life before transportation; colonial experience tended to be contained in a glib coda. In subsequent sections it will be seen that the experience before transportation becomes increasingly reduced to a short preamble, while the coda expands as writers become more accustomed to dealing with life in Australia. Ultimately the concluding moral lesson will either be discarded or transmuted into a new statement of values.

While a number of the accounts written between 1788 and

1829 merit scant attention, there are a few which require closer observation.

Writings of some early convicts

It is difficult to explain the fascination that George Barrington exerted on the imagination of eighteenth- and nineteenth-century writers. The first chap-book about him appeared in 1777 and there has been what can only be described as an astounding number of publications about him since then.[115] Barrington's contribution to works attributed to him is obscure. His *Voyage to Botany Bay* is written from the official viewpoint: he is represented as being aloof from the convicts, and in tone and observations his work smacks more of the journals than of the Australian convict biographies. Nevertheless his was the first account to use the traditional formula, and given the widespread dissemination of books about him, his influence is likely to have been considerable.

To James Hardy Vaux[116] must be attributed the honour of being the first to flesh out the convict experience. Barron Field believed that Vaux's perception was tainted:

> The religion, indeed, (if it can be so called) of Mr Vaux is, like that of most convicts, a low sort of fatalism, which may be called *a fatalism after the fact*. The followers of this sect do not connect predestination with "foreknowledge absolute", but merely comfort themselves with the truism, that when their *misfortunes* have happened, nothing can prevent them having happened.[117]

In addition to this outlook, Vaux had an eighteenth-century literary sensibility that was mediated through a rogue's mind. The prose rhythms, literary allusions and ironic tone of his work substantiate his claim to have read widely. The *Memoirs* have much in common with Head's *Meriton Latroon,* but whereas the latter was frequently coarse, and the hero's conduct promiscuous, Vaux is never coarse and he asserts that he never indulged in complete debauchery. His work is at its best when he deals with the subterfuges and vicissitudes of a London thief. His portrait of colonial life is notable for its vignettes, rather than for a sustained account. Indeed, the texture of Australian experience is frequently almost indistinguishable from the English:

> By degrees, however, I began to degenerate. I increased my acquaintance among the Commissary's and some other clerks, most of whom lived an expensive and dissipated life. All that I can say in my own favour, is that I continued to be regular in my attendance at the office, and was never found defective, or incapable of my duty; but no sooner was I at my own disposal than I eagerly sought my dissipated companions, and spent the rest of the day in drinking, and other irregularities, sometimes at public or disorderly houses, and frequently at my own.

Dickens found Vaux "unwholesome". H. M. Green called him "a smug and sanctimonious hypocrite", but the convict came closer to achieving an imaginative synthesis of life in the colony than had any of his predecessors.

Thomas Wells's life of Michael Howe is the precursor of many lives of bushrangers. In this account we find a sustained ferocity coupled with a certain galmour suffused by shades of the tragic, which characterize so many of the biographies of these tormented and lawless men.

It will be noted that when the convict experience was taken up by the writers of chap-books and broadsheets a standardized formula quickly developed; it is this formula which served as the basis for many subsequent works.

There are some examples of other types of convict writings that must be referred to. Thomas Watling, one of the first artists to arrive in the Colony, possessed the skill and the inclination to describe the new environment, something which other convicts had neglected for lack of that skill. His descriptions express an eighteenth-century artistic sensibility:

> Perhaps nothing can surpass the circumambient windings, and romantic banks of a narrow arm of the sea, that leads from this to Parramatta . . . The poet may here descry numberless beauties; nor can there be fitter haunts for his imagination. The Elysian scenery

of a Telemachus, arcadian shades, or ecstatic bowers, present themselves at every winding to the ravished eye.[118]

Two ex-convicts left general accounts of the colony: Daniel Mann[119] and Edward Eagar.[120] The former's work is said to have influenced later writers.[121] Eagar was an ardent supporter of the emancipist cause and he took some pains to demonstrate that convicts *had* been reformed:

> Here the reformation that has taken place among the convicts, transported to New South Wales, appears both in its nature and degree: of 17,000 persons transported in thirty years, nearly 5,500 have died; 3,300 are still convicts; 1,700 are so far reformed as to have obtained the first degree of reward and indulgence, and 6,067 have become heads of families, householders, and proprietors of landed and other property. [They] have upwards of nine thousand children, who are in the course of being educated in industrial habits. Whatever the private morals or failings of these people may be, they have been politically, and as far as human laws are concerned, morally reformed.

Reformation, then, for Eagar took place in the moralist's "external forum". The means to this end were the isolation of the convict from his confederates, and employment in domestic or agricultural labours so that he could acquire "habits of useful industry". The convicts' fate may have been gratifying, and the way to it salutary, but transportation

> is in itself certainly the most severe punishment, next to death, that can be inflicted. It is banishment from family, home, friends. [A man] has to undergo a six months voyage over boisterous seas ... during which he is subjected to every privation consistent with the preservation of life, to strict control and summary punishment in chains and irons.
> On his arrival in the colony he is put to hard labour; placed under the most rigid controul [sic], subjected to summary punishment, flogging, working in irons, solitary confinement for every instance of disobedience, idleness or neglect.

Eagar, the successful ex-convict, could not forget the familiar formulation of woes.

Henry Savery was still a convict when he adopted the pseudonym of Simon Stukely to write a series of essays known as *The Hermit in Van Diemen's Land*.[122] Reportedly based on the model of Felix Macdonough's *The Hermit in London or Sketches of English Manners* (1821), these essays appeared in the Hobart *Colonial Times* in 1829. One of them attracted a libel suit. *The Hermit* contains a series of vignettes, some lively, others dull. Essay no. 26 is noteworthy in that it is one of the first Australian pictures of a retired serviceman now "devoted to pastoral pursuits". He "counts his flocks and his herds by the thousands" and reproduces in Tasmania the decorum, hospitality and domestic economy that was idealized as the lot of the country squire.

We hear of a less opulent master discussing a military magistrate:

> "What I likes 'em [military magistrates] for is," said the countryman, "they be so used to hear talk about and see the poor fellows as gets the four or five hundred lashes, they don't think nothing of giving a man five and twenty — so I always knows how to manage my servants, for if they don't please me, or if they be surly to my wife when she's got a drop or so, I have only to take 'em to the office and it don't seem nothing to give them a couple of dozen or so, 'tis only a taste like."

The satire is heavy, but the point is nevertheless made. The literary essay, which requires fine perception, restraint and a fastidiousness in style, was rarely employed by the convicts, who preferred to daub with glaring colours.

Few examples of another genre, the ballad, can be traced with certainty to the period 1788-1830; nevertheless there appears to be little doubt that variations of treason songs and parodies of popular ballads provided some solace to the convicts as they meditated upon the conduct of their superiors.

The most general convict response to life during the first forty years of the existence of the penal Colony was to complain about its severity. Many observers believed, however, that transportation had been shorn of its terrors, and some convicts awaiting transportation entertained the same notion:

> Whilst the judge most solemnly exhorts the criminal to prepare for

an hereafter, his [the convict's] mind is perhaps employed in contemplating a voyage of pleasure. It is only the other day that an offender, on being sentenced to transportation, thanked the judge with an appearance of sincerity for sending him to a much better country than this.[123]

However, under Governor Arthur in Tasmania and Governor Darling in New South Wales, the life of the convict was becoming increasingly subject to scrutiny and control. The exuberance and resilience of a James Hardy Vaux gradually disappeared from convict writing, as it probably did from convict life.

The period 1788-1830 provided a literary model, a vocabulary and an oral tradition that would enable later convicts to describe the sombre details of their lives.

3
1830-68: The End of Transportation; The Beginning of Fiction

> Merrily, Merrily do we live now,
> Jolly Bush-rangers here, under the Bough.
> T. C. Moncrieff, *Van Diemen's Land* (1830)

Between 1830 and 1868 Australian society underwent a transformation. Social institutions continued to be moulded around the control and reformation of British convicts, who arrived in greater numbers. However, the influx of free settlers also increased, and as the Colony prospered its citizens turned their attention to gaining political autonomy. Transportation came to be seen as an obstacle to attaining this objective, yet some colonists were loath to forgo their supply of cheap labour. The convict was thus viewed simultaneously as a profligate, a political impediment and a hierodule in the temple of gain. He continued to see himself as a slave enchained by tyrants.

In one guise or another he still preoccupied officials, observers and the community at large. The first province of the convict in literature is thus accounts of the development and state of the colonies.

Personal narratives about the experience of transportation were still being written: broadsheets, chap-books and more substantial accounts were based upon the formula discussed in the first two chapters of this study. In addition, some of the more educated convicts used their autobiographies to launch a polemic against the penal system.

The first Australian works of fiction appeared at a time when there was a change of emphasis in the graphic arts:

> Before 1821 the main occupation of artists in Australia had been to portray the curiosities of nature, the life of the Aborigines and the progress of the small settlements. But a new range of subjects became increasingly popular. Colonials on horseback hunting the emu and kangaroo, bivouacking around an evening campfire, or attacked by Aborigines or bushrangers: these were the themes which came to symbolize the adventurous colonial life and to attract migrants to the country.[1]

Convicts were the subject of relatively few paintings and engravings, but they dominated the early works of fiction, for which the public were as ready as they were for the new focus in art.

In England and France, there was an upsurge of interest in writings about criminals, whose minds Hugo, Ainsworth, Bulwer Lytton and Dickens began to probe. These novelists strove to explore more fully the components of the traditional formula. Writers of Australian convict fiction showed an awareness both of the formula and of its new development. They were also conscious of the taming of the wilderness, so that the convict story became more and more bound up with the story of the settlement of the land.

While this story has been invested with great significance by later writers, at the time expansion was caused by the needs of primary industry and of an increasing population. Approximately three-fifths of convicts sent to Australia arrived after 1830. To this influx was added increasing numbers of free settlers and, after 1851, droves of gold-diggers.

It will be obvious that, with the increase of free immigrants and the end of transportation, the proportion of convicts in the community dwindled considerably. Whereas in 1830 convicts made up forty per cent of the population of New South Wales, they formed only three per cent of it in 1847. In Van Diemen's Land the proportion slipped from forty-two per cent in 1830 to thirty-eight per cent in 1848 and three per cent in 1861. In Western Australia, where transportation continued until 1868, convicts obviously made up a great proportion of the population of 24,300.[2]

If at first glance it appears that in the period 1830-68 the convict element was swamped, Professor Russel Ward has argued that an alignment of interests among the native-born, convict and emancipist populations preserved the social impact of convictism in the Australian community and that this combined group tended to form a numerically significant part of the population.[3]

It is obviously true that a sense of common purpose and interest will unite various groups, particularly if they are faced with an identifiable opposition. This solidarity is well illustrated by an event in penal history which took place outside Australia: during the American War of Independence there were, in the prison ship *Jersey* in New York and in various prisons in England, between ten and thirty thousand American seamen. These men came from a wide variety of backgrounds. United by the fervour of new patriotism, they saw themselves oppressed by England in general and their gaolers in particular. This group of men "governed themselves in accord with abstract notions of liberty, justice and right" so that

> the prisoners articulated a collectivist ethical code. Their government was egalitarian and in their culture and conduct they showed a high degree of awareness of themselves as a group and a loyalty to that group. There is a distinctive flavour about this egalitarianism seeming to set the seamen's values apart from the individualism and hierarchism of the leaders of the revolution.[4]

The experience of the American seamen would thus seem to demonstrate that Ward's hypothesis is feasible. However, it is appropriate to recall that the American prisoners were geographically concentrated, animated by a common revolutionary fervour, and confronted by a visible opposition during a limited period. It is problematical whether for any length of time the same loyalty to an ethos could be maintained by a faction-ridden population scattered over the Australian continent.

The problem of what became of the Australian convicts and their putative ethos is most important for the study of Australian convict fiction for the simple reason that a work of fiction must have a conclusion – the conflicts in the work must be resolved, or declared to be beyond resolution. To see whether fictional conclusions correspond with historical reality, the latter must first be examined in outline.

In real life the tale of each individual was played out against the background of developments in the colonies: immigration; the rise of the squatters; emancipation; responsible government; penal reform; and the abolition of transportation.

The social background of convict literature

The need for immigrants was explained with single-minded simplicity by Dr Turnbull: "The Colony is poor because it cannot export and it cannot export because it cannot produce cheaply and it cannot produce cheaply because labour is dear and labour is dear because it is scarce – therefore a supply of efficient labour will enrich the Colony and make it prosperous."[5] Unfortunately, while enlightened immigrants like Mr Micawber struck out for the bush, the less enlightened tended to stay in the city, so that it was the convicts and former convicts who served the Micawbers. Dr Lang drew comfort from importing "superior Scotch mechanics" who displaced "drunken ticket-of-leave men or emancipated convicts",[6] forcing them into exile in the bush.

Survival in the bush, and prospering there, required prodigious acts of will. Those powerful enough to carve out distant holdings became known as squatters, who had emerged as a class by 1846, when the Waste Lands Occupation Act was passed. While accounts of benign squatters are not unknown, the majority are depicted as using "slave labour" and "the lash" to carve out their "princely domains".

The squatters were not the only group to attract opporbrium. They were joined by the emancipists, at least in this respect. As a class, Dr Lang believed, they tended "if possible to dispossess the whole convict population of all sense of criminality and degradation".[7] In 1836 Attorney-General Plunkett refused to "risk the administration of justice" in the hands of an emancipist jury.

The taint of convictism was also seen as an impediment to self-government: "Your colony is a penal settlement . . . administered on the principle of a gaol . . . in a place in which the first care of government must be the security and coercion of prisoners [who cannot] enjoy the full liberty of Englishmen".[8]

While the distant colony grappled with the problems of the convicts, the Mother Country was reviewing the lot of the prisoners in its own gaols. There were rapid reforms: in the period 1818-32 public decapitation after execution and public floggings were abolished; the criminal's corpse was delivered from the dissector's hands (doubtless to the joy of the resurrectionists) and the number of capital offences was reduced. Concurrently there was a transformation of the penal system.

In fact it was in the conduct of the prisons that change was most visible. Millbank Prison had been established in 1821. Here prisoners were kept in separate cells for the first part of their sentence and set to work with their fellows during the second half. George Holford wrote lyrically of the benefits of this system.[9] He tells the story of the young man who, while blessed with good parents, allowed himself to be seduced by bad companions. He stole, was caught during his first offence, and resolving to reform was thrown into the hulks in 1815. His resolutions were sorely tested by the coining, obscenity and blasphemy that flourished

> Where Vice unblushing tells her grossest tale
> And images obscene are made for sale.

He was transferred to Millbank, where reformation could be far more easily achieved (Holford believed) through reflection and friendship with the Chaplain:

> Here every action is by rule defin'd;
> To each its proper time and place assign'd,
> Oft sounds the prison bell, and as it rings,
> Its brazen voice a known commandment brings;
> By rule our several duties we fulfil,
> Now throw the shuttle, and now turn the mill,
> Now, march'd in pairs, the beaten circle trace
> Around the gravell'd courts, with measur'd pace.

The reality appears to have been somewhat different.

In 1835 William Crawford filled the newly-created position of Inspector of English Prisons. He visited the Eastern Penitentiary in Pennsylvania, where the separate system (complete cellular isolation) prevailed; he also saw the silent system in operation at Auburn Penitentiary, New York, where prisoners were separated at night and worked together by day. The result of his inspection and the triumph of theories of the day led to the construction of Pentonville Prison in 1840. It received its first inmates in 1842.

Prisoners were subjected to a detailed set of regulations which fell into the following general pattern:

(i) The prison was for convicts between eighteen and thirty-five years of age who received sentences of transportation for fifteen years or less.

(ii) Eighteen months were to be spent in secular and religious instruction. The prisoners were to be given sufficient "privacy" to allow them to reflect. After this time they were to be transported.

Ernest Teagarden has tabulated the improvements which this system is supposed to have effected in the first thousand prisoners to experience it. Whatever else was achieved, the prisoners definitely improved their ability to read, write and count.[10]

In 1844 *Blackwood's Magazine* severely criticized the new scheme; it will be seen later that Dickens and Reade were also hostile to it. One contemporary complained that the prison "took all the starch out of the prisoners' characters and rendered both their wits and their wills limp and flabby".[11]

Mayhew felt that the Pentonvillians suffered from "mental and moral anaesthesia" and believed that lunacy among them was increased tenfold.[12] He also believed that the "reformation" of many prisoners was sheer hypocrisy. Roger Therry (1863) was struck by the "abstracted and eccentric habits"[13] of the Pentonvillians who came to Australia. It is difficult to account for the unfavourable opinion held by reliable witnesses when Teagarden asserts that the records do not substantiate the charge that the silent system engendered more madness than could be expected in the prison sample of population.

By 1845 fifty-four prisons had been built on the new lines. Conditions were not always elysian. Chatham Prison became notorious: even the deliberate self-amputation of an arm was insufficient to deliver a prisoner from a severe flogging. The crank (so vividly described by Reade), the treadmill and the systematic handling of a heavy shot were part of hard labour. Dickens, who is usually held to have been humane, remarked

> And to such useless work I plainly say, I desire to set that determined thief, swindler, or vagrant *for his punishment.* I have not the least hesitation in avowing that it is a satisfaction to me to see that determined thief, swindler, or vagrant, sweating profusely at the treadmill or the crank, and extremely galled to know that he is doing nothing all the time but undergoing punishment.[14]

Prisons are thus children of their times, and when the horrors of the Australian system are recalled, it is appropriate to remember that they were not confined to this country.

In 1858 the hulks were demolished; after 1865 prisoners were no longer employed as warders. In 1868 transportation to Australia ceased, and six years later Britain ended transportation completely by sending no more prisoners to Gibraltar.

Before transportation to Australia ceased, the system was examined and modified.

In 1847-48 one such examination was conducted by a committee chaired by Sir William Molesworth. He was assisted by men of the calibre of Lord John Russell, Sir George Grey, Sir Robert Peel and John Buller. Groups such as the Australian Patriotic Committee and the Petition Committee had lobbyists who appeared before the Committee. To their voices was added the testimony of noted colonists like John Dunmore Lang, James Macarthur and William Ullathorne.

The findings of the Committee are set out in what is usually called the Molesworth Report.

The Commissioners found that material conditions on the hulks and the convict ships had improved, but that coarseness of manner and conservation still prevailed. They also discovered that the convicts conversed "much of their crimes" and entertained high hopes for their careers in the colony. There was some disagreement about the reason for this sanguine outlook. James Macarthur and William Ullathorne both agreed that the Australian convicts sent home glowing accounts of the colony, but John Ward, a Newgate official, disagreed: "The letters which are sent home do not really produce much effect; they do not come in sufficient numbers, I mean, to influence the people in general".

Nevertheless, a Newgate prisoner, Thomas Dexter, testified that his brethren did not fear transportation. The fact is that prisoners had knowledge of the colony: those convicts who wrote uncensored letters home, and returned expirees and absconders, no doubt recounted their exploits with bravado. Probably tales of horror were also told, but as we have seen, there was always the hope that there would be a "good run". Ullathorne also testified that the convicts' conversation contained the inversions that were typical of cant.

The Committee learned that once the convicts had arrived in the colony, the majority were assigned. Considering the lot of master and servant (which even Arthur described as a master-slave relationship) as being one in which the only constant characteristic was caprice, Molesworth and his colleagues could find little to applaud or even condone in assignment. The report and other contemporary records demonstrate that summary convictions and punishments, favouritism in the distribution of assignees, stinting of clothing and rations, and the overbearing, callous attitude of some masters were among the hazards that convicts were likely to encounter.

Even before the publication of the Molesworth Report, Sir John Franklin was instructed to suspend assignment in Van Diemen's Land, and it was stopped in 1841 in New South Wales, whither, for the time being, the last convict ship had come in 1840.

The Committee found that the road-parties (comprising those who had no discernible talents and those returned by disgruntled masters) were demoralized, vicious and criminal. The misery of some of these men was increased by their obligation to work in irons, a punishment said by Arthur to be "as severe a one as could be inflicted on man". The torments of the day over, these convicts were locked up in "caravans or boxes" far too small to contain them.

The convicts were said to be subject to overseers "a great many of (whom) were men who cannot succeed in other occupations", and to constables who exerted "the most tyrannical discipline that can be imagined".

Refractory female convicts were sent to a female factory where they could undergo punishments like solitary confinement, picking wool, breaking stones and laundering. It was widely believed, nevertheless, that discipline was light in this kind of institution, which was held to be "in reality a lying-in hospital".

Males who were not amenable to the rigour described above could be sent to agricultural settlements like Wellington Valley or Emu Plains, or to one of the penal settlements. In the period 1830-68 the chief of these were Norfolk Island and Port Arthur (Point Puer was always dedicated to the reclamation of juvenile offenders). Although it has been suggested that "the convict dossiers are not full enough to test the truth of the horrifying pictures painted of" Norfolk Island,[15] almost every witness throughout this period confirmed Molesworth's opinion that life in the penal settlement was "one of unmitigated wretchedness".

The more fortunate convicts were found to gain tickets of leave and then afterwards, conditional or absolute pardons. Some freed convicts became wealthy (very suspiciously according to Dr Lang) but most ex-convicts were thought to "retain the habits of profligacy which led them into crime and became still more worthless and dissipated". The committee had "no doubt . . . of the moral corruption of the free by the criminal proportion of the community" and believed that continued transportation would corrupt the children of emigrants.

The committee recommended that transportation to New South Wales and the settled parts of Tasmania be discontinued: henceforth penal settlements were to be isolated from the community.

In 1842 the Probation System was introduced. It was to include five stages: "1st Detention at Norfolk Island; 2ndly the Probationary Gang; 3rdly the Probation Passes; 4thly Tickets of Leave; and 5thly Pardons".[16]

The need for economy underlay this system, which was meant to be characterized by "invigorating hope and salutary dread" at every stage. Instead, it was dogged by misfortune. It was implemented in the middle of the depression of the 1840s; Van Diemen's Land was swamped by a new wave of convicts who could not be employed when their entitlement came; and it was to be organized by Sir John Eardley-Wilmot, who (whatever his other accomplishments) was unequal to the formidable administrative task. "The worst effects of sensuality were the most alarming feature of this system, but even they were probably only more flagrant because the extent of transportation gave them wider range".[17] With the new system in dissaray, transportation was suspended for two years until a solution could be devised.

Plans to found a new penal settlement in the far north were tentatively drawn up and then discarded. In 1847 Grey announced a new scheme: initially prisoners would be closely confined in England in Pentonville. After employment on public works they would be "exiled" with conditional pardons. The exiles had a mixed reception, as the colonies were divided over the anti-transportation debates. The last convict ship bound for the eastern states departed in 1852 and in 1853 the order-in-council constituting Van Diemen's Land a penal colony was revoked; Norfolk Island was abandoned as a penal colony in 1856.

Financial problems and the lack of labour led the settlers in Western Australia to request the transportation of convicts to that colony. The first of these arrived in 1850. Apart from a grim period (1866-67) under Governor Hampton, transportation in the west appears to have benefited convicts and colonists alike. Though in 1863 a Royal Commission recommended the continuation of the system, it had run its course. New penal policies in England were in consonance with anti-transportation sentiments in the colonies. The last convict ship left England late in 1867. In 1868, the year public executions were abolished in England, the last transported convict arrived in Australia. The last convict on the roll had been sentenced to fourteen years at a court martial. We are told that he was born in 1845, that he was Presbyterian and literate. The date of his death has not been determined.

In the eastern states transportation, as we have seen, had ceased earlier, despite the clamour of conflicting interests. When the *Hashemy* arrived in Melbourne in 1849 with a band of "exiles", a tumult prevented their disembarkation. Sent on to Sydney, they were greeted by a large and excitable crowd. One cannot help wondering what the exiles thought of schemes for their reformation.

When gold was discovered many people remarked that it was ridiculous to transport convicts to the diggings when others had to pay their own way. Some colonists were threatening secession if transportation continued. A new government in England bowed to the pressure, and transportation to the eastern states ended in 1853.

John West saw the struggle against transportation as a purifying experience: "The strenuous resistance to transportation had cleansed the character of the colonists, and proved that the feelings harmonised with the universal and unchangeable convictions of mankind. The first news of this great discovery was accompanied by the strongest evidence of Australian loyalty to the common law of nations".[18]

A more recent historian sees it differently: "The anti-transportation movement was a specific reason why moral enlightenment became accepted in eastern Australia".[19]

"Moral enlightenment" or the "new faith"

> arose on foundations laid by the *philosophes* and reinforced by Jeremy Bentham — individualism, rationality, man's power to control his environment, the need for reform, the concept of progress . . . the quest for perfection became the keynote: man should cast off all vice, stupidity and selfishness as he created an earthly Utopia . . . every person can and must join in the advance.[20]

In 1850 Palmerston was remarking that England was a nation "in which every class of society accepts with cheerfulness the lot which providence has assigned to it",

> while at the same time each individual of each class is constantly trying to raise himself in the social scale, not by violence and illegality, but by persevering good conduct and by the steady and energetic exertion of the moral and intellectual faculties with which his creator had endowed him.[21]

In Australia, John West wrote an epitaph on transportation in his *History*:

> Nearly 120,000 prisoners have landed in these colonies: of these, the major part have passed into eternity. Thousands have died in chains. Thousands and tens of thousands perished by strong drink. Their domestic increase, compared with equal numbers of free persons, is insignificant — partly from the effects of vice, and in part by the impracticability of marriage: they melt from the earth, and pass away like a mournful dream. In every parochial burial-ground there

is a large section of graves, where not a tomb records who slumbers there.[22]

How accurate is it? The records in New South Wales are not sufficiently complete to allow a full analysis of the fate of convicts there; the Tasmanian records are more extensive.[23] It will be recalled that of convicts transported to the eastern states, no more than fifteen per cent went to penal settlements and that most were not flogged. The latter statement represents, of course, an average. One must remember that in New South Wales in the 1830s one convict in five was flogged, the average punishment being forty-five lashes. Ten per cent of convicts served out their sentences without incurring additional penalties. Most convicts who did not die in captivity regained their freedom. In 1851 "there were about 80,000 convicts and ex-convicts in the Australian colonies, or about ninety per cent of those who had been transported and were still alive".[24] Thus, about one person in five of the total European population (437,665) was a convict or an ex-convict.

In Tasmania in 1857 the census revealed that fifty per cent of adults and sixty per cent of adult males were convicts or ex-convicts.[25] In that colony forty-four per cent of crimes committed in 1875 (over twenty years after the end of transportation) were attributed to emancipists, who as late as 1889 also numerically predominated among the inmates of institutions for the disabled and needy.

Moreover, "the workhouse Depots were the final retreat for the British convicts; the final stage in that long line of humiliating institutions from lockup in British shire town, through prison hulk and convict ship, penal station and chain gang to probation station."[26]

More fortunate "*Van Demonians* merged quietly into the Australian population, where their origins soon became lost in the general confusion of immigration and movement". Therry informs us that "humane treatment in Tasmania made the survivors from Norfolk Island more manageable and civilized".

In Tasmania few convicts achieved social prominence. One exception was John Davies: an ex-convict, he was a brother of Edward Davies, the "Jewboy bushranger" and the son of Michael John Davies, also a convict. John Davies became a member of the legislature and founder of the Hobart *Mercury*. His son, John George Davies, was knighted and was speaker of the House of Assembly.[27] In New South Wales it was perhaps easier to gain distinction: the Lords, the Pyes, the Reibeys and Drys managed to become enrolled among the "ancients".

Some convicts attained notoriety. Apart from the bushrangers and others whose lurid crimes attracted attention, there were yet others who achieved their own form of singularity. Thomas Soulsby Wright, for example, died in captivity at Norfolk Island in 1843. He was 105 years of age. He had been sentenced to transportation for life in 1799. In 1839 (aged 98) he was sentenced in Sydney to fourteen years' transportation to Norfolk Island for possessing forged notes.[28] Samuel Levy arrived in Sydney in 1810; he received a conditional pardon in 1847. In the interim he had been sent to Hobart, where he was soon sentenced to death; the punishment was commuted and he spent thirteen years at Newcastle, followed by two years at Port Macquarie. He was then assigned, reconvicted and condemned to serve in a chain gang; a further sentence took him to Moreton Bay; upon his release, only the intercession of his fellow Jews preserved him from further imprisonment for vagrancy. When Trollope met the convict Doherty at Port Arthur in the early 1870s the latter had been in detention for forty-two years. He claimed to have received almost 3,000 lashes. He had just been recaptured after one of his many attempts at escape. Trollope "was assured that (Doherty) was thoroughly bad, irredeemable, not to be reached by any kindness, a beast of prey, whose hand was against every honest man, and against whom it was necessary that every honest man should raise his hand. Yet he talked so gently and so well and argued his case with such winning words".[29]

What happened to the majority of convicts who were neither great saints nor great sinners, neither celebrated nor notorious? We are told that by 1860 eighty per cent of convicts in Tasmania were emancipated or free from servitude, that three per cent had absconded and that twelve per cent "were not recorded as being freed; one per cent were imperial paupers".[30]

In his *Catholic Mission in Australia* (1837)[31] William Ullathorne made a generalization about the fate of convicts which may be as accurate a statement as any about the experience of the "silent majority".

In homiletic style he selects convict types and traces their fortunes. First, there is the footman who has been "brought up in a good family, well instructed" and well-housed and fed. Upon arrival in Australia "he is a prize quickly drawn" by a wealthy master, whom he robs. He is flogged, sent to the treadmill, falls in with bad companions and returns from the iron-gang "a hypocrite and a conscientious thief". He receives his ticket, marries and becomes a publican.

Next comes a carpenter and a blacksmith, who have been apprentices "amidst domestic comforts and the good example of the painstaking middle class". They have been transported for making "burglarious implements" and for burglary. Assigned to master-mechanics, they are looked upon as valuable property and work well or badly, according to the way their masters treat them. They are joined by their wives who come out "by a compromise with the law". They become master tradesmen and "solace their cares from morning to night with potations of rum".

Next Ullathorne distinguishes a "man in black" transported for forging a bill for fifty pounds. He is assigned to an ex-convict publican. Being literate, the former keeps accounts, writes prisoners' petitions, and is called upon to assist in entertaining more important guests. He lords it over a lad who, having lost his parents and fallen among thieves, has been transported for stealing a pheasant. He seduces a female servant transported for stealing trifles "through vanity". He lends money at forty-five per cent interest . . . Here, surely, Ullathorne is delineating that element of the convict population that became the nucleus of the Australian underworld. Certainly, it seems that after 1830 the more engrained type of criminal was transported: an examination of the records of ships arriving demonstrates that many convicts bore the tatoos and scars that were recognized as the distinguishing marks of the felonry.

By the 1840s "pushes", or gangs of larrikins, were identified in Sydney. It is said that the first "push" was founded by the ex-convict, Stick, at the Rocks in 1841.[32] The "Cabbage Tree Mob" was an early example of such a "push".[33] In 1858 a witness said of the Rocks "I am acquainted with some of the worst parts of London such as Jacob's Island, Golden Square, Lambeth, Drury-Lane, Gravel-lane, etc., and with the most unhealthy parts of Liverpool, Paris and other towns, but nowhere have I seen such a retreat for vice and filth as the 'Rocks' of Sydney".[34]

In 1860 a Select Committee of the Upper and Lower Houses of the New South Wales Parliament was requested by the Lower House to examine the "condition of the Working Classes of the Metropolis". One of the Committee's findings was that "Prostitution amongst the lower girls — some only just thirteen or fourteen — was strongly impelled by the old female convict element, who are often out of gaol in areas where growing females are to be found".[35]

It is odd that with the exception of Nat Gould, Ambrose Pratt and Louis Stone, few writers have dealt at length with this part of the urban convict legacy.

We are told that when gold was discovered in Victoria "ex-convicts in hundreds and thousands concentrated for loot and plunder in the weeks before the police were detailed to a new rush". And further that "probably the great majority of the criminals on the fields were from Van Diemen's Land". Hence the contentious (Victorian) Convict Prevention Act which excluded from Victoria all holders of conditional pardons.

We do not know whether the goldfields criminals ever forsook their lawless ways. It is certain however that at least some of the convicts became members of the underworld. Modern groups like the "Toecutters" are their lineal descendants.

The last category described by Ullathorne was "a number of hapless wretches" lacking the footman's "ability in service or crime" who were either "dragging carts all day and locked up at night" or "hastening up the country".

Convicts in the bush

Those who hastened up the country have come to be considered an important group. In the 1830s there were twice as many assigned convicts as free hands outside the nineteen counties. It has already been noted that emigrants were usually unwilling to go to the bush. In the late forties, one quarter of the adult males in the Port Phillip district were ex-convicts. Convicts formed an important part of the labour force in the Moreton Bay district. Tasmania, of course, did not have the territory to admit of large runs, and most assigned convicts were employed in the town districts.

Initially, convicts (legally) found their way to the outback because they were assigned. Later, their services were at times sought in preference to those of emigrants. Ward argues that once there, convicts tended to stay, and that those liberated elsewhere often migrated to the bush. For these choices he suggests a number of social and economic reasons.[36]

It is impossible to generalize about the fate and conduct of convicts and ex-convicts assigned to, or living in, the outback. Some fell in with tyrannical masters like James Mudie or those described by Harris.[37] Others could have the good fortune to serve a man like Charles Sturt (not, of course, as pastoral workers). Some convicts behaved very well, while others were considered refractory.

The solitary shepherd has emerged from this period as an established type. Charles Bean tells us that the shepherd was

> A tall gaunt figure in a long frayed overcoat, a shabby felt hat half hiding the sunken cheeks, a thin grey beard, and hard lines drawn as with a ruler across his face. One can see the round backs of a hundred sheep feeding in the hollow below him. And motionless as a statue on the hill there, the ragged edges of his overcoat showing against the yellow sky, with his stick and his pipe and his dog — the old man himself. With no other companions, he lived year in and year out — twenty, thirty, forty miles from the homestead. Once in three weeks or more a cart would turn up with his rations. But seeing men so seldom, he came not to wish to see them — a "hatter" they called him for his madness. That man was the shepherd.[38]

In 1846 Wentworth had felt that where there were two or three men in a slab hut they could steadily contemplate "the power and beneficence of the Great Author of the Universe". Surely, he told his fellow legislators, this opportunity could "soften and humanise and restore a fallen being to his primitive condition". The Molesworth Committee, a very long distance away and eight years earlier, knew better. The condition of the "hatters" was a travesty of that reformation which life in the wilderness was meant to produce.

Far from elevating the mind, the convict condition is often stated to have caused sullenness, despondency and a consequent docility. One record at Norfolk Island may speak for many: Charles Daley died there in 1841, aged forty-one. His record says: "13 years on the Island. Some time previous to decease, being refused by the Judges he fell into a melancholy and never recovered".[39]

It is likely that the mental capacity of some convicts was never great. "Arthur complained that a quarter of his convict labourers were idiots and the convict stations did indeed maintain a large crop of mental defectives."[40] The phrenologists held that "in some cases the moral and intellectual organs were so deficient that the minds were incapable of improvement". These were "irredeemables", a relatively small number, who represented "the very worst strain of the British race".[41]

The commission of crime by "irredeemables" and others in Australia was relatively high during the transportation era: as Glenelg observed, given the nature of the population, a higher crime rate was inevitable.

The outback also had its recognizable convict element, which Henry Lawson found in

> hundreds of out-of-the-way places in the nearer bush of Australia — hidden away in unheard-of "pockets" in the ranges; on barren creeks . . . up at the ends of long dark gullies . . . where families live for generations in mental darkness almost inconceivable in this enlightened age and country. They are often in a worse condition mentally than savages to the manner born . . . Some of these families are descended from a convict of the worst type on one side or the other, perhaps on both, and, if not born criminals are trained in shady ways from childhood. Conceived and bred under the shadow of exile, hardship, or "trouble", [theirs is the] sullen brooding spirit which enwraps their lonely bush-buried homes . . . There are things done in the bush . . . which would make a strong man shudder.[42]

Whether in the metropolis or the bush, surviving convicts became an embarrassment as the century drew to its close.

Marcus Clarke tabulated the categories of inmates he found at Port Arthur in 1870:

Convicts	301
Do, invalids	13
Do, insane	8
Paupers not under sentence	116
Lunatics do.	86

These persons, Clarke believed, constituted the "jetsam of the great transportation wave". He was affected by the "general scowl of depression on the fellows' faces" and applied to the whole institution what a prisoner said of an empty rum bottle: "Ay, only the smell of it [is] left".[43] Shortly afterwards Trollope also found there the "odour and flavour" of the convict days.[44]

When the establishment was broken up in 1878 there were only seventy convicts in custody. Some of these no doubt later joined

> noble swagmen, inefficient emancipist beggars or depraved social

outcasts . . . the burden of the ex-penal community. The spectre of the old, hairy beggar was a reality of life, an impediment which it was believed disgusted many visitors and discouraged immigrants. The silent mercy came to be the element of time, for every year the community was able to bury more or its paupers, and the understanding grew that if one could wait long enough this particular problem would solve itself.[45]

Some of the institutionalized ex-convicts showed a reluctance to co-operate in this method of solving the problem they posed. At the end of the century Twain visited the Refuge for the Indigent and found

> a crowd there of the oldest people I have ever seen. It was like being set down in a new world — a weird world where youth has never been, a world sacred to age, and bowed forms and wrinkles. Out of the 359 persons present, 223 were ex-convicts, and could have told stirring tales no doubt if they had been minded to talk; 42 of the 359 were past 80, and several were close upon 90; the average age of death there is 76 years . . . There were 185 women in that Refuge and 81 of them were ex-convicts.[46]

At least one of the Tasmanian ex-convicts lived long enough to receive an old age pension when the Commonwealth Government introduced that system of assistance in July 1909.

English troops were withdrawn from Tasmania and Western Australia in 1870. In the latter state, the closing-down of outlying convict depots began in 1872. By 1874 there were only 324 imperial convicts in custody; the number shrank to 75 in 1886 and the last six convicts were released in 1906. By 1891 many ex-convicts were in institutions, like that at Toodyay where some dead ex-convicts joined lunatics in being buried in unhallowed ground.

Occasionally, if only at death, some ex-convicts emerged from the obscurity into which they had sunk. Thus, memories of Joseph Bolitho Johns (the original Moondyne Joe), who had long been lost from public view, were revived at his death in 1900, and the bushranger, William Day, left his self-imposed seclusion to die in the Bathurst Hospital in 1898.

All in all, Trollope's observation does not appear to be unduly melodramatic: "men remember whence Bill Sikes came and why; but they forget how they got the roads and buildings".

It will have become obvious in this survey of developments in the colony and in its increasingly melancholy tone, that the convicts moved with increasing acceleration to the periphery of society and the institutions it cherished. The writings, the "convict literature", that we have been examining testify to this shift. Generally speaking, those convicts who wrote about themselves had a different perspective.

There are many surviving accounts of their experiences written by the convicts themselves. Details of these publications will be found in the bibliography and summaries are included in appendix IV.

Eyewitness accounts of the convict experience

There is little point in summarizing each account here. Some of the more prominent examples will be discussed. This discussion will disclose common preoccupations and convey an idea of the types of convicts who wrote their accounts.

Isaac Solomons (1830)[47] attained considerable notoriety during his lifetime. It is said that Dickens used him as a model for Fagin and Thackeray sardonically ascribed the authorship of *Catherine* to Ikey Solomons Jnr. Several pamphlets appeared about Solomons; that schematized in appendix IV (item 1) takes him only as far as his trial. Elsewhere we learn that he escaped from the hulks and paid his own fare to join his wife who had been transported. He was apprehended, sent back to England, and transported; he arrived in 1831 and received a conditional pardon in 1844.

W— (1937) provides us with an American's view of transportation.[48] Travelling as a passenger, he was disgusted by the indiscriminate mixing of young and old convicts in "tumultous confusion". Most convicts appeared to be "reckless of either body or soul". The voyage was eventful: cholera wrought "terrific havoc" among the convicts; a re-transported convict fomented two abortive mutinies and "punishments were frequent but indispensable". W— mixed with the convicts, whom he found generally sullen and resigned; two of them told him their stories, which adhere to the traditional formula.

Snowden Dunhill's reminiscences (1834)[49] were edited by the printer who admitted suppressing "many anecdotes and many adventures" to preserve the reputation of living persons. With the help of an amanuensis, Dunhill told his story as "a warning to others who may possibly be deterred from a life of crime by a relation of my present miseries and misfortunes". The causes of his downfall were many: chance, cards, his wife, the "Squire-archy" and the laws which inhibited the "natural desire" to poach. The printer tells us that when freed, Dunhill became an habitual drunkard, while his wife enjoyed a "reputation for religion and sanctity". In the printer's opinion, the colonies could be "deemed prototypes of the bottomless gulf of perdition".

Before coming to Australia, Dunhill had "heard much about the easy lives led by convicts in New South Wales". A broadsheet published in 1835[50] was designed to disabuse the public of this false impression. It purports to reproduce a letter written by a convict in the ninth year of his imprisonment. The horrors of the iron gang, flogging, extension of punishment, hard labour and poor rations and accommodation are the substance of this account, the writer of which concludes that it would have been better had convicts not been born. W. Dickson's letter[51] from "Mangrove Plantation, Van Diemen's Land" conveys similar sentiments.

William Ross wrote *Fell Tyrant* (1836)[52] "to undeceive such as entertain these ideas [transportation is scarcely a punishment] and to deter others from the committal of crimes". Excessive labour, starvation and flagellation were the "manner of treatment of the unfortunate settlers in this settlement [Moreton Bay]". It was with gratification that he reported that "most of the high authorities in New South Wales [who] have been conspicuous for tyrannical proceedings have died an unhappy death". With some justice he remarks that it was iniquitous to expect the same amount of labour from those who had never used a spade as from those born and bred as agricultural labourers. The afflicted convicts "soon forget they ever had been men, their spirits seem to have fled from them, they begin to neglect their persons, become slothful, giving themselves up as lost for ever, and by their continual fretting and cruel treatment linger into the grave".

Fell Tyrant begins in conformity with the traditional formula, but is one of the first accounts to devote more space to the colonial than to English experience. The vocabulary and perspective are the same as those adopted in the 1790s, but the account is more substantial.

There were eight editions of George Loveless's *Victims of Whiggery*.[53] He was one of the Tolpuddle Martyrs; if his account and that of his "companions in persecution" is tendentious, the tone is nevertheless undramatic: the memorialists were content to let the colonial experience speak for itself.

James Mudie's *The Felonry of New South Wales* (1837)[54] is a master's view of the convict experience. Mudie was overbearing and quarrelsome: his treatment of convicts at Castle Forbes provoked an official enquiry, and he seems to have engaged in continuous litigation with other colonists. He believed that "conviction of a felony renders a man for ever infamous in England — infamous in *law* — and attaches to him for life certain disabilities which incapacitate him for exercising some of the rights and duties of citizenship". It is not surprising that he found the convicts to be "generally profligate, treacherous, dishonest and mutinous". He has left us an account of the life of one convict, William Watt, which is schematized in the appendix.

Francis Xavier Prieur was one of a group of Canadian rebels who were transported to Australia. Although his memoir was not published until 1869, it was based on a journal made in the thirties, and it provides a first-hand, outsider's view of the assignment system.[55]

Upon arrival the Canadians were told that they might be sent to Norfolk Island, a place which had already been represented to them as that "to which were sent the most depraved and incorrigible of the convicts. Every day the most atrocious crimes were committed there, and the treatment to which these wretches were subjected was in keeping with the behaviour of the inhabitants of this frightful locality".

The Canadians were spared the ordeal of further transportation, but assignment in Sydney was galling enough. Their prospective masters "opened our mouths so as to examine our teeth, employing in the process almost the same formalities and the same amount of gentleness as a horse dealer uses when ascertaining the age of a horse he thinks about buying".

At Longbottom their superintendent was a "coarse, brutal" cashiered officer, who laid traps to catch his prisoners out. However, he became more tolerant of them after they helped him to arrest the guards who fell into a drunken brawl. Being granted a ticket of leave, Prieur joined his compatriots in various unsuccessful business ventures. Their attempts to be sawyers, candlemakers and bakers were thwarted by natural disasters and their inexperience. One of his fellows escaped, but Prieur decided to remain in the colony until his sentence expired.

Possibly because he knew so little English and was therefore little acquainted with the oral traditions, Prieur's account affords us a fresh and ironic appreciation of the convict experience.

Joseph Holt's *Memoirs* were written in the early nineteenth century but they were not published until 1838. In the first volume he recalls his part in upheavals in Ireland. In the second, he provides us with some graphic and pungent descriptions of personalities and events. The "very irritable"

Margarot's house was pointed out to Holt as "the most seditious in the colony". Marsden was "a busy meddling man of shallow understanding"; King had "a violent and intemperate disposition" while Foveaux was a "monster worse than that ogre the seed of Abarcurtinea, and the offspring of the Patagonians, that eat human flesh and drink blood". Norfolk Island was "a barbarous island, the dwellingplace of devils in the human shape, the refuse of Botany Bay, the doubly damned". Overseers like Bob Jones (who had informed against his own father and brothers, so that they were hanged) "have been criminals themselves and have neither prudence, honesty or humanity". The most frequently quoted part of the *Memoirs* is the description of the flogging of Maurice Fitzgerald and Paddy Galvin in 1800.

Holt saw himself as "the victim of tyranny and oppression" and the plaything of fortune. He decided that "resolution and good conduct should be my motto".

In tone and level of perception Holt's *Memoirs* distil the essence of many convict narratives, and bring to mind the influence of the early convict memorialists.

Edward Lilburn felt that "the alarming progress of crime in every part of the empire is a sufficient reason for calling the attention of Parents and Guardians to the certainty and excessive severity of legal punishment". His *Exposure* (1841),[56] schematized in appendix IV, concludes:

> Ah! if my friends and neighbours knew a guilty convict's woe
> Or witness half the misery I daily undergo
> They'd never tread the paths of vice and while they are yet free
> They'd think on Edward Lilburn's fate
>   an strive to happier be.

John Knatchbull's *Life*,[57] which is virtually a last dying speech, is an excellent example of the way in which the gallows literature became combined with accounts of the Australian convict experience.

John Knatchbull, a psychopath, was a stumbling-block to his contemporaries and remained as such to many subsequent commentators.

While many aspects of his life were contentious, the fact remains that he traced out the familiar dreary path from good parentage and education through colonial tyranny and treachery to conversion before he died on the gallows. More eloquent than most convicts, whatever his aberrations may have been, Knatchbull has left some memorable sketches of convict life. For example, shortly before he left Norfolk Island (his sentence had expired) he was (unjustly, he says) loaded with irons. He refused to co-operate with the authorities and was haled before the commandant:

> A carriage, a large wheelbarrow, was brought to the door, and your humble servant safely lifted into it, but not in the most polite and gentle manner possible; but one at my head, and another holding my legs by the irons, was dropped into this most delightful vehicle, ready to knock my wind out, when a great he-monster, the cook, drove off towards the court-house.
>
> Fully expecting the easy manner I should be assisted out, I prepared for the worst by holding fast to both sides. Nor was I deceived in my conjectures, for as soon as my carriage drew up to the court-house door, I was turned out like a lump of dung would have been.

Knatchbull's life is schematized in appendix IV (item 15).

James Connor's *Recollections* (1845),[58] transcribed by an amanuensis, is one of the few accounts which deal with Maria Island, where, as coxswain, he enjoyed the benevolence of "Captain W.", to whom he was assigned, and in whose company he warded off an attack by Aborigines. When the captain died, Connor's good fortune deserted him, and his life became a series of escapes, adventures in the wilds, recapture and punishment. During one of his escapes he met a mother and son whose story he relates: the mother had been ruined "by a villain who insinuated himself into her favour"; she "led a life of sin" which "contaminated" her son. They were both transported for stealing and receiving. She "sincerely repented her misconduct" and hoped that her son might "by an exemplary life atone for the failings of himself and his parents". She "breathed her last amongst the wood-covered mountains of a penal settlement as a runaway convict". After suffering from his fellow-convicts and an "alcoholic tyrant" at Macquarie Harbour, Connor made his escape by sea, when that establishment was broken up.

W. H. Barber's *Case*[59] deals at some length with "all the horrors" he experienced. His legal friends summarized them:

> the ruin of his fortunes, the mental torture, the bodily restraint, the trial, the unjust conviction, the title of felon affixed to him, the prison, the convict ship, the companionship of the vilest of mankind.

Barber was a solicitor, convicted (he asserts) through a conspiracy of his enemies for forging a will. He was sent in chains from Newgate to Millbank and thereafter spent some time on a hulk. He was transported to Norfolk Island, where he endured the enmity of Major Joseph Childs.

> The *reason* assigned for thus singling me out as an object upon whom to inflict, in a concentrated and aggravated form, all the horrors of Norfolk Island was, that I am a prisoner of "great notoriety" ... [and] in pursuance of "instructions"!!

He was favoured with the constant attention of the police ("a viler set of miscreants . . . could scarcely be collected from the regions of darkness"), and subjected to hard labour and abuse. He was sent to Tasmania, where upon his receipt of a conditional pardon, his fellow prisoners "clubbed together such few odd articles of wearing apparel they happened to possess" to get him as far as Sydney, where a public subscription enabled him to get to Madras, whence he went "home" aided by similar means.

Margaret Catchpole's *History* (1845),[60] based on her letters in the early days of the colony, is both the traditional moral tale and a form of novel. The "root of all the evil that befell her" was that her early impressions of religion "had been of a very desultory kind". Her early love was thwarted, and she was hounded by the villainous John Luff, with whom she escaped from prison only to be apprehended on the beach while on the point of leaving England. Transported to Australia, she was assigned to kindly masters and married a prosperous settler who had long cherished a love for her: "the remaining history of this singular individual was one of quiet calm, and yet benevolent exertions in all good works of faith and love".

John Mitchell's *Jail Journal* (1854)[61] records some of the misfortunes of an Irish political prisoner. Tried for sedition, he was transported first to Bermuda, then to the Cape and finally to Tasmania, where he arrived in 1851. In 1853 he escaped, eventually reaching San Francisco. In later life he returned to Ireland, where he was elected to parliament. The journal is a mixture of natural description, anti-British sentiment, escape plans and caustic observations:

> "Rural population!" It is almost profane to apply the title to these rascals. All the shepherds and stock-keepers without exception are convicts, many of them thrice-convicted convicts: there is no peasantry, very few of them have wives; still fewer have families, and I say the fewer the better. The wives are always transported women too, shoplifters, prostitutes, pick pockets, and other such sweepings of the London pavements . . . the best shepherds in Van Diemen's Land are London thieves . . . And what is stranger still many of them grow rather decent — it would be too strong to say honest . . . They are friendly to one another, hospitable to strangers . . . yet human they are not. Their training has made them subterhuman, praeterhuman; and the system of British "reformatory discipline" has gone as near to making them perfect fiends as human wit can go.

Rev. Colin Browning (1856) espoused the opposite view.[62] as chaplain on nine convict ships between 1831 and 1842, he believed that at least some convicts were converted and reformed. Once prisoners were put on board "with the greatest possibly solemnity" he carefully inquired about their level of education and divided them into graded classes. "An abundant variety of religious tracts, and of valuable works published by the Tract Society, were in constant circulation and diligently perused" so that "from the commencement of a voyage to its termination, the persons breathed a moral and spiritual atmosphere."

Although he viewed any sign of repentance with "great suspicion", he was gratified when on one voyage "*eleven* men voluntarily formed into a Christian Society for the worship of God".

Rev. Charles B. Gibson was another clergyman who spent some time with the convicts. He found that assignment was a lottery and a state of slavery, and that Macquarie Harbour was a hell on earth.

John Leonard (1859), suffered from treachery, brutality, flogging, venal overseers, corrupt magistrates, tyranny, impossible tasks and repeated convictions.[63] Swamped by this sea of troubles, he at one time concluded: "It's no use striving; I'll let things take their course, for what is lotted to a man he must put up with."

His lot led him to Port Arthur where two of his fellow prisoners were Frank the Poet and Cavanagh. Leonard was as free in admitting his crimes as he was in denouncing tyranny. Eventually he gained his "ticket of freedom" and became a "prosperous gold-digger".

Joseph Platt (1862) also seems to have suffered a range of enormities, but his story[64] is far less credible. After undergoing the customary horrors, he absconded and roamed with Aborigines from "the Snow Mountains" to "Cape York where Captain Kennedy was killed". Morgan's *Life of William Buckley* is a far more credible description of life with the natives.

J. F. Mortlock brought to his *Experiences*[65] a wry detachment:

> Such numbers of prisoners having suddenly been poured into the country, the Commissariat Department found itself temporarily unable to provide sufficient clothing, in consequence of which, men clad in one sole garment formed out of the rug belonging to his pallet would now and then make their appearance on the muster ground; — looking like New Zealand Chiefs in court costumes.

This mood he dropped only when he recalled the iniquities of his relatives or remarked with compassion upon the sufferings of others. He knew everything of legal complexities except how to escape their rigour. His sentences led him to Norfolk Island, Van Diemen's Land, Millbank and Western Australia. As the recipient of a pass and conditional pardon he wandered in Van Diemen's Land and Sydney. His account is one of the most restrained and "literary" that has survived.

Soon after transportation to Tasmania ended, James Bonwick recalled an earlier observation made about the role of a clergyman in the convict days: "In Hobart Town he had to grapple at the very gates of hell if he would rescue a soul; he had to struggle with the enemy in close combat, face to face, and foot to foot". This statement expresses the moral squint with which convict society was regarded in the factual accounts, and it contains something of their intensity.

The schematic table in appendix IV indicates that most convict accounts concentrated on hardships experienced. These components were used at times to draw a moral, which has been called the "social myth": "Even if one knows society's rules of decorum, gentlemanliness and order to be wrong and repressive in any given situation those rules are essential to society's survival".[66]

Many convicts were no doubt unaware that they were perpetuating a myth. The schematic table makes it plain that they drew upon the traditional formula, which also provided them with their perspective: they were to concentrate on the most startling details and to express edifying sentiments.

Other convicts used the same components as reasons for inveighing against the iniquities of the legal system and society or as new grounds for denouncing perfidious Albion.

Whatever their motives — and one must not exclude that of writing to make money — the convicts and other observers showed a progressively greater ability to explore the area of their limited range of interest: they preserved the vocabulary and accents of their predecessors, but they were able to express more clearly the substance of "tyranny, oppression and fraud".

The convict in fiction

It was perhaps inevitable that the incongruity of founding a new colony with convicts as the majority of settlers would mark out the new settlement as a subject for parody. Even before the First Fleet set out, the burlesque *Botany Bay* was staged at the Royal Circus; and mention has already been made of "The Prologue", of Field's poems and of the early pipes which circulated in the colony. *Giovanni in Botany* (1822)[67] was written in the same vein; its general tenor may be gathered from the *dramatis personae* (with Jonathan Wild as Governor and Don Giovanni, Leporello and Dive as convicts) and from Dive's outburst:

> For seven long years transported.
>   That is the time o' day!
> With *kiddy coves* assorted
>   I drive all cares away.
> Though now I'm up the spout,
> My time will soon be out;
>   Then I'll sail
>   With the gale
> From the Bay of Bot'ny, O!

The shift in British taste which began, in the 1820s, to demand descriptions of the more adventurous aspect of life in Botany Bay has already been mentioned. The focus of the traditional formula, the continuing popular appetite for the macabre, and the doleful emphasis of the first convict biographies all indicated to the early writers of fiction that seriousness, not facetiousness, was the tone they should employ.

It is difficult to say which was the first novel about Australian life. Dr Morris Miller bestowed that honour upon Mary Leman Grimstone's *Woman's Love*.[68] During her relatively brief residence in Tasmania, Mrs Grimstone had attracted criticism over some comments she made about the colony.[69] As a consequence, she apparently decided that *Woman's Love* would contain only oblique references to it.

The anonymous *Alfred Dudley*, published in England in 1830, is of little importance in itself; however, in stressing the role that the landed gentry could play in the reformation of the convict and in asserting the worth of virtues like benevolence, fortitude and perseverance, it anticipated the subject matter and perspective of later novels.

John Howison's *One False Step* (1830)[70] is possibly the first novel which grappled with the problem of finding the convict a place in society. The hero of the novel, Deveral Hermsdill, has a familiar background:

> He was twenty-six years of age, and his early life had been passed under circumstances favourable to the development and mixture of the best qualities of the human character. But on the death of his father, which occurred before he reached manhood, he came into the possession of a considerable patrimony, and being entirely his own master he quickly dissipated it by a course of extravagance and debauchery, in which he was, as usual, encouraged and assisted by the companions of his pleasures.

To extricate him from his troubles his mother impoverishes herself and Hermsdill tries to succour her by forging a bill. He is apprehended, tried and transported. He is disgusted by his voyage: "Though accustomed to the society of profligate characters, he was unprepared for the bold and disgusting depravity of his fellow convicts".

Being thoroughly ashamed, and having no negotiable skills, he is happy to be assigned to Mr Bronde, whose farm is remote from Sydney. Hermsdill's charms attract the attention of the convict servant Rachel (who displays "marks of former profligacy and dissipation") and of the fair Harriet Hasmere, Bronde's niece.

Hermsdill is a tainted man: "What are the pains of hard labour, privations and tyranny to the tortures of being deemed capable of committing any and every crime?"

The author allows his hero to explore a number of means of ridding himself of his taint: Hermsdill incurs the enmity of Bronde and he flees to join some bushrangers he has encountered. These men display "a type of gallantry that more or less hides their coarseness"; but tiring of their villainy, Hermsdill resolves to become a solitary: "'Hail! earth, skies, woods and waters!' exclaimed he, 'you are henceforth to be my only companions. I utterly renounce all future sympathy, intercourse and communion with my own species. I now regard every man as hostile and treacherous'". This option fills him with disillusion: "better to be a convict and feel and arouse passions".

His mother arrives in the colony with a conditional pardon for her son, who then finds himself shunned by the "exclusionists" and by Bronde in particular. When Bronde is murdered, suspicion wrongly falls upon Hermsdill, who seeks to fly the colony. The boat in which he is escaping is pursued, and he jumps overboard. He is dragged up into the pursuing boat in which his mother waits to tell him that he has been exonerated. "We shall yet be happy!" she cries,

> "No! No Mother", replied he faintly and almost inarticulately: "your hopes are vain — *One false step in the path of crime seldom can be retrieved.*"

Under these circumstances, death is a good solution.

If much of this novel appears contrived, we can yet be grateful to Howison for the following passage which suggests the substantial reality of the society he described:

> His fellow passengers from Sydney to Parramatta were convicts both male and female, all of whom seemed to regard their situation with the utmost indifference, and one of the latter made many advances towards making an acquaintance with Deveral, singing fragments of love songs with an affected air, leaning her head upon her hand and sighing, and then breaking out with loud fits of laughter. Two of the men amused themselves playing picquet, one receiving from his partner the title of your grace, and the other that of your lordship throughout the game. A third held a fragment of an old newspaper in his hand, and talked to those next to him of the necessity of parliamentary reform; and another, not far off, was complaining of the clumsiness of the fetters at that time in use throughout the colony and suggesting how they might be improved.

Before writing his play *Van Diemen's Land*[71] (1831) W. T. Moncrieff read widely to ensure that "a correct picture of the conduct and treatment of the convicts and the actions, feelings and peculiarities of the Caffres and Bush-rangers" would be conveyed to the audience. The play swings uneasily from the farcical conduct of Darby Ballylaggan, "an Irish convict transported by mistake", through the complaints of

"Ben-ni-long" to the melodramatic plight of Agatha, who was "transported for a trifling theft". Absconding, improbable bushrangers, and perfervid outbursts against tyranny are often features of this type of drama.

David Burn's play, *The Bushrangers*,[72] was written in Van Diemen's Land in 1829, first presented in Edinburgh in the same year, and re-written about 1835. Colonial society, from the Governor down, teems with treachery in this play. Survival is difficult for the wronged convict, guileless settlers and the Aborigines. Brady, the hero of the play, is forced to use a spy system which is "a capital trade in Van's Land, and I've taken a leaf out of His Majesty's representative".

The only humane official is Captain James, yet even he, while being "kind and merciful, cannot feel the convict's woe". Brady, on the other hand, is a lover of liberty, a pardoner of his enemies, and the protector of female virtue. The question is, how does Brady's heroism profit him?

> BRADY: No. Bravely the game's been played — most nobly. The reign of tyranny cannot last. Mac Cabe, I follow . . . friends during life, in death we . . . have . . . have . . .

Comradeship? notoriety? vindication? eternal bliss? Burn cannot say. Indeed, who can?

There is no ambiguity about the ending of Henry Savery's *Quintus Servinton* (1830-31),[73] the first novel printed in Australia. Apart from its historical distinction, the novel has considerable merit, given the mode in which it is written and the lurid interests of contemporary writers. Volumes I and II treat Servinton's advantageous parentage, education, early career and marriage. It appears that he was doomed to undergo "great reverses of fortune" through "a train of unforeseen circumstances" and "the capaciousness of his mind to get the better of his judgment". His lot was forecast by gipsies at his birth: "Sweet and sours — more sours than sweets — / A newborn Son your Honour greets."

He overreaches himself in business and seeks to extricate himself through uttering forged bills, but he is detected. Apprehended while fleeing, he attempts suicide. His is condemned to transportation. His voyage to Australia and his experiences on the hulk are relatively pleasant.

Once in Australia his hopes of "more ease, happiness, and contentment than had long fallen to his lot" are baulked by his being enrolled "in the common herd", so that "society he could not keep, because to that alone, of which he had always been a member, he could no longer be admitted". His defects "still were green and flourishing in his heart" and he again engaged in imprudent transactions. This folly and the machinations of "a faction" cause him to be sent "to the interior, where he [is] deprived of every mark of favour, and placed upon a severe system of convict discipline".

Even the prospects of domestic bliss are thwarted through the designs of a specious friend: Quintus's wife, recently arrived in the colony, is persuaded to return to England. He again attempts suicide. Imprisoned once more, he probes "the seat of his disease" and gains wisdom from a fellow convict: "Be contented therefore, and receive everything as designed for your good."

While his wife labours in England for his pardon, Quintus, upon his release from prison, retires into seclusion provided by his friends. He comes to see the truth of his wife's admonition: "We all know that you are fully competent to any moderate pursuits you choose to adopt; but by trying to do too much, you diminish your own value and create for all of us, much unhappiness."

Reunited with his wife, he leads a quiet, retired life and works to acquire a competency. An absolute pardon enables him to return to England, to be "greeted by all [his] surviving relations with the most affectionate and hearty welcome".

Savery chose not to write about religious reformation. Servinton nevertheless experienced a change of heart whereby he became content with "moderate pursuits". In return he was blessed with the love of his wife, a sufficiency of means, a prosperous son and the birth of a grandson. *Quintus Servinton* contains little brutality. Guilt was expiated by the gaining of wisdom, and freedom came not by flight but through an official pardon. Rehabilitation by being admitted to colonial society was impossible: it came through interior peace, living in retirement, and returning "home" with the fruits of colonial labour. The novel exhibits a restraint, and occupies a middle ground, that has been adopted by few of those who have written about the convict experience.

In real life, Savery's own fate was far different. He was found dead in his cell with his throat cut. The reality pricks the bubble of enchantment. We are reminded that Servinton's modest happiness was difficult to attain and that death was a tidier — and more frequent — solution.

In 1843 Charles Rowcroft's *Tales of the Colonies*[74] appeared. In tracing the fortunes of the emigrant, William Thornley, Rowcroft was one of the earliest writers of fiction to concentrate on the life of a free settler and to set the convict on the periphery of this experience.

In the introduction Rowcroft set out his frame of reference:

> In resuming the occupations of the patriarchs of old, the emigrant may be said to recover the natural dignity of man ... He stands on his own land, the source of certain subsistence, and of almost certain wealth for himself and for his children ... going forth to his cheerful labour with the full reliance that, from the bounteous earth, he may always produce the abundance which nature never refuses to her industrious children.

This novel-cum-emigrant's manual records the growth in prosperity of two emigrants, Crab and Thornley. Crab's life-long antipathy to the colony is reflected in his dying words: "I am — going — at last — out — of this — wretch — wretch — wretch-ed — country — home — at — last."

Thornley believes that he himself exemplifies what may be achieved by "industry, frugality and perseverance". In garnering his abundance Thornley clashes with bushrangers and Aborigines; he is lost in the bush; his house is burned down; he hunts; he masters the convicts; he rescues a convict's daughter ... there is no end to his resourcefulness.

The latter comment is not meant to be patronizing; such were the difficulties immigrants faced; if some settlers broke under the strain there were others who triumphed. If the vision of the successful gentleman settler now seems fusty and smacking of arrogance it was nevertheless a sustaining vision for those who aspired to realize it. Moreover, the catalogue of obstacles Thornley had to overcome became part of the formula to be used when describing a settler's life.

When Marsh, a new settler, arrives, the record of his instruction provides something of a catechism for the colonies. To the newcomer's question, Thornley replies that the convicts are "imperfect labourers . . . but somehow amidst scolding, and teaching, and occasional mishaps, the work is done". A magistrate's sitting is described. Against his wishes, the magistrate condemns a convict to be flogged but upholds another convict's complaint against the same master: in the eyes of Rowcroft, the ex-magistrate, justice was even-handed.

At one time Thornley finds himself thrown with a bushranger, Gypsey, who tells his story: The son of a well-to-do family, he was poaching with friends when they were discovered by some keepers, one of whom was killed. Although innocent of the murder, Gypsey was transported for life. After some time he "got his liberty" and married. Knowing that the welfare of his family was dependent on the "caprice" of his master, Gypsey tried to flee the colony. He was caught and sent to Macquarie Harbour for life. He heard that his wife died and he absconded; he became the head of a gang of bushrangers, with the prospect of perishing "miserably in the bush (or being) betrayed, shot or hanged". (In the event, he fell over a precipice.)

Thornley promises to rescue Gypsey's daughter from the clutches of her uncle, who is seeking to defraud her of an inheritance. Honouring this promise leads Thornley to adopt a disguise and to insinuate himself into a gang's headquarters. After many adventures he saves the girl, secures her inheritance, and brings her up as his own daughter until he has the good fortune to see her happily married.

In *Tales of the Colonies,* therefore, we find the components of plot that were popular in contemporary English literature, with the substitution of settlers for squires and convicts for English thieves and criminals.

James Tucker's *Ralph Rashleigh* was being written two years after *Tales of the Colonies* appeared. Tucker's novel centres on the convict experience, but, like Rowcroft, Tucker's ideal was domestic bliss achieved in rural order. Amid the horrors of the novel, the Marshall's home becomes a haven and a symbol:

> Small, indeed, was the extent of that little parterre, and very, very common were its plants; yet from its extreme rarity, it breathed the balmy breath of old England's cherished homes around the travellers as sweetly as if it had contained many acres and had been appended to a palace . . .
>
> The floor, 'tis true, was only made of cow dung and ashes trod into a solid and firm mass, but then, it was level and clean-swept. The stools and tables, though all the coarsest make, being apparently the handwork of the settler himself, were scoured until they were perfectly white . . .
>
> The appearance of both father and children told that the hand which thus laboured for their creature comforts also extended its attention to their personal wants. Rashleigh noticed as they came in that the children washed themselves in water set ready near the back door, even to their feet . . . [75]

The house and its occupants are the antithesis of the squalor of the Hibernian's dwelling (though their gaiety and benevolence in some measure atone for it) and that of Arlack's house, where filth and boorishness bespeak the crass and greedy spirit of the proprietor.

When Rashleigh's heroism has provided the grounds for his readmission into society, it is in "recently opened pastoral country" that he achieves peace:

> The sufferings of his early career in the colony produced such an effect of reformation in his mind that he was ever after respected as a man of scrupulous integrity by all that knew him, who united sincerely in lamenting his premature death.

The novel is a combination of the traditional formula and the oral traditions of the convicts. Rashleigh, whose parents "were of decent rank as London shopkeepers", gave him "a good plain English education". He falls a victim to a bad companion, Hartop, and then embarks on a career of theft which leads to his transportation. This journey frequently lands him in prison, where the customary profligacy and obduracy of the prisoners and the ineptitude of the ordinary are depicted.

Before his voyage he ruminates on "his probable fortune in Australia". An abortive mutiny and a threatened attack by Portuguese enliven the "dreary voyage".

Rashleigh's early colonial career embraces assignment, hard labour, sufferings at the hands of "tyrants" and the horrors of Emu Plains and Newcastle. These hardships and his macabre adventures with the bushranger Foxley are depicted with an imaginative intensity which distinguishes Tucker from contemporary writers. Cruelty and gratuitous savagery are not horrific appendages tacked on to pander to a kind of voyeurism. They form part of a world which also includes the Emu Plains theatricals and the ironic asides of the author.

Tucker, a convict, did not personally experience many of the hardships he described, but he has obviously used the traditions and the anecdotes circulating in the colony to convey the texture of experience of some convicts.

Tucker's account is written from the inside. Unlike many of the other memorialists, he does not consider himself superior to the general run of his companions. For him, there are evil convicts and evil authorities, just as there are decent people in each category. Whether it be in his depiction of the terrors of Newcastle or in Rashleigh's capitulation to the system and prevailing ethos which enables the convict to quit his troubles, Tucker has created a credible picture of the penal settlement which in tone and imaginative detail is unequalled in contemporary works.

The perfunctory nature of the latter part of the novel (where the writer very obviously relies upon the oral tradition rather than upon personal experience) is a serious flaw in the work. Nevertheless, when one considers the blending of the traditional tale with an unique treatment of colonial experience, it is obvious the novel has a merit above that of most other such novels. In addition, Tucker showed a sureness of touch in realizing that, regardless of Rashleigh's later irreproachable behaviour, the hero could more safely be venerated as a dead hero.

Charles Rowcroft's second book, *The Bushranger of Van Diemen's Land* (1846),[76] also tells the story of an Englishman in search of colonial prosperity. In this case it is Major Horton, who is accompanied by his daughters Louisa and Helen, and by a "pretentious cockney", Jeremiah Silliman.

The arrival of the Major's brig in d'Entrecasteaux Channel is observed by the bushranger Mark Brandon and his gang. By stratagem they take the brig. A party of soldiers arrives; among them is Trevor, who cherishes a love for Helen Horton. The plot then revolves around skirmishes, captures and escapes. Brandon saves Helen from rape, and when she is caught by Aborigines, he sets out to rescue her. Success in this venture would no doubt have been sufficient to rehabilitate him, but he is marked out for destruction. His confederates prove treacherous and he is obliged to murder Gough, who had betrayed him. Brandon is shot by the soldiers and speared by the natives. He writes his confession in his own blood, and being attacked by an eagle, he falls over a precipice to his death.

After this introduction to the colony, it is small wonder that the girls beg their father to return home. He decides to stay: "According to the doctrine of chance, the extraordinary events which have happened to us once will not happen again."

His calculations prove to be correct: he and his family attain bliss and prosperity.

Mark Brandon is a complex figure, but the complexity proceeds from Rowcroft's inconsistent presentation and the exigencies of the plot, rather than from an attempt to plumb the depths of the outlaw's soul. He appears not so much as a hero in his own right, but as an obstacle to the progress of the Hortons. The novel thus reflects the trend to displace the convict from the centre of the stage. The novel also contains some remarks which may be pointers to general contemporary attitudes: "We must use our clubs; one white man is enough for half a dozen natives any time," and "The devil is never so black as he is painted; and the convicts are not so bad as some people say."

Edward Dudley, the well-educated but impoverished hero of R. James' *The Convict* (1857),[77] is not bad at all; he is the innocent victim of circumstances which include smuggling, chartism, thwarted love, and the machinations of a Jesuit in mufti. The latter suborns one of his flock to perjure himself, and on this evidence Dudley is transported.

We first find him in Australia at Mount Gambier, where he has absconded. "Australia", he tells Captain M— , who has chanced upon him, "is a land where nature seems to have planted fraud and enmity among the human race and to which other countries send the offscourings of their population to propagate new crimes, and even degrade the barbarous wickedness they find."

This degradation is caused, according to Dudley, by the indiscriminate mixing of new arrivals with hardened offenders. Nevertheless, even some of the latter can be humane, as the hero finds when he is kindly treated by the bushranger, Brady.

A chain of coincidences leads to Dudley's exoneration. Thereafter he becomes "engaged in sweeping the last trace of convict from his name, and recording the proofs of his innocence in such a manner that doubt or shame could *never* visit him".

Alexander Harris's *The Emigrant Family* (1849),[78] makes a far more perceptive examination of the convicts' situation:

> As the lower [colonial] order generally is that one which in common civil society rebels the most recklessly against control, the collision between it and the law thus interpreted [i.e., by military magistrates]

became still more harsh, rash and desperate:— the superior [military magistrate] mingling, but too commonly, with his investigations and judgments the caustic and irritating sneer; the inferior passing into furious defiance. And it was by these means that a vast amount of the benefit to the criminal's morale, which should have resulted from his seclusion in a new country, was prevented; or even after it was commenced, neutralized.

In accordance with this principle, the convicts in *The Emigrant Family* are generally alienated from, and hostile to, the society in which they live. They are predators living on the outskirts of society and respectability.

At the centre of the social circle depicted in the novel are the emigrants, Lieutenant Bracton, his son Willoughby, his daughter, Katharine, and their Australian friend, Reuben Kable. Kable is not the degenerate offspring of convicts or a pretentious colonial oaf. In bravery he is the Bracton's equal; in the management of colonial affairs he is their superior. He eschews their artificial refinement:

> "I say, Reuben", said Charlie, "that Miss Katharine, as they call her, would make you a rattling fine wife: and she seems the most sensible of the lot."
>
> "Ha! I don't suppose she would have me, Charlie," replied his countryman. "They are brought up in such a fantastical, fol-de-rol way, that a man is nobody in their eyes if he can't cut as many capers as a dancing master..."

Kable's gentlemanliness and good breeding are never doubted by his English friends. However, his dwelling and land exhibit taste adapted to Australian conditions:

> A fine square-sided tract of cultivated ground... It was about a quarter of a mile in length along the water-side and about half as much in depth... On the upperside, nearly or quite in the middle, stood a bush cottage, with that appendage almost universal throughout the colony, as a protection from the sunbeams during the hottest period of the day, a verandah.

The mistress of this house is Kable's sister, Mary, who shares her brother's "simplicity of character". The old convict servants are loyal and devoted pensioners of the establishment.

Elsewhere, harsher treatment leads convicts to exasperation:

> Such is the actual character of the felon population:— a word — a whisper — a whim often suffices to decoy them into dangerous positions, which carry them on through the impetus of their own downhill tendency, and eventually involve loss of liberty and life.

The leader of one group of convict predators is Martin Beck, a half-caste and a former colonial convict. He is resourceful, brave and intelligent; qualities which have become misdirected through harsh treatment. His wiles and stratagems are eventually defeated by Kable. The Bractons and the Kables become united in marriage, bliss and modest prosperity: "Willoughby has very properly concluded . . . that it is better to have a wife and plenty to live on, than lose wife, and self, and all, in trying to get too much."

This novel is one of the first to accord pride of place to an Australian hero. Its emphasis is on colonial experience. The antecedents of the Bractons are cursorily sketched in, while those of most of the convicts are like the servant Margaret's: "a leaf in the book of her life, pasted down; a page defaced, and for some untold reason, not readable". *The Emigrant Family* denotes a further drift in the preoccupation of colonial fiction.

However, the old moral tale was not forgotten, as Mrs Vidal's *The Convict Laundress* (1852),[79] indicated. In this story, retribution falls upon two generations. Grace Allen (the central figure) is the daughter of a Protestant girl who married a Roman Catholic and reared their children in his religion. The mother is punished for her share in this by seeing her husband and son killed and her daughter transported. Grace becomes a faithful servant, but her heterodoxy and her love of opium and grog lead to her death in an asylum.

John George Lang related many stories about the early days of the colony, without, however, seeking to draw a moral. His interests run rather to devising a neat or surprising ending. Lang's use of Israel Chapman, the thief-taker, whom he depicted under the name of George Flower, allowed him to rehearse many surprising stories of roguery. For example, Flower paid £335 to help a convicted earl-elect to return to England. On being asked how he raised the money, Flower replied that some of it was blood money:

> "The rest I borrowed from four Jews, receivers of stolen property, on these easy and quiet terms: my verbal promissory note, payable with interest at one thousand per cent per annum — the account to be settled on the great day of judgment, and the money to be forthcoming on the day after."
> "And did they consent to these terms?"
> "Consent, sir! Why, there is not one of them that I could not transport to Norfolk Island for life, at any moment that I like."[80]

Lang is prolix, and the movement of his plots is turgid, but his stories and novels are important for three reasons: they record some of the oral traditions (he claimed that *Botany Bay* contained "True Tales"); they illustrate the perspective of a dispassionate observer; and they contain a change in the tone of humour. In Vaux's and Tucker's work we find an ironic commentary possessing affinities with the tone of eighteenth-century writers. Lang's humour is less buoyant; it veers more towards the sardonic mode that was to characterize later Australian writers. It is not claimed that he inaugurated this mode in Australia, merely that his work attested to its existence in the mid-nineteenth century.

Much as he disliked *Geoffry Hamlyn* by Charles Kingsley (1859), it did not ever occur to Joseph Furphy to describe the novel as a story about a transported convict, yet that is precisely how the novel was summarized early this century:

> An important character is a transported criminal who is followed to Australia by a number of his connections. A fascinating picture of bush life and adventures with bushrangers. The Colonial scenes are the fruit of personal experience.[81]

Although it would be a distortion to make George Hawker the focus of *Geoffry Hamlyn,* yet it is undeniable that his career has important repercussions on the Buckleys and the Thorntons. The son of a gipsy who had "a sort of double first at Satan's university", Hawker is transported to New South Wales, which Robert Lowe categorized as "the university where . . . scholars in vice and iniquity . . . finish their course of instruction".[82] In the seduction of Mary Thornton and in his other acts of villainy, Hawker showed that he reached an advanced standing before transportation. In the colony he finally murders his old enemy, William Lee. Retribution follows: he is apprehended and he learns that he has killed his own son. Before his execution he repudiates the twenty years of Lee's penitence; he refuses to receive the consolation proffered by the chaplain, but he experiences a rough kind of relief in his camaraderie with Major Buckley and Hamlyn: "I feel more kind and hearty towards you and Hamlyn for coming to me this day, than I've felt toward any man this twenty year."[83]

What is adjuged the frank manliness of Buckley and Hamlyn also enables Frank Maberly to achieve some rapport with the desperate inmates of a convict shepherd's hut.

However, important as Hawker is to the plot of *Geoffry Hamlyn,* he and other convicts are incidental to the burgeoning of the Buckley interests, that is, to the reproduction of an English gentry mode of living in Australia.

Like Mary Thornton, Martha Grylls, the heroine of *The Broad Arrow* (1859),[84] was ruined by a faithless lover. The novel is one of the few which concentrates on a female convict. Martha is seduced by Norwell, who abandons her. When her child dies she is convicted of murder, and under the name of Maida Gwynnham she is transported for life. When the author, Caroline Leakey (Oliné Keese, in reality), depicts Martha in assigned service and suffering in the convict hospital the novel has some vigour and perception.

Melodramatic contrivances of plot tend to dissipate these attributes. Nevertheless, there is an undeniable poignancy about Gwynnham's life that cannot be entirely obscured by melodrama and maudlin sentimentality.

B. L. Farjeon's *Grif* (1866),[85] is as improbable and as sentimental as *The Broad Arrow,* but the inset of the story of

"Welsher", a convict "falsely convicted and transported for burglary", demonstrates that the traditional formula was as vigorous at the end of the transportation era as it had been at the beginning.

Australian fiction written between 1830 and 1868 contains little that is intrinsically worthwhile as literature. Nevertheless, its subject matter indicates colonial preoccupations and attempts to translate colonial experience into fiction.

If early Australian fiction was not rich in quality, life itself was rich in variety. In the years 1830 to 1868 there were major developments in every sphere of Australian life, and as the summaries of convict writings show, even the lot of transported felons exhibited a fascinating diversity. The energies of our forbears were absorbed in survival and social development. The period was not conducive to innovations in the arts. It is not surprising, therefore, that early Australian fiction was based on the traditional formula, and that it shared the pieties of contemporary fiction elsewhere. Australian novels differ in the kinds of experience through which these pieties were examined. The possibilities of fiction were widening, but the convict experience was still described in harrowing terms and writers became increasingly adept at describing convict life within this framework.

As the thrust of Australian life became more and more directed to the settlement of the land, the life of the settlers became a more acceptable subject of fiction. In literature, as in life, convicts came to play an increasingly subordinate role.

4
After 1868: Transportation in Retrospect

> Tell me about that world of shadows I loved so much. And about the life and the soul tell me also.
> Oscar Wilde, A Letter to Robert Ross, September 1896, in *De Profundis*

> The soul, too, has its history.
> Benedetto Croce, *Aesthetic: A Science of Expression and General Linguistic*

> The difficulty is that the history is interior — no documents can give sufficient intimation: the novel must replace history at precisely that point where experience is sufficiently emotional, spiritual, psychical, moral, existential or supernatural to expose the fact that the historian in pursuing the experience would be obliged to quit the clearly demarcated limits of historic inquiry.
> Norman Mailer, *The Armies of the Night: History as a Novel. The Novel as History*

It has been seen that the state of the convict's immortal soul attracted a great deal of attention throughout the transportation era. Submission to, and revolt against, the civil law were taken as indices of his inner life. In the same way the anti-transportation movement and the behaviour of native-born Australians were taken as symptoms of the quickening of the spirit of a new people.

Since the end of transportation, those who have written about Australia have explored many interests. One of them was to examine more closely both the collective and the individual inner life. Whether in pursuit of this objective, or for other reasons, writers continued to deal with the convict experience. When they were used for investigations of the life of the spirit, tales of crime and punishment were invested with a wider meaning than they had hitherto been called upon to convey. Before examining this, and other, uses of the genre, it is useful to consider its treatment by an author who worked outside the English and Australian tradition: Herman Melville.

During the last five years of his life Melville (1886–91) worked on his short novel, *Billy Budd*.[1] Its background is the mutiny at the Nore, for participation in which some sailors were transported to Australia as convicts. *Billy Budd* tells of the interaction of Budd, the Handsome Sailor and the natural innocent, John Claggart, the naturally-depraved master-at-arms, and Captain Vere, who is learned, austere and a victim of the political upheavals of his time.

Through "the arch interferer, the envious Marplot of Eden [who] still has more or less to do with every consignment to this planet of earth", Budd is afflicted with a stammer which leads him to express himself through a blow rather than words when Claggart accuses him of fomenting mutiny. Claggart, who nurses a "spontaneous and profound" antipathy for the innocent Budd, is killed by the blow.

With the memory of Nore so fresh, Captain Vere cannot condone Budd's act, even though "at the last assizes it shall acquit". Budd is tried and condemned to death. In the brig he experiences an agony which "mainly proceed[s] from a generous young heart's virgin experience of the diabolical incarnate and effective in some men". He is visited by the chaplain, who, feeling that "innocence was even better than any religion wherewith to go to judgment", refrains from offering any spiritual advice either there or at the execution. Budd's last dying speech is "God bless Captain Vere!"; the cry is involuntarily yet spontaneously taken up by the whole crew.

When it is remembered that Budd is unable to give an account of his parentage or education, the components of his story (the absence of a ruling passion, evil companions, and wicked deeds; his compassionate treatment by the court-martial; his lack of orthodox repentance, and his unusual dying speech) make it obvious that on the basic narrative level Melville deliberately departed from the traditional formula.

There are many levels of significance imposed on this narrative basis. First, the novel is an "inside story". We penetrate the characters' consciousness, but only to a certain extent. Much remains inexplicable, even to Melville: "But there is no telling the sacrament, seldom if in any case revealed to the gadding world, whenever under circumstances at all akin to those here attempted to be set forth two of great Nature's nobler order embrace". Second, through allegory (the ships mentioned are *The Rights-of-Man, Bellipotent* and *Athée*) and authorial speculation, the novel grapples with what Captain Vere calls the "mystery of iniquity". Third, there is the polemical and false version presented to the world at large by the garbled account printed in the "News from the Mediterranean". Fourth, among the sailors there is an oral tradition of the incident which finds sustenance in their veneration of the spar from which Budd was hanged. They follow it from destination to destination until it is "reduced to a mere dockyard boom". This tradition is, naturally enough, "in a measure mysteriously gone". Fifth, Budd's story becomes enshrined in a ballad, "Billy in the Darbies". It contains a grim humour:

> O, 'tis me, not the sentence they'll suspend.
> Ay, Ay, all is up; and I must up too,
> Early in the morning, aloft from alow.

It expresses a rough camaraderie:

> But Donald he has promised to stand by the plank;
> So I'll shake a friendly hand ere I sink.

Yet it fails to convey the truth of the inside story.

Billy Budd thus comprehends the following levels: the traditional formula; the oral tradition; the ballad; the garbled printed version; the inside story and the metaphysical discussion.

In considering Australian convict literature before 1868 we have seen examples of the first four levels. There were few attempts to portray the inside story, and the metaphysical was expressed through lip service to religious tenets or by an invocation of chance or probability. After 1868 the convict story continued to be told on the first four levels; we shall also find more determined attempts to grapple with the last two.

Later nineteenth-century writings about the convicts

The year after transportation ended, Thomas Huxley coined the term "agnosticism", and a few years later Sir Leslie Stephen wrote "An Agnostic's Apology". There was a great deal of late nineteenth-century literature that dealt with religious faith and doubt. Nevertheless the traditional story of crime, punishment and repentance was still written and read. In 1881, for example, Thomas Bastard wrote his autobiography[2] "to leave to a large circle of cherished friends, acquaintances and relatives the exact memorials of a life marked by more than ordinary vicissitudes, and also of the manner in which it is intended to illustrate how possible is the growth of evil habit, upon a genial social disposition, and how equally possible an absolute reformation."

After 1868 many convicts wrote of their experiences. Some accounts were published; others remain in manuscript. Martin Cash, Mark Jeffrey, and Jorgen Jorgensen wrote autobiographies that have remained in print ever since they were written. Cash's narrative gives a general idea of their scope and attainments.

James Lester Burke played some part in the writing of Cash's *Narrative*[3] (1870), so that it is difficult to know how much of the real Cash is portrayed in the work. Even his fellow convicts appear to have doubted Cash's bona fides:

Lawrence Kavanagh told him " 'Martin, they have got you', implying by that observation that [Cash] had become a tool in the hands of government officers". Cash asserts that Kavanagh later apologized for this accusation, but Kavanagh's suspicions and Cash's reprieve suggest that the latter's reminiscences may be somewhat distorted.

The *Narrative* begins with an account of Cash's parentage and of his "early habits of dissipation . . . folly and misconduct". An ill-fated love affair leads him to shoot a rival, for which he is transported to "that much dreaded receptacle of all human depravity, Botany Bay". We are told nothing of his life in prison, and "nothing remarkable occurred" during his voyage to Australia, where he arrived in 1828. He is assigned to various masters, his account illustrating the vicissitudes that the assignment system entailed. He spends nine years in New South Wales, during which he engages in "business, not always on the right side of the law". He goes to Van Diemen's Land. After some physical encounters with the constabulary (in which he is invariably victorious) and a period of honest labour, he is sentenced (unjustly, he maintains) to seven years' transportation for robbery. At Port Arthur under O'Hara Booth he works in a chain gang with Kavanagh, Jones and Frank the Poet.

With some vigour, he relates his attempts at escape and his life as a bushranger, laying stress upon his resolve not to molest women and his determination to avoid gratuitous violence like flogging the "tyrannical master" McKay. Jealousy again leads to his apprehension. He is sentenced to death, reprieved, and sent to Norfolk Island. He witnesses the administration of Price and Childs and the revolt of 1846, in which he refuses to participate. He stays on the island until the settlement is broken up. After returning to Tasmania he regains his freedom and buys an orchard.

He makes no pretence of undergoing a religious reformation, though he admits that he could feign contrition when it suited him. He admits his hypocrisy in assuring Booth, after an unsuccessful attempt at escape, that "it was the first, and should certainly be the last, time I should ever be guilty of a similar indiscretion, which entailed so much misery upon the unhappy offender ... and ... I should feel it my duty to point out to my fellow prisoners the folly and absurdity of the proceeding". Yet, in the end, he died a free man, and as far as one can judge, he was not engaged in any criminal activity.

Cash experienced the extremes of the convict's experience: the chain gang, Port Arthur, escape, bushranging and Norfolk Island. He witnessed some of the most celebrated events of convict history, and he knew some of its most notorious characters. Although he was one of the survivors he displayed none of the sullenness and moroseness usually attributed to that remnant. His *Narrative* is full of the verve, irony and resilience that go back through Tucker and Vaux to Carew and Head: Cash possessed all the vitality of the archetypal English rogue.

In his bushranging days he exhibited the restraint and quaint nobility that was to become embodied in Boldrewood's Starlight and in Tom Robert's painting "Bailed Up".

He was a rogue whose adventures were calculated not to alienate the reader, so that, recording as it does the extremes of the system, his *Narrative* corroborated the fictional experiences of Rufus Dawes, and other heroes of convict novels and tales.

* * *

"It would be interesting to traverse the field of fiction," A. G. Stephens wrote, "and show the singular force of the death climax where the plan permits it to be used."[4] He went on to consider death climaxes in novels like *Madame Bovary* and *The Story of an African Farm*. Yet, as I suggested in chapter 3 of this study, the death climax is particularly suited to the Australian convict story: it is a good arrangement whereby the hero or heroine can escape the convict taint. If the author opts for another ending, the hero must be allowed to achieve some kind of *modus vivendi* within the community. We have seen that it was difficult to be identifiably an ex-convict and still enjoy the unalloyed esteem of the populace. The writer's dilemma appears most clearly in the two versions of *His Natural Life*, but all writers had to face it. We have noted that, although transportation was a closed system, it effectively lingered on and people found it impossible to view the period dispassionately or as an historical curiosity.

Death as a conclusion presented itself as an obvious solution for those writers who were aware of the traditional tale and for those who sensed that such was the most fitting culmination of a life of suffering.

It was also the ending usually employed by those writers who are sometimes known as the Newgate School.[5] It was the ending deemed most fitting by Hugo's Jean Valjean (1862). In his various disguises the convict had demonstrated that he was a fine citizen. Considered as an ex-convict, he realized he was an embarrassment: ≪Il est utile que je m'en aille. La mort est un bon arrangement≫.[6]

While the conclusion is at hand, the novelist who would treat crime and punishment must decide what pattern he will impose upon other events. A writer even of the calibre of Solzhenitsyn is conscious that impelling some order into the moral and emotional chaos of people in captivity is a demanding task, one that is central to the success of the artistic presentation.[7]

In Australia, a number of unifying patterns and themes have been adopted. For example, in his series of macabre and strident tales Price Warung subsumed treachery, cruelty and perversity in his concept of the system. In a string of pioneering novels writers like Miles Franklin, M. Barnard Eldershaw, Brian Penton and Katharine Susannah Prichard included components of the convict past in a rhetoric devised to express their perception of the national spirit. In Roy Connolly's *Southern Saga* (1940) the rhetoric becomes so dense that it collapses in upon itself like a black hole. More recently popular interest in the graphic, not to mention lurid, depiction of brutality is reflected in films and mini-series about "our past".

To provide an outline of the ways the traditional tale has been developed it is pertinent to survey some examples of related fiction written since 1868.

* * *

It is probably true to say that for generations of Australians Marcus Clarke's *For the Term of his Natural Life*[8] has been the primer of the convict system, just as *Robbery Under Arms* has been that of bushranging. The triumph of this novel is a triumph over problems inherent in the author and in his work.

In the first instance, Clarke's brilliance was not readily harnessed. He found difficulty in meeting deadlines. There was little in his previous writing career that indicated he would be able to sustain his efforts over a lengthy period. In fact, in its first, serialized form, the latter parts of his novel are sluggish at best. The public tired of it, and Clarke was dissatisfied. Sir Charles Gavan Duffy provides us with some insights into Clarke's somewhat impulsive efforts at revision,[9] so that artistic instinct seems to have triumphed over the rationale for a "high and adequate motive".

There also seems to have been a triumph over Clarke's previous attitudes to the convicts. He claims to have come across disturbing "settlements" of them in Melbourne;[10] he had had a fight with an old hand at a station;[11] the convicts who appear in his writings as he began *His Natural Life* are grotesque. He expressed the matter well himself: "I do not have any maudlin sentimentality for convicts",[12] and by implication: "an old lag, with a forehead like an ape and ears like a dog".[13] At best, particularly in *Old Tales of a New Country* (1871),[14] he displayed a dispassionate facility, with a certain wry amusement never far away.

Whether it was solely the need for money that inspired

Clarke to go to Tasmania "to write up the criminal records", we cannot really know. We learn that he claimed to have been working on criminal documents for three years; we also learn that he claimed to have read no other works similar to that which he had in hand.

It is usually agreed that John Price served as a model for Maurice Frere (though one suspects that Javert also figures in the lineage). There have been numerous attempts to trace the original Rufus Dawes. (A review of the novel in 1886 asserted that "its two principal characters, 'Rufus Dawes' and 'Lieut. Frere' are said to be still alive".[15]) In fact, while many convicts shared the range of punishments inflicted on Dawes, unfortunately, few, if any, were men as he was a man.

Clarke has left us two reasons for writing the novel. In his preface, he asserts that his intention was to demonstrate "the general inexpediency of again allowing offenders against the law to be herded together in places remote from the wholesome influence of public opinion". Later, he wrote to Duffy of his wish " . . . to show that in many instances the *law* makes the criminal".

As early as 1810 John Grant had resolved to convey the enormities of transportation by writing a biography: "At times the Idea comes to me of writing the first 15 years of my life in which to assemble all the sufferings of the convicts sent from England".[16]

Clarke, of course, did not know of Grant's journal. He did, however, adopt biography as a unifying force, and he also assembled many of the convicts' sufferings. To name these components points in the direction of, but understates, the achievements of the novel.

Although even after revision, the original motive for Dawes's heroism is confused, it is plain that his background is similar to that of the Buckleys, the Brentwoods, the Bractons and the Thornleys: the pastoral heroes whose careers form the substance of many nineteenth-century novels. Dawes shares their upbringing, their decency, their resolve, but his courage rises far above their pluck. One of the reasons for diminished interest in the serialized form may have been the public's recognition that this kind of hero was an improbable participant in events on the goldfields and at the Eureka Stockade.

The sufferings of Dawes and his stature have suggested parallels to Christ and his sufferings.[17] In essence, the parallel may more properly be understood if we concentrate on the nature of each protagonist. In the traditional Christian view, Christ was both God and man: in some mysterious manner the riches of the godhead were united with the frailty and vulnerability of the human being. In Pauline terms there was an emptying followed by an exaltation.

As far as Dawes is concerned, there is the outward aspect of the criminal, but the reader and the hero know that there is another, rich dimension of which the tormentors are unaware. This richness is maintained until Dawes reaches his breaking point, his emptying. This point of the novel leads us to another perception of the author's intent.

As we have seen, Christian reformism underlay the implementation of the transportation system. We have also seen how far practice strayed from intent. One of the most forceful expressions of the disparity may be seen in an outburst from William Westwood, or "Jacky-Jacky". When the first stage of the orgy of slaughter at Norfolk Island in 1846 had satisfied his immediate thirst for vengeance, Westwood cried "Now for the Christ killer!": Barrow, the magistrate, whose cruelty annihilated any semblance of Christianity on the island.

If we can believe Price Warung, the convicts substituted Satanism for Christian worship, and the rites were "too terrible" to be described. Presumably, sodomy figured in them somewhere.

It is sodomy and the annihilation of the relevance of Christianity that lies at the heart of Dawes's emptying. The incidents occupy chapters XIII to XVI of book 3.

Young Kirkland, the son of Methodists, and perhaps unjustly transported, is offended by the blasphemy of

Captain Burgess, commandant of Port Arthur. For remonstrating, he is sentenced to the chain gang and locked up at night in the yard with his formidable and lascivious companions. "What is he more than anyone else?" Dawes asks himself.

North, the chaplain, seeks to intervene; but Burgess and his minions, Troke and Hailes, refuse to stop the rape which they know will occur. The next day Kirkland (now "Miss Nancy") attempts suicide. He is stopped by one of his grotesque paramours, Gabbett. Kirkland is sentenced to a flogging. Mr Meekin — the exemplar of the simpering, ineffectual clergyman — arrives. He is too purblind to understand what is happening, and North, an alcoholic, sinks into a debauch so that he fails to protect Kirkland.

Dawes is appointed flogger. He demurs and Kirkland ironically remarks: "Go on Dawes ... you are no more than any other man". Kirkland swoons under the lash; Dawes refuses to flog any further, so that he is strung up and flogged by Gabbett. Physical pain, official connivance, the powerlessness of the cloth and Kirkland's degradation all combine to wring from Dawes an outburst which no previous sufferings had done:

> Having found his tongue, the wretched man gave vent to his boiling passion in a torrent of curses. He shrieked imprecations upon Burgess, Troke and North. He cursed all soldiers for tyrants, and all parsons for hypocrites. He blasphemed his god and his Saviour. With a frightful outpouring of obscenity and blasphemy, he called upon the earth to gape and swallow his persecutors, for heaven to open and rain fire on them, for hell to yawn and engulf them quick . . He seemed to have abandoned his humanity.

The divine and the human are thus crushed in him.

Kirkland dies. Dawes and North confront each other and participate in one of those sacraments of which Melville was to write; in this instance it is a sacrament of humanity: "Forgive me brother!" says North, and Dawes "seemed to catch a glimpse of misery more profound than his own, and his stubborn heart felt human sympathy with this erring brother. 'Then in this hell there is yet a man,' said he."

As he leaves Port Arthur, North speaks with the "narrow-minded, conscientious, yet laughter-loving" Father Flaherty, who would have done well enough "where men live too easily to sin harshly". Clarke comments: "He [North] was right. He who would touch the hearts of men must have had his own soul seared". North's own soul is seared again in his love for Sylvia.

On Norfolk Island, North later resolves to save Dawes with his [North's] "own blood". The clergyman loathes his own sinfulness and degradation. Like the gringo and the priest in Greene's *The Power and the Glory*, North fails to realize that in the relinquishing of one's own chance of life and salvation through love of another — however incoherent and poorly understood the love may be — there is a saving power that transcends the orthodox canons of salvation.

North gives Dawes the chance to escape from servitude, but in the cyclone and the swirling sea, which acts as a means of regeneration, the outraged manhood of Dawes and the outraged womanhood of Sylvia find healing by slipping the bonds of the flesh: "They felt as beings whose bodies had already perished, and as they clasped hands their freed souls, recognizing each the loveliness of the other, rushed trem-blingly together." They appear destined neither for heaven nor for hell, but for a state of transcendent bliss that will atone for all that man, and God through man, have inflicted upon them.

This ultimate exaltation (possibly suggested by Wagner's *Der Fliegende Holländer* [1843] or Heine's earlier treatment) is a significant variation on the theme of reformation. Dawes is "saved" but not in a Christian sense. His final state is not heaven but a world of myth. This transposition is in keeping with the irrelevance of Christianity as presented in the novel and it certainly is a truer statement of Clarke's own world view.[18]

In an impressive manner, therefore, Clarke resolved two basic dilemmas. In the first instance, Clarke portrayed a convict hero, a hero of the kind acceptable to the Australian public: the English gentleman, but with two important modi-modifications. First, he was shorn of the mannerisms and aspirations inherent in Furphy's abhorred "virgin-souled slender-witted overgrown schoolboys". Even with these excisions, however, the hero-figure remains substantially the same. His courage, dignity and humanity in the face of unmerited suffering borders on the sublime. In this way he solved his second dilemma by contriving to salvage integrity from the ritual of reformation.

Clarke described his novel as *His Unnatural Life* and "a chamber of horrors".[19] Undoubtedly the novel is full of horrors, and at times it does not lack melodrama. Nevertheless, the power and imaginative strength of many descriptions of suffering and cruelty cannot be denied.

The novel provides a synthesis of many themes of convict writing. For over one hundred years this synthesis has been accepted as an artistic truth, regardless of its departures from the historical truth of the average convict experience. *His Natural Life* succeeded in articulating an acceptable understanding of the convict era.

For the sake of completeness, it should be noted that there is a variant of *His Natural Life*, but a watery grave and the title are the only ways in which Elizabeth Winstanley's *Her Natural Life*[20] resembles Clarke's work. Margaret Shirley, Winstanley's heroine, is an orphan. She is seduced by a squire's son, Nesbitt Aubert, who is "full of mischief and wickedness". Abandoned by him, she is pursued by other lechers, even after she is transported (her baby had died and she attempted suicide). She is followed by the faithful love of Jack Hatchell, who eventually presides over her sea burial after she dies escaping from Sydney.

* * *

When Captain Charles Fitzgerald was appointed Governor of Western Australia in 1848 he was told that only the Emperor of Russia had charge of a larger area than he. No doubt Fitzgerald came to perceive some irony in this description, but the statement expresses the sense of vastness that pervades convict literature set in that state.

The best known of these is John Boyle O'Reilly's *Moondyne*,[21] which involves escape, adventures in the desert, scenes of London life, gold, alliances with the Aborigines, penal reforms and heroic death.

The novel is based loosely on the exploits of Joseph Bolitho Johns. *His* death was not heroic: destitute, he died of senile decay in the Freemantle Asylum.

The wider significance of the convice experience

Some writers have striven to rise above the welter of cruelty and sufferings to examine its underlying principles.

One of these writers was William Hay, who approached his writing with the zeal of a plastic surgeon who is so bent on altering the patient's appearance that he breaks and resets every bone. That Hay's approach was just as painstaking is reflected in the tense and often difficult style in which he wrote *The Escape of the Notorious Sir William Heans* (1919).[22] In reflecting on the achievement of his novel Hay asked "what about the *artistry* that has managed to avoid the sordid in telling of those days?"[23]

As we have seen, it was indeed difficult to avoid the sordid in dealing with the convict days. Hay attempted to do more than avoid the sordid: he sought to explore the motivation of the principal agent of his convict's sufferings. It became traditional, as we have seen, to depict those set in authority over the convicts as tyrants: Maurice Frere is the fictional embodiment of a type that goes back to Foveaux. In seeking to unravel the mystery of Hean's tormentor, Mr Daunt, Hay tried to determine whether seemingly harsh officials could have been prompted by any motives other than sadism:

> Last, Daunt's show of friendliness! What did the forgiveness of a man like Daunt mean? He might well have asked "Did Daunt credit

him with the weakness of being confused by compliment? Was Daunt at the old game of stripping a foe's heart of armour for the next man's sword to play upon? Had Daunt at sight of him forcing his way through that sea of police, been startled into one of his half-friendly moments? Or, more likely had the man's mistrust been allayed by his [Heans's] reply to Lady Franklin?" (Devil or philanthropist, which was Daunt?)

Herein lies the mystery of Mr Daunt, a mystery which Hay left unsolved. While Daunt lay dying of a malignant disease, he summoned Heans to make a final statement about the convict in the presence of the governor. Daunt died before he could unburden himself:

> With the gentlemen gathered in that remote room, we can but wonder what was his intention. We may choose to think with his Honour and Captain Garian that Mr Daunt meant to act as became his station, and acknowledge to Captain Shaxton before he died that he had mistakenly traduced his wife, and credited the prisoner with the lowest of all thefts. We may think with Magruder, and possibly old Oughtryn, that Daunt was ashamed of the character of the billeted soldier, and would even have cleared Sir William Heans of his own carelessness; or go to Shaxton's extreme, unquiet and suspecting of the dead man after two engagements with him; or even feel relief with poor, sad Heans that those yet smiling lips had been unable to announce the capture of his friends. Nay (for how could he know Carnt was in the coach at that moment?), he has as much as expressed a doubt whether Daunt knew something of their plot, and, in love with his "lightning and sunshine" to the end, would have thus authoritatively disclosed and stopped them. To these fevered accusations let us add our private contributions: that if he knew their plans, it were the better revenge upon the one to have permitted the two other parties to go free . . . Indeed, that he expired with a look of hate upon his face may seem to some that he died according to his will and intention at the end, even in the manner of his silent death.
>
> We may think with any one of these. Or we may think with the Government Surgeon that Commandant Daunt must have been painfully ignorant of his interior. Or with Karne and Kent — here was a fine bitter man caught by Death.
>
> Or, with Mr Craye, we may pray unmoved above the pretty murmur of the music.

Hay also managed to convey Heans's sufferings without

subjecting him to physical torture. Heans was transported for attempting the abduction of Lady Charlotte S—t. While his culpability is frankly admitted, it is somewhat attenuated by the remark that "it is a fair comment on the case that the lady was in after life again in the Courts". Nevertheless, Heans continued to try to manipulate women's affections: he enlisted Matilda Hyde-Shaxton to help him to escape, and he proposed that they should elope together. When this attempt was thwarted, he used Abelia as a go-between with Matilda, and he did not hesitate to hide incriminating evidence in Abelia's saddlebag. Such were his charms that women helped him unsolicited: the normally-cautious Mrs Quaid took risks on his behalf, and his successful escape was conceived by Abelia, furthered by Matilda, and accomplished with the help of Conapanny.

For a man of a degree of elegance and sophistication sufficient to appeal to Matilda Hyde-Shaxton, the association with less-refined convicts would obviously have been a keen trial. During a visit to "Fraser's Rooms", Heans became the butt of crude humour: "A funny fellow with a strange unsmiling face had placed a paper eyeglass in his eye, and was cutting a jocose caper in the shadow of a friend. They would ponder with a burlesque heaviness when Sir William pondered, and nearly collapse in their ecstasies of wild anticipation when Sir William elected to play". His keenest sufferings came from subjection to authority:

> "You have been suffering, Sir William Heans," she said, breathless yet eager. "I am afraid you are finding – finding the life difficult." Sir William did not answer for a moment. He dropped his head and tapped his cane upon the wooden rail.
> "These men are voracious against misfortune – against a sentence – in one of my standing," he said, in a quiet voice. He went on to tell how Head-Warder Rowkes or Captain Jones, who had raised themselves, and from whom temper and selfishness had barred the goal of their ambition, oppressed him with a secret and careful resentment. In the strangest way did the most successful, commanding men disclose some private disappointment by a severity or a grim snub which they knew he was powerless to return. "The resentment of the prisoners in the Hulk, when I go to report myself, against my

clothes" (he looked upon his gauds with a sighing laugh) "is kinder than the hate of these deluded men."

From these and similar torments he earns deliverance by adopting a more selfless attitude towards women. Homely O'Crone, who knew Heans in England, was grieved to find Heans "so unchanged": " 'How little can the world change us! It has no respect for difficulty; but with a gentleman's heart it can do but little' ". Indeed, Heans reached the depths of his despair when he feared that the female convict, Madame Ruth, would escape, leaving him behind:

> "Else she'll go, sir, and we're left," said Sir William, trembling in his saddle.
> "This may be false; you and that man — "
> "False!"
> "You and that man — "
> "It is all false — false as life itself! There's not a word of truth in it, or in any of us, or Life sir — in man, woman or child. It is a lie. You and I are a lie, sir; and that prison; and the confounded, jangling bell. Everything — hurt or joy, or faithfulness like yours, or hope like mine, Carnt's generosity, Islip's spying deference — all a damnable fancy! Why should I be brave enough to hope — or you mad enough to care!"
> "Hold!" snarled O'Crone, touching his arm, "I believe in your bitterness."

Heans triumph over his despair and self-love by rescuing Albelia at the price of ruining another attempt at escape. His change of heart is represented in modest terms:

> Writing to his friend Sir Charles of his future prospects and the things a man may do, he reflects incidentally how "a fellow may engage himself in being simply a generous, temperate, and noble person, passing his leisure in reading and talking for entertainment and yet fall short of a difficult ideal". It will serve our turn to suppose he engaged himself in some effort of this nature.

It is woman who exhibits nobility: she is too good for man:

> What a poor thing — this woman — at which the ages rail! Pray, let us fashion a better and more miraculous gift from God and the spirit; from darkness, gloom and dust! Empty the world of her airs, and her hair, and her loning, ironic, slightly wearied eye! Take her away, with her music, her wit, her strangeness, her frail body and her

pain, her brave little feet walking beside us. Give us — the road without her.

The themes of the novel — the sufferings of the refined convict, the mystery of authority and the fidelity of womankind — are united in an intricate structural framework.

The novel is divided into three books: "High Water", "Neap Tide", and "Low Water of Spring Tides". These titles were no doubt suggested by the fact that escape from Tasmania was possible only by sea, and also by Brutus's famous sentiments:

> There is a tide in the affairs of men
> Which, taken at the flood, leads on to fortune;
> Omitted, all the voyage of their life
> Is bound in shallows and miseries.

Heans's fortunes are at their lowest ebb in the second book, "Neap Tide"; when later he takes the current when it serves, he escapes, but not with the same high hopes and exaltation as he had entertained in book 1.

Heans resembles other convict novels in that it purports to be based on documents — not on the criminal records — but on Heans's letters to his friend, Sir Charles Scarning, letters to Heans from people like Jarvis Carnt; the hieroglyphs of the lavender pad; Sir William's private album; messages written in the "jailed volumes" of Plutarch's *Works,* and in a hat, and engravings upon a stable wall.

Quite literally at the centre of the novel stands Carnt's message written on a cancelled ticket; it is enclosed in the lavender pad, which in turn is in one of the volumes of Plutarch. The Plutarchs contain brief notes about the convict, Walter Surridge, whose full story is written on a hat band. These documents bind the novel together. The Plutarchs had belonged to Governor Collins, in whose time Surridge had suffered the grosser cruelties of the penal system. The past still lives in Surridge's engravings on the stable wall and in his escape tunnel, which Heans himself planned to use. The stable adjoins Oughtryn's house, which was the scene of the murder of Collins; it is also the house in which Daunt dies. The treacherous Spafield, who is a survivor and quasi-symbol of the early days, is killed in the stable. Oughtryn's house is thus the means of setting Heans's sufferings against the background of the traditional physical torments, which are thus skilfully contained.

Heans's escape is effected by the women of Oughtryn's house who are legatees of the convict system: Conapanny (who as Moicrime was Surridge's lover) and Abelia, the daughter of an ex-convict.

Hay has thus synthesized the past and present as well as external and internal sufferings. The labours of reconstituting the components of the convict narrative are reflected in Hay's Meredithian style. Throughout the novel, he used shades like "pallor" and "lavender" to convey mood. At the end of the novel, these shades are reassembled to denote the final synthesis: as Heans waits for the boat which will carry him away,

> he would stand, in the half-dusk, an ignoble and tattered object, sick with the deferred hope of fruitless days, staring with a shred of obstinacy into that wan opening in the walls. He describes the hot sunrises, beautiful enough. This one, "a splash of red currant on a silver plate"; that one "a badly trimmed oil lamp on a damask cloth"; and another, Heaven knows, in less sad circumstances a pretty thing! It was a sky of mighty lavender clouds, backed with remote pale alps, and fired with a rifling of pink. A grey satin sea, lit very bright and pale, especially near the cliffs and fall, where the glassy path was bestrown with lavender and carnation.

In structure, perspective, themes and style, *The Escape of the Notorious Sir William Heans (and the Mystery of Mr Daunt)* is an unique achievement in Australian convict literature.

From the 1950s onward, writers have invested the convict experience with a much wider significance. For example, while the former convict, Judd, in Patrick White's *Voss* (1957) "had been subjected to the greatest brutality and most rigorous kinds of physical labour" it is not because of this background that his contribution to the novel is important. Rather, burdened with an "empirical nature", which leads him to reject the Kierkegaardian call, he becomes the embodiment of all who renounce it:

> Since his own fat paddocks, not the deserts of mysticism, nor the transfiguration of Christ, are the fate of the common man, he [Judd] was yearning for the big breasts of his wife, that would smell of fresh-baked bread even after she had taken off her shift.[24]

Some members of the expedition had been unaware of the call; others, as Le Mesurier said, had experienced a form of damnation. All except Judd perished. He became a species of scapegoat. "Tired and confused", he survived to wander about with a garbled recollection of the mysteries in which he had participated.

If "All that was essential, most secret, was contained for Judd, like his own spring water, in a nest of ferns," the treasure of Ellen Roxborough, heroine of White's *A Fringe of Leaves* (1976) was similarly concealed:

> Not by any lucid flesh, but working her way towards a solution, she strung the ring on one of the runners straggling from her convolvulus girdle, and looped the cord, and knotted it, hoping the gold would not give itself away by glistening from behind the fringe of leaves.[25]

The metaphysical gold which is the object of her intuitive, if not fully-conscious, quest, is more carefully hidden from her. Her journey takes her through the thickets of civilization, where the insensitive and the pompous lurk, and through the Australian bush where she suffers from the peremptory, but not artificial, attentions of the Aborigines. Her deliverance comes through Jack Chance, a bolted "miscreant" (as Mr Roxborough called the convicts). Chance had been convicted for the murder of a London prostitute:

> "Oh, Captain Lovell," [Ellen Roxborough] cried, "most of us are guilty of brutal acts, if not actual murder. Don't condemn him simply for that. He is also a man who has suffered the brutality of life and been broken by it."[26]

Despite his sufferings or (as White would say) possibly because of them, Jack the convict becomes Ellen's "saviour-lover".

In these two novels, therefore, the traditional convict story is transcended, and convicts are caught up in speculation about the possibilities and contingencies of the human condition:

> For however much crypto-eagles aspire to soar, and do in fact through thoughtspace and dream, their human nature cannot but grasp at any circumstantial straw which may indicate an ordered universe.[27]

An aside in *Happy Valley* (1939) and the treatment of Judd and Chance reveal White's awareness of the traditional tale. Other writers have chosen to set it aside to tease out the drama inherent in the suffering and cruelty of the convict era. These components are given a focus by reference to a sample of works related in some way to that era.

In *The Tilted Cross* (1961) for example, Hal Porter found inspiration in writings about the transported artist Thomas Griffiths Wainewright (1794–1852), who serves as a model for the Judas Griffin Vaneleigh of the novel.[28] The baroque and heightened tone of Wainewright's writings are in consonance with Porter's own style. Moreover, given Porter's ability to perceive the malice and hypocrisy that hide behind a civilized veneer, Tasmania of the penal era is an apt subject. It is a world where the convict Christ-figure, Queely Sheill, is an embarrassment, so that he is drawn into his inevitable passion and death. It is an horrific end, the details of which were drawn from an early surgeon's manual.

An equally-graphic climax brings Thomas Keneally's *Bring Larks and Heroes* (1967) to a close. In this case, the novel is built around an incident in Watkin Tench's journals and the writings of the transported artist, Thomas Watling. The setting of the novel is the coastal area which figures prominently in Keneally's first two novels. While this background is powerfully presented, the penal society imposed upon it is shadowy and uncertain. This forms a fitting milieu for the hero, Phelim Halloran. A transported Irish Catholic, he is equally a Catholic of the 1960s transported into the past. The sixties, the period of the Second Vatican Council, was a period in which the conscience of the individual and the requirements of Church laws — the validity and authenticity of which were questioned — were much-debated issues. In fact it is the incisiveness with which Keneally analyzes Halloran's threshing about in the thicket of conscience that is the major achievement of the novel. It is ironical that its final question: "he being borne presiding through so many constellations that he asked himself, panic stricken 'Am I perhaps *God?*' ", appears to echo a passage written by that champion of orthodoxy, G. K. Chesterton.[29]

In the writings of Porter and Keneally, the world of the convict era is not re-created. Rather, various beams and bricks are taken and a new edifice is built around them.

As the bibliography shows, it is possible to cite many other treatments of the convict experience. It is likely that it will be a minor but continuing preoccupation of Australian, and other, writers. People in bondage, abuse of authority, capitulation, treachery, heroism: these are universal themes and unfortunately, Mark Twain's perception is equally applicable to all cultures:

> When death sets open the prison door of life there the band salutes the freed soul with a burst of glad music.

In many cases in life and art, death remains a good solution.

Appendixes

Appendix I   A Schematic Presentation of the Components of Some Factual British Criminal Biographies, Numbered to Conform with the Notes to Appendix I

AUTHOR AND YEAR OF PUBLICATION	SHORT TITLE	EARLY LIFE	INTRODUCTION TO CRIME	PROGRESS IN CRIME	CAPTURE	PRISON
1. BALDWIN	IACKE CADE		LED BY "FORTUNE". "FROWARD FOLLY".	REBELLION. MURDER.	THROUGH TREACHERY OF COMRADES	
2. ORDINARY OF NEWGATE (N.D.)	SARAH MALCOLMSON	"HONEST CREDITABLE PARENTS". GOOD EDUCATION. WENT INTO SERVICE	LED BY BAD COMPANY	JOINED CONSPIRACY TO ROB HER MISTRESS WHO WAS ALSO MURDERED	DUE PROCESS OF LAW	SHOWED G... PENITENC...
3. ORDINARY OF NEWGATE (N.D.)	WILLIAM RAY	"HONEST PARENTS". "GOOD EDUCATION". BECAME A FARRIER.	BEGAN TO DRINK. JOINED BAD COMPANY.	IN A DRUNKEN RAGE HE MURDERED HIS WIFE		SHOWED PENITENC...
4. ANONYMOUS (1783)	'JOHN AUSTIN' (BROADSHEET)		BAD COMPANIONS	HIGHWAY ROBBERY AND ASSAULT	DUE PROCESS OF LAW	
5. ANONYMOUS (1783)	'SIX UNFORTUNATE MALEFACTORS' (BROADSHEET)			CRIMES INCLUDED ASSAULT, ROBBERY, IMPERSONATION.		
6. ANONYMOUS (1752)	'JOHN SWAN & ELIZABETH JEFFREYS' (BROADSHEET)			CONSPIRACY TO ROB AND MURDER		
7. ANONYMOUS (N.D.)	'WILLIAM NEVISON' (BROADSHEET)	"GOOD PARENTS". "GOOD EDUCATION".	"BADLY DISPOSED".	ROBBERY. EXTORTION. HIGHWAY ROBBERY.	DUE PROCESS OF LAW	
8. KNAPP & BALDWIN (1811)	'JOHN DONELLAN' (NEWGATE CALENDAR)	GOOD EDUCATION AND PARENTAGE IMPLIED. JOINED ARMY.	CASHIERED FOR LOOTING. HE WAS GREEDY AND AMBITIOUS.	ELOPED WITH A RICH GIRL; POISONED HER BROTHER.	DUE PROCESS OF LAW.	
9. ANONYMOUS (1781)	'JOHN DONELLAN' (GENTLEMAN'S MAGAZINE)			MURDER		
10. BORROW (1825)	'SAMUEL HAYWARD' (CELEBRATED TRIALS)	WELL EDUCATED	ASSOCIATED WITH "NOTORIOUS COURTEZANS" AND GAMBLED.	FREQUENTED A GAMBLING HOUSE AND BROTHEL. JOINED A GANG OF THIEVES.	THROUGH TREACHERY OF ACCOMPLICES	
11. ANONYMOUS (N.D.)	'BAMFYLDE MOORE CAREW' (CHAP BOOK)	SON OF CLERGYMAN. WELL EDUCATED.	JOINED GYPSIES. SWINDLING. IMPOSTURE. VAGRANCY.			
12. ANONYMOUS (N.D.)	'BLOODY TRAGEDY - JOHN GILL' (CHAP BOOK)		LED A WICKED LIFE.	MURDERED HIS PARENTS. RAPED A SERVING MAID. ROBBERY. ARSON.	DUE PROCESS OF LAW.	
13. ANONYMOUS (N.D.)	'DICK TURPIN' (CHAP BOOK)	SON OF AN INNKEEPER. AVERAGE EDUCATION. INDULGED BY PARENTS.	BAD COMPANIONS.	JOINED GANG OF THIEVES. STOLE SHEEP. HOUSE BREAKING. TORTURE. HIGHWAY ROBBERY.	DUE PROCESS OF LAW.	
14. ANONYMOUS (N.D.)	'JAMES WARD' (CHAP BOOK)			MURDERED HIS WIFE.	CAPTURED IN A PUBLIC-HOUSE.	LETTER THE CON... CELL REPRODU...

Appendix I   149

AL	SENTENCE AND EXECUTION	ADDITIONAL MATERIAL OR COMMENTS
	HANGED, DRAWN AND QUARTERED AT TYBURN.	ENDING OF PLAY MEANT TO DEMONSTRATE THAT GOD HAS "ORDAYNED THE POWER" SO THAT HE WHO RESISTS AUTHORITY RESISTS GOD. ALL ARE EXHORTED TO AVOID CADE'S VICIOUS COURSES
	DIED EXCLAIMING 'LORD HAVE MERCY' BUT REFUSED TO ADMIT COMPLICITY IN THE MURDER.	ORDINARY INCLUDED SUMMARY OF SERMON TO CONDEMNED; THE SUBJECT: "GOD'S VENGEANCE UPON MURDERS". HE INSISTS HE HAS TRANSMITTED TO PRINTER TRUE ACCOUNT OF SARAH MALCOLM'S CRIME AND PUNISHMENT.
	AT HIS EXECUTION THE ROPE BROKE; STRUNG UP AGAIN.	ORDINARY STATES RAY BELIEVED HIS SENTENCE WAS JUST CONSEQUENCE OF MURDER, SABBATH-BREAKING, IDLENESS AND NEGLECT OF RELIGIOUS DUTIES
'S ED	PENITENT. EXHORTED SPECTATORS TO SHUN BAD COMPANY AND HIS BAD EXAMPLE.	LAST SENTENCE OF THIS BROADSHEET PROVIDES SENSATIONAL DETAIL: "THE NOOSE OF THE HALTER HAVING SLIPPED TO THE BACK PART OF HIS NECK, IT WAS FULL TEN MINUTES BEFORE HE WAS DEAD".
ED	PENITENT. CONFESSED THEIR GUILT.	EXECUTION DELAYED BY VIOLENT STORM. A POEM, "THE LAMENTATIONS OF A SINNER", ADDED TO THIS ACCOUNT.
DE AND	BOTH ACKNOWLEDGED THEIR GUILT.	JEFFREYS FAINTED MANY TIMES; BECAUSE SHE WAS SO SHORT SHE HAD TO BE STOOD ON A CHAIR. EXECUTION WITNESSED BY "THE GREATEST CONCOURSE ... THAT HAD EVER BEEN SEEN IN THE MEMORY OF MAN".
NT	PENITENT. ACKNOWLEDGED THAT HIS SENTENCE WAS JUST.	PROSE ACCOUNT RECAPITULATED AND EMBELLISHED IN BALLAD "BOLD NEVISON THE HIGHWAYMAN".
E WITH TION ITIONS ERS	AT SCAFFORD HE SWORE THAT "HE FELL A SACRIFICE TO THE MALICE OF HIS PROSECUTORS".	ACCOUNT MUCH MORE RESTRAINED THAN THAT WHICH FOLLOWS. VICTIM'S "VENEREAL COMPLAINT" AND AUTOPSY GLOSSED OVER.
E T		DONELLAN'S SLANDERS AGAINST HIS VICTIM RECORDED. LURID ACCOUNT OF THE AUTOPSY. GENERAL TONE OF ARTICLE ONE OF GRATIFICATION THAT A PARVENU HAS BEEN PUNISHED.
	DIED "WITH A FIRMNESS THAT ASTONISHED EVERYONE PRESENT".	BORROW DENIED THE USE OF EXISTING MODELS BUT IT IS OBVIOUS THAT HE WROTE WITHIN THE ESTABLISHED TRADITION.
		CAREW WAS ELECTED KING OF THE GYPSIES.
D T.	EXECUTED	THERE ARE ADDED "SEVERAL OTHER THINGS, WORTHY THE OBSERVATION OF YOUNG PEOPLE".
E UCH T ERS".	DEATH. BEFORE HIS EXECUTION HE SPOKE FOR HALF AN HOUR WITH THE HANGMAN AND THEN JUMPED OFF THE LADDER.	"HE BEHAVED WITH AMAZING ASSURANCE AND BOWED TO THE SPECTATORS AS HE PASSED".
MANY SPEECH	DEATH. THE EXECUTION IS DESCRIBED IN DETAIL.	CHAPBOOK CONTAINS WOODCUTS ILLUSTRATING THE MURDER, WARD'S APPREHENSION AND EXECUTION (WITH THE LEGEND, "A TRIPLE CORD IS NOT NOT EASILY BROKEN"). STORY IS RECAPITULATED AND ENLARGED UPON IN CONCLUDING POEM.

Appendix II: A Schematic Presentation of the Components of Some Fictional British Criminal Biographies, Numbered to Conform with the Notes to Appendix II

AUTHOR AND YEAR OF PUBLICATION	SHORT TITLE	EARLY LIFE	INTRODUCTION TO CRIME	PROGRESS IN CRIME	CAPTURE	PRISON LIFE
1. HEAD (1665)	MERITON LATROON	RESPECTABLE PARENTS EDUCATED. INDENTURED.	LED ASTRAY BY AN EVIL COMPANION	DRINKS. WHORES. JOINS A GANG OF THIEVES AND GYPSIES.	DUE PROCESS OF LAW.	i) A HELL, A SCHOOL VICE. ii) HE REFO
2. DEFOE (1722)	COLONEL JACQUE i) JACQUE ii) TRANSPORTED FELON pp. 152 ff	i) ILLEGITIMATE. RAISED IN POVERTY ii) POOR. DISREPUTABLE.	LED TO STEAL BY NECESSITY	JOINED A GANG OF THIEVES; INCREASING SOPHISTICATION OF CRIME. INCREASINGLY SOPHISTICATED CRIME	CAUGHT BY CHANCE	A SCHOOL OF AND MISERY
3. DEFOE (1722)	MOLL FLANDERS	POVERTY. DISGRACE.	CORRUPTED BY HER BETTERS, HER RULING PASSION AND BY NECESSITY.	ASSOCIATED WITH RECEIVERS, INCREASINGLY SOPHISTICATED CRIME.	DUE PROCESS OF LAW	GARNISH, E' ASSOCIATES INEFFECTUA ORDINARY. COMPUNCTIO
4. GAY (1728)	BEGGAR'S OPERA (MACHEATH)			INVOLVED IN ORGANISED CRIME. VIEWED VICTIMS CALLOUSLY.	THROUGH TREACHERY OF ASSOCIATES.	GARNISH. OFFICIALS ASSOCIATES ESCAPE ATT
5. LILLO (1731)	LONDON MERCHANT	BARNWELL MILLWOOD	LED BY PASSION LED BY RULING PASSION AND NECESSITY	DEFRAUDED MASTER - COMPASSION ON VICTIM GOADED BARNWELL INTO CRIME; NO COMPASSION.	CAPTURED THROUGH TREACHERY DUE PROCESS OF LAW.	HELPED BY DISSENTING MINISTER, P
6. FIELDING (1743)	JONATHAN WILD	PROSPEROUS PARENTS NEGLECTED SCHOOLING	LED BY OWN WILFULNESS	ORGANIZED HIS OWN GANG OF THIEVES. ACHIEVED PROMINENCE AS A RECEIVER.	DUE PROCESS OF LAW.	GARNISH. OF CORRUPT. OF VICE AN INEFFECTUA ORDINARY.
7. HOGARTH (1747)	IDLE PRENTICE		FRITTERED AWAY MASTER'S TIME	NEGLECTED DIVINE SERVICE. GAMBLED WITH BAD COMPANIONS. ROBBED IN COMPANY.	BETRAYED BY HIS WHORE.	
8. GOLDSMITH (1760)	T - C -	"CREDITABLE PARENTS". "VERY GOOD EDUCATION".	"LEWD COURSES" "CARDS ON SUNDAY". LIVES OFF CREDIT.	HIS SKILL IN LIVING OFF CREDIT EXCEEDED THAT OF ALL OTHER ENGLISHMEN		
9. GOLDSMITH (1760)	CITIZEN OF THE WORLD	ORPHAN. POOR EDUCATION.	LED BY DEVIL - KILLED A HARE.		CAUGHT BY MAGISTRATE WHO OWNED HARE.	HE BELIEV WAS WELL- IN NEWGAT

Appendix II   151

TRIAL	SENTENCE	CONSEQUENCES	ADDITIONAL MATERIAL AND COMMENTS
	TRANSPORTATION	CAPTURED BY TURKS IN TRANSIT	TO LATROON'S TALE IS ADDED THOSE OF A BOON COMPANION AND THOSE OF "TWO DOXIES" WITH WHOM THEIR LOT IS CAST.
	TRANSPORTATION	WELL TREATED. FELT COMPUNCTION. PROSPERED.	HE IS KIDNAPPED AND SENT TO AMERICA WHERE HE IS TREATED LIKE A TRANSPORTED CONVICT. HE PROSPERS AND REPORTS THE PROSPERITY OF MANY TRANSPORTEES.
WAS JUST. SSES WERE LE	TRANSPORTATION	CREW WERE KIND. FELLOW PRISONERS COMPRISED A COLLGE OF VICE AND CRIME. THROUGH BRIBERY, EFFECTS OF TRANSPORTATION WERE AVOIDED.	MOLL EVINCED A COMPUNCTION OF SORTS. ESCAPED MOST RIGOURS OF TRANSPORTATION.
SSES LE.	DEATH	REPRIEVED	CONCEPT OF PENITENCE IRONICALLY TREATED.
WAS JUST.	DEATH	DIED REPENTANT	
	DEATH	DIED OBDURATE	MILLWOOD BELIEVED SHE WAS PREDESTINED TO DAMNATION: "I WAS DOOMED BEFORE THE WORLD BEGAN TO ENDLESS PAINS".
RED SSES: AN SIONED CE.	DEATH	DIED OBDURATE AND HATED BY THE SPECTATORS.	WILD'S LAST ACT WAS TO PICK THE ORDINARY'S CORKSCREW FROM HIS POCKET
CHED BY PLICES	DEATH	EXECUTED	IN THIS SERIES HOGARTH ILLUSTRATED THE PATH OF CRIME AS IN THE COMPANION SERIES, THE "INDUSTRIOUS 'PRENTICE", HE ILLUSTRATED THE PATH TO PROSPERITY.
		DROWNED	SATIRICAL TREATMENT OF THEOPHILUS CIBBER DEMONSTRATES HOW ORDINARY'S SPEECH HAS DEGENERATED INTO PATTER.
CTED OF POOR	TRANSPORTATION	ILLNESS & STARVATION ON TRANSPORT SHIP. HIS SENTENCE EXPIRED, HE WORKED HIS PASSAGE HOME.	GOLDSMITH AGAIN USED THE TRADITIONAL TALE FOR SATIRE; ON THIS OCCASION HE TOOK AN IRONIC VIEW OF A VETERAN'S LOYALTY TO THAT COUNTRY WHICH HAD TREATED HIM SO POORLY.

Appendix III: A Schematic Presentation of the Components of Factual Convict Accounts and Biographies (1792–1830), Numbered to Conform with the Notes to Appendix III

AUTHOR YEAR OF PUBLICATION OR WRITING	TITLE	EARLY LIFE	INTRODUCTION TO CRIME	PROGRESS IN CRIME	CAPTURE	PRISON LIFE	TRIAL	SENTENCE
1. JAMES LACEY. (1792)	LETTER.							
2. ANON. (1792)	LETTER.							
3. T.F. PALMER. (1795)	LETTER.							
4. GEORGE BARRINGTON. (1795 - 1801)	VOYAGE TO BOTANY BAY. I + II	PROSPEROUS PARENTS. CHANCE OF GOOD EDUCATION.	PERVERSITY & BAD COMPANY.	INCREASING SOPHISTICATION & AUDACITY IN CRIME.	DUE PROCESS		CHIEF BARON'S SPEECH RECORDED. ELOQUENT DEFENCE.	SEVEN YEARS
5. JAMES MARTIN. (1796)	MEMORANDOMS.			THEFT.		TWO MONTHS.		SEVEN YEARS.
6. J.A. SEMPLE. (1799)	LIFE.	ENLISTED. ACCOUNT OF HIS AMOURS & TRAVELS IN EUROPE.	SWINDLED TO PAY HIS WAY.	CONTINUING THEFT & IMPOSTURE.	CAUGHT FOR STEALING A SHIRT.	TWO YEARS. COMFORTABLE QUARTERS. PEREMPTORY REMOVAL TO TRANSPORT.	SUPPORT FROM BOSWELL & BURKE.	SEVEN YEARS.
7. JAMES GROVE (1803)	LETTERS.	A DIE-SINKER. MARRIED.	ENGRAVED A PLATE FOR FORGERY.		TRICKED BY BANK SPIES.	CONVERTED, HORROR OF FELLOW CONVICTS. EXPIREE TOLD HIM ABOUT COLONY.	PLEADED GUILTY.	LIFE.
8. JOHN GRANT. (1804 - 1811)	JOURNAL; LETTERS.	RESPECTABLE PARENTS. EDUCATED. APPRENTICED.	SEDUCED A SERVING MAID. BANKRUPT.	SHOT A SOLICITOR.	DUE PROCESS.	REVOLTED AT CRUDITY OF PRISON LIFE. REJECTED RELIGON.	LAWYER TRIED TO PLEAD MENTAL INSTAB-ILITY.	DEATH COMMUTED TO LIFE IMPRISON-MENT.
9. JOHN SLATER. (1819)	CHAPBOOK.							
10. JAMES HARDY VAUX. (1819)	MEMOIRS. (I)	GENTEEL FAMILY. EDUCATED. APPRENTICED.	BAD COMPAN-IONS & HIS OWN "INSTABILITY"	INCREASING SOPHISTICATION. JOINED GANG OF THIEVES.	CAUGHT FOR CRIME "HE DID NOT COMMIT".	SCHOOL OF VICE VENAL OFFICERS. GAOL FEVER.	CONVICTED THROUGH PERJURED WITNESSES.	SEVEN YEARS.
	(II)			ASSOCIATED WITH CRIMINALS & EXPIREES.	CAUGHT THROUGH HIS RECKLESS-NESS.	SHARED CONDEMNED CELL.	BETRAYED BY HIS LAWYER.	DEATH, COMMUTED TO TRANSPOR-ATION FOR LIFE.

Appendix III 153

	COLONIAL EXPERIENCE	END OF SERVITUDE (AS RECORDED IN TEXTS)	REMARKS
ENT. RUMOR OF TS MED H DUTY.			
LY WITH N.	PROSPERED IN COLONY AS A TAILOR. SOME CONVICTS WERE WORKED HARD. PRICES & NATURAL DESCRIPTIONS GIVEN.		
D OF NG A	HIS LIFE WAS "A REGISTER OF VEXATIONS AND PERSECUTIONS". HE COMPLAINED OF INJUSTICES OF THE MILITARY AND OF BRUTALITY TO ABORIGINES AND CRITICISED HIGH PRICES.		
SED BY ERS. TABLE RS. IN	SHORTLY AFTER ARRIVAL MADE SUPER-INTENDENT OF CONVICTS. STORIES OF ABSCONDING CONVICTS; RESTLESSNESS OF IRISH; DIFFICULTIES OF CONTROLLING CONVICTS; CHANGE FROM CIVIL TO MILITARY GOVERNMENT.		PART II IS OBVIOUSLY A PARAPHRASE OF COLLINS' ACCOUNT.
TEN ON E NED.	EMPLOYED CLEARING GROUND. FULL DESCRIPTION OF ESCAPE WITH BRYANTS.	<u>MEMORANDOMS</u> ENDS WITH REIMPRISONMENT IN NEWGATE.	
D BY CORPS RIFT URES.		EVENTUALLY APPREHENDED, HE WAS IMPRISONED IN BRIDEWELL. HE DEPLORED THE EFFECTS OF VIOLENT PASSIONS.	
WITH S. ANIED ILY. NT E.	PROSPERED IN COLONY. HELD HIMSELF ALOOF FROM CONVICTS. REGARDED TRANSPORTATION AS BLESSING.		
ED AT IONS K. ED TO N'S RS.	ARRIVED WITH FAVOURABLE INTRODUCTIONS. BECAME ALIENATED FROM OFFICIALS BY PURSUING CONVICT'S CAUSE. IMPRISONED. SENT TO NORFOLK ISLAND. MAROONED ON ISLE PHILIP. HEALTH FAILED. RETURNED TO MAINLAND. ACTED AS CHAPLAIN AT NEWCASTLE.	ABSOLUTE PARDON. (RECOMMENDED BY BLIGH). RETURNED TO ENGLAND. (WITH REFERENCE FROM MARSDEN).	
REMOVAL ULK. CY, EMY & Y OF ERS. LEASANT E.	INSPECTED BY GOVERNOR'S SECRETARY. "HARD WORK AND HARD FARE IS GENERALLY THE LOT OF THE SETTLER'S MAN". DESCRIPTION OF PUNISHMENTS AT NEWCASTLE; FLOGGING ON THE BREECH; GENERAL DISSOUTE CONDUCT. "INDUSTRIOUS ATTENTIVE PEOPLE DO WELL".		
RTABLE E.	CAME WITH LETTER OF INTRODUCTION; COOLLY RECEIVED BY KING; ASSIGNED WELL TREATED; GOVERNMENT CLERK; FRAUD - GAOL GANG; MARSDEN'S CLERK; FLOGGED.	SENTENCE REMITTED SO THAT HE COULD ACT AS KING'S SECRETARY ON VOYAGE HOME.	
FIED LKS. MURDER, R. RTABLE E.	FOUND TYRANNY PREVALENT. WRONGLY CONVICTED, SENT TO NEWCASTLE; SYDNEY; ATTEMPTED TO ABSCOND; NEWCASTLE; FLOGGED.	THE ACCOUNT ENDS WITH HIM STILL IN SERVITUDE, BEMOANING HIS CRIMES, RESOLVING TO REFORM AND WITH HINTS OF SERVING AS A WARNING TO OTHERS.	VAUX WAS TRANSPORTED A THIRD TIME. A CANT VOCABULARY IS ADDED TO THE MEMOIRS.

Appendix III (cont'd)

AUTHOR YEAR OF PUBLICATION OR WRITING	TITLE	EARLY LIFE	INTRODUCTION TO CRIME	PROGRESS IN CRIME	CAPTURE	PRISON LIFE	TRIAL	SEN
11. THOMAS WELLS. (1819)	MICHAEL HOWE.	APPRENTICED.	ABSCONDED. ENLISTED IN NAVY.	HIGHWAY ROBBERY.	DUE PROCESS.		IRREGU- LARITY IN INDICTMENT.	SEV YEA
12. ANON. (C.1820)	UNHAPPY TRANSPORT WILLIAM DALE (BROADSHEET)	HONEST FARMER'S SON. APPRENTICED.	BASE COMPANIONS. NEGLECT OF DUTY.	DRUKENNESS. IDELNESS. THEFT.			"LEARNED COUNCIL."	DEA COM TO FOU YEA
13. ANON. (C.1822)	GENTLEMAN CONVICT.	GOOD FAMILY.	LED INTO "DEBAUCHERY & VICE" BY HIS TUTOR.	ROBBERY.	DUE PROCESS.	ESCAPED; CLOSELY CONFINED; THEREAFTER, PLEASANT.	FATHER DIED OF A BROKEN HEART; MOTHER INSANE.	TRA ATI
14. JAMES MACKENZIE. (C.1825)	LIFE.	POOR BUT HONEST PARENTS. "SUITABLE EDUCATION". APPRENTICED.	BAD COMPANY.	DRINKING. SWEARING. STEALING. SABBATH- BREAKING. JOINED GANG OF THIEVES. REPEATEDLY IN GAOL.	DUE PROCESS.			FOU YEA
15. - MELLISH. (1825)	RECOLLECTIONS							
16. JAMES REVEL. (1824)	"UNHAPPY TRANSPORT". (BROADSHEET)	POOR & HONEST PARENTS. EDUCATED. APPRENTICED.	WICKED COMPANY.	JOINED A GANG. DRUNKENNESS & THEFT.	BETRAYED.	VISITED BY GRIEVING PARENTS.		FOU YEA
17. JOHN JACKSON. (1825)	"JAMES KEVEL REMARKABLE NARRATIVE". (BROADSHEET)	MERCHANT'S SON; HONEST PARENTS. GOOD EDUCATION. APPRENTICED.	WICKED COMPANY.	THEFT; JOINED GANG. DRUNKENNESS.	BETRAYED.			FOU YEA (AG FOU
18. AUGUSTUS H. (C.1830)	THE CONVICT.	RESPECTABLE PARENTS. WELL EDUCATED. ARTICLED. MARRIED.	SPENT RECKLESSLY.	FORGED BILLS.	CAPTURED WHILE FLEEING.	GOVERNESS WAS COMPASSION- ATE.		DEA COM
19. ANONYMOUS. LIFER. (C	MEMOIR.							
20. ANONYMOUS (C.1830)	"CONVICT MAID CHARLOTT W" (BROADSHEET)	HONEST PARENTS. SCHOOLED IN VIRTUE.	STOLE TO FINANCE MARRIAGE.					SEV YEA

Appendix III   155

	COLONIAL EXPERIENCE	END OF SERVITUDE (AS RECORDED IN TEXAS)	REMARKS
IOUS PASSAGE ED	ARRIVED 1812; PUBLIC LABOUR; ASSIGNED; ABSCONDED; JOINED OUTLAWS; SURRENDERED AT AMNESTY OF 1814; OUTLAWS AGAIN: ROBBERY, INCENDIARISM, MURDER; PURSUITS & ESCAPES; SENT THREATENING MESSAGE TO GOVERNOR; MARTIAL LAW; SURRENDERED; ESCAPED; BETRAYED; KILLED.	DEATH.	HOWE SHOWED A TREMENDOUS, IF MISDIRECTED, FORTITUDE AND RESILIENCE. HE ACQUIRED SOMETHING OF THE AURA OF THE GOTHIC HERO AS HE WANDERED IN THE WILDS, TORMENTED BY DREAMS WHICH HE RECORDED IN KANGAROO BLOOD.
ED BY KABLE PS".	UNCEASING LABOUR; WORK IN CHAINS; POOR FOOD & ACCOMMODATION; CONVERTED.	FREE BY SERVITUDE. RETURNED TO ENGLAND. EXPRESSED GREAT REMORSE. PRINTED AS A WARNING TO MANY.	THE ACCOUNT AND LETTER ARE RECAPITULATED IN A BALLAD.
ABLE S.	RECOMMENDED TO GOVERNOR WHO DISPENSED WITH HIS "PERIOD OF SERVICE"; TOOK FARM; PROPERED; OVERSEER OF ROAD GANG.	REMAINED IN COLONY; REPENTED; CAUTIONED YOUTH TO AVOID HIS EXCESSES.	
R NTH	ASSIGNED; STOLE; FLOGGED; STOLE; 500 LASHES; COAL MINES; WORKED IN CHAINS; SEVERE LABOUR; FREQUENT PUNISHMENTS; REPENTED.	FREE BY SERVITUDE. RETURNED TO ENGLAND.	
S	DESCRIPTION OF CLOTHES, FOOD NATURAL PHENOMENA.	RETURNED TO ENGLAND; ADVENTURES EN ROUTE; RECONVICTED & SENTENCED TO TRANSPORTATION.	RECOLLECTIONS WRITTEN TO AMUSE GAOLER'S WIFE.
	ON ARRIVAL, PRISONERS WERE INSPECTED LIKE HORSES; "BOUGHT" FROM CAPTAIN; HARD LABOUR; NO SHOES; ILL, BUT NO RESPITE; "BOUGHT" AGAIN; A "SLAVE"; REPENTED.	FREE BY SERVITUDE; RETURNED TO JOYFUL PARENTS; ADMONISHED ALL TO AVOID HIS FAULTS TO AVOID GAMBLING. "AMONG THE NEGROES TO WORK WITH THE HOE".	THE HACK WHO WROTE THIS BALLAD OBVIOUSLY DREW ON AMERICAN PRECEDENTS: "PLANTER" "PLANTATION", "NEGROES" TO WHICH HE ADDED SOME AUSTRALIAN MOTIFS.
NGS.	ASSIGNED; NO SHOES; AXE AND HOE; WORKED DAY AND NIGHT; FLOGGED; REPENTED.	RETURNED TO ENGLAND; PARENTS HAD DIED OF A BROKEN HEART; WARNS YOUTH TO AVOID HIS ERRORS.	WRITTEN TO COUNTERACT FALSE IDEAS ABOUT TRANSPORTATION, THIS BALLAD PLAGIARISES REVEL'S, BUT ALL AMERICAN REFERENCES ARE EXPUNGED.
	THE LIFE OF AUGUSTUS WAS SPARED; AND HE NOW LIVES IN A FOREIGN LAND, BANISHED FROM HIS HOME AND COUNTRY, WHERE HE MUST END HIS DAYS A WANDERING EXILE. LET THOSE WHO WOULD AVOID HIS FATE SHUN HIS FAULTS.		
DNEY OLK	THIS FRAGMENTARY ACCOUNT DESCRIBES SUFFERINGS AND HORRORS AT NORFOLK ISLAND, WHERE THE WRITER BAITED AUTHORITY AND WAS MADE "THE FINGER POST OF REVENGE FOR EVERY ADVERSE WIND THAT BLEW".		CONTAINS MANY SUGGESTIONS ABOUT PENAL REFORM. SPEAKS OF "LEAGUE OF WICKEDNESS CEMENTED TOGETHER". MANY CRYPTIC REFERENCES TO SCRIPTUAL VERSES. SUFFERINGS APPEAR TO EQUAL RUFUS DAWES', BUT RELATED WITH A GRIM HUMOUR.
	CONSTANT TOIL; KEENLY FELT SEPARATION FROM FRIENDS; REPENTANCE.		THE BALLAD WAS WRITTEN, AT HER REQUEST, TO DETER FEMALES FROM CRIME.

Appendix IV: A Schematic Presentation of the Components of Factual Convict Accounts and Biographies (1830–1868), Numbered to Conform with the Notes to Appendix IV Colonial experience (undergone or witnessed) included in text, indicated by "X".

AUTHOR AND YEAR OF PUBLICATION	SHORT TITLE	EARLY LIFE	INTRODUCTION TO CRIME	PROGRESS IN CRIME	CAPTURE	PRISON LIFE	TRIAL
1. ISAAC SOLOMONS (c. 1830)	IKEY SOLOMONS	BORN 1787. ONE OF 9 CHILDREN.	BEGAN SELLING STOLEN GOODS AT THE AGE OF 9.	PLUNGED "HEEDLESSLY AND FEARLESSLY" INTO EVERY SPECIES OF ROBBERY.	CAUSED BY WIFE'S JEALOUSY OF HIS MISTRESS.		DETAILS OF INDICTMENTS. VERDICTS ON 5 INDICTMENTS.
2. W. DICKSON (c. 1833)	A COPY OF A LETTER... (BROADSHEET)						
3. SNOWDEN DUNHILL (1834)	LIFE	WANDERED AWAY FROM HOME AS A SMALL BOY. THE VICTIM OF FATE.	PLAYING CARDS.	THEFT. COWARDICE. VANITY.		PRISONERS WERE THE SCUM AND OUTCASTS OF SOCIETY.	TRANSPORTED FOR A CRIME HE "DID NOT COMMIT".
4. "H.W.D." (1835)	STATE OF CONVICTS (BROADSHEET)						
5. WILLIAM R—SS (1836)	FELL TYRANT	WEALTHY FATHER. ENTERED MERCHANT NAVY.	DISSIPATED LIFE; LIVED BEYOND MEANS.	EMBEZZLED, RETURNED FROM TRANSPORTATION.			
6. WILLIAM THOMPSON (1836)	AWFUL EXECUTION (BROADSHEET)						
7. W— (1837)	VOYAGE IN A CONVICT SHIP						
	i) ANONYMOUS CONVICT			RETURNED FROM TRANSPORTATION.		ATTEMPTED ESCAPE.	
	ii) YOUNG POOLE	NATURAL SON OF WEALTHY FATHER. INDULGED BY MOTHER.	PETTY THEFTS.	JOINED GANG OF THIEVES. FLAGRANT ROBBERIES.			
	iii) LAD FROM LANCASHIRE. (WILKINSON)	RESPECTABLE PARENTS. SOUND EDUCATION.	BAD COMPANY. EVIL HABITS.	JOINED GANG OF THIEVES.		VISITED BY HIS MOTHER WHO DIED OF GRIEF.	
8. GEORGE LOVELESS (1838)	SUFFERINGS OF JAS. LOVELESS, JAS BRINE JAS BRINE:						
9. JAMES MUDIE (1837)	FELONRY WILLIAM WATT.	CLERK IN SCOTLAND.		"SERIOUS DELINQUENCIES" OUTLAWED. FLED TO ENGLAND.	"THROUGH SAGACITY AND EXTRAORDINARY PERSEVERANCE OF AN OFFICER".	"PROFLIGATE AND ABANDONED CONDUCT REVEALED".	

Appendix IV

	ASSIGNED	PROBATION GANG	NO PERSONAL HARDSHIPS RECORDED	FLOGGED	POOR CLOTHING RATIONS, FOOD ACCOMMODATION	HARD LABOUR	IRONS/ROAD GANG	ARBITRARY TREATMENT BY AUTHORITY	ABSCONDED	LIVED WITH ABORIGNES	GAOLED	WITNESSED BRUTALITY	EXPERIENCE AT NORFOLK IS.	EXPERIENCE AT MACQUARIE HBR	EXPERIENCE AT PORT ARTHUR	BUSHRANGING	PENITENT	IMPENITENT	ADMONITIONS DELIVERED	EXPERIENCE AT MORETON BAY	END OF SERVITUDE	ADDITIONAL DETAILS AND COMMENTS
S	X				X	X													X			
OF LIFE S.W." AND ST.					X	X									X						BY SERVITUDE, WENT FROM SYDNEY TO HOBART. DRUNKARD.	ONE SON EXECUTED, ANOTHER SON, A STEP SON AND HIS WIFE WERE ALSO TRANSPORTED AS WERE 2 OF HIS DAUGHTER'S LOVERS.
				X	X	X	X												X			
				X	X	X	X	X		X		X	X				X		X	X	BY SERVITUDE.	SETTLERS DIVIDED INTO 4 CLASSES: "SWELLS", "DUNGAREES", "SOUGES" AND "STRINGYBARKS" LATTER MOST HUMANE TO CONVICTS. SYDNEY A SINK OF INIQUITY.
	X				X	X	X	X										X				THERE APPEARS TO BE NO HISTORICAL BASIS FOR REBELLION DESCRIBED. THE "MERCURY MINES" WERE MOST DREADED PUNISHMENT.
PT- INY PTED ER NERS																		X				REFUSED TO DIVULGE MEANS USED TO ESCAPE FROM TRANSPORTATION.
TENT ENTLE OCILE																						
S A TO SE.																						
	X				X	X	X	X		X											BY SERVITUDE	HIS MASTER, A MAGISTRATE BELIEVED UNIONISTS PLOTTING ROBBERY AND MURDER. WARRATIVE PUBLISHED AS WARNING TO WORKING CLASSES.
			X																			BY "PLAUSIBILITY OF ADDRESS AND MANNERS" HE "PROCURED" A TICKET THROUGH "LAX AND UNWISE POLICY". APPOINTED EDITOR OF THE SYDNEY GAZETTE.

Appendix IV (cont'd)

AUTHOR AND YEAR OF PUBLICATION	SHORT TITLE	EARLY LIFE	INTRODUCTION TO CRIME	PROGRESS IN CRIME	CAPTURE	PRISON LIFE	TRIAL
10. FRANCOIS-XAVIER PRIEUR (1838)				CANADIAN REBEL.	THROUGH TREACHERY	WELL-TREATED BY CLERGY AND OFFICIALS	DEPOSITIONS RELATED. CONDEMNED TO DEATH SENTENCE COMMUTED.
11. CHARLES ADOLPHUS KING (1840)	LIFE AND SUFFERINGS	BORN 1818, APPRENTICED. (i)	BAD COMPANIONS	NUMEROUS CONVICTIONS			AGED 18, SENTENCED TO 14 YEARS' TRANSPORTATION.
		(ii)			THROUGH TREACHERY	5 YEARS IN MILLBANK	TRANSPORTED FOR LIFE
12. JOHN FROST (1840)	MEMOIR	"ONE OF THE PEOPLE" "HONEST PARENTS" EDUCATED.	DECLARED BANKRUPT.	INCITED A RIOT.			"A MISCARRIAGE OF JUSTICE"
13. EDWARD LILBURN (1841)	COMPLETE EXPOSURE						
14. JAMES BACKHOUSE (1843)	NARRATIVE OF A VISIT: ROBERT KING A PRISONER	RESPECTABLE PARENTS. GOOD EDUCATION. CAREFULLY BROUGHT UP. EDUCATED.	BAD COMPANY. PUBLIC HOUSE. BAD COMPANIONS.	"MUCH EVIL" INTEMPERANCE JOINED GANG. HOUSEBREAKING.	ARRESTED BY "STRONG ARM OF THE LAW". THROUGH VIGILANCE OF A WATCHMAN.		
15. JOHN KNATCHBULL (1844)	LIFE	NOTABLE FAMILY. EDUCATED. "DISTINGUISHED" NAVAL CAREER.	PICKING POCKETS.		BETRAYED BY HALF-BROTHER		
16. JAMES CONNOR (1845)	RECOLLECTIONS		"ONE LITTLE ACT"				
17. LINUS MILLER (1846)	NOTES OF AN EXILE		PARTICIPATED IN CANADIAN REBELLION.			EMPORIUM OF VICE.	LENGTHY ACCOUNT; BELIEVED HE WAS VICTIM OF INJUSTICE
	"HENRY WILLIAMS"	RESPECTABLE, WEALTHY PARENTS. LIBERAL EDUCATION. DISINHERITED BECAUSE OF MARRIAGE	STOLE TO FEED STARVING WIFE AND CHILD.		CAUGHT BY A POLICEMAN. WIFE DIED OF SHOCK		PLEADED GUILTY
18. JOSEPH LINGARD (1846)	NARRATIVE OF A JOURNEY	COTTON WEAVER. MARRIED.	WRONGLY CHARGED WITH STEALING KEYS.				SENTENCED TO TRANSPORTATION FOR SEVEN YEARS.
19. CHARLES COZENS (1848)	ADVENTURES OF A GUARDSMAN	WELL-TO-DO FAMILY. ARMY.	STRIKING AN OFFICER.				

Appendix IV   159

ASSIGNED	PROBATION GANG	NO PERSONAL HARDSHIPS RECORDED	FLOGGED	POOR CLOTHING RATIONS, FOOD ACCOMMODATION	HARD LABOUR	IRONS/ROAD GANG	ARBITRARY TREATMENT BY AUTHORITY	ABSCONDED	LIVED WITH ABORIGNES	GAOLED	WITNESSED BRUTALITY	EXPERIENCE AT NORFOLK IS.	EXPERIENCE AT MACQUARIE HBR.	EXPERIENCE AT PORT ARTHUR	BUSHRANGING	PENITENT	IMPENITENT	ADMONITIONS DELIVERED	EXPERIENCE AT MORETON BAY	END OF SERVITUDE	ADDITIONAL DETAILS AND COMMENTS
X				X			X				X									ABSOLUTE PARDON.	REFUSED TO PARTICIPATE IN AN ATTEMPTED ESCAPE.
X			X		X	X		X													ESCAPED FROM COLONY, RETURNED TO ENGLAND AFTER AMAZING ADVENTURES.
																					DECLARED HE PREFERRED DEATH TO TRANSPORTATION.
		X												X							FROST WROTE HE WAS SATISFIED WITH SITUATION AT PORT ARTHUR. SPIRITS WERE "VERY GOOD".
			X		X		X				X	X				X	X				INCLUDED STORIES OF CONVICTS WHO MURDERED TO BE HANGED, SPOKE OF "PROVERBIAL DEPRAVITY" ON NORFOLK ISLAND.
		X															X			DIED.	HEALTH WAS IMPAIRED BY DEPRAVITY, BUT HE DIED REPENTANT. BACKHOUSE ADDS THAT KING'S LIFE WAS SUBJECT OF A TRACT.
X			X					X	X								X				THE PRISONER WAS TRANSPORTED TO BERMUDA, SYDNEY AND NORFOLK IS. HIS REPENTANCE LED OTHERS TO CONSIDER HIM A "BAD MAN".
X						X		X		X	X	X					X			EXECUTED.	
X					X	X		X				X		X						ESCAPED	CONNOR WROTE OF MARIA IS. AND MACQUARIE HBR. RECORDED MANY ADVENTURES IN THE BUSH
	X			X	X		X	X			X	X			X					ABSOLUTE PARDON.	MILLER VIEWED THE MORAL FAULTS OF FELLOW-CONVICTS WITH HORROR BUT EXPRESSED NO REGRET FOR PART IN REBELLION AND FOR ABSCONDING.
																				DIED IN AN ASYLUM.	IN TONE AND CONTENT THIS NARRATIVE SUITABLE FOR TRACT.
X	X																			TICKET OF LEAVE, FREE BY SERVITUDE. WORKED HIS PASSAGE HOME.	ENJOYED CONSIDERABLE FREEDOM ON SHEEP STATION.
X	X																			TICKET OF LEAVE, RELATIVES SENT PASSAGE MONEY.	FOR MOST OF HIS COLONIAL CAREER COZENS WAS A CONSTABLE.

Appendix V: A Schematic Presentation of the Components of Fictional Convict Accounts and Biographies (1830 to the present), Numbered to Conform with Notes to Appendix V. Colonial experience (undergone or witnessed) included in text, indicated by "X".

AUTHOR AND YEAR OF PUBLICATION	SHORT TITLE	EARLY LIFE	INTRODUCTION TO CRIME	PROGRESS IN CRIME	CAPTURE	PRISON LIFE	TRIAL
1. HOWISON (1830)	ONE FALSE STEP	RESPECTABLE FAMILY. GOOD EDUCATION.	BAD COMPANIONS.	DISSIPATION. EXTRAVAGANCE. DEBAUCHERY. FORGERY.			
2. HENRY SAVERY (1830)	QUINTUS SERVINTON	RESPECTABLE FAMILY. GOOD EDUCATION.	OVERREACHED HIMSELF IN BUSINESS.	FORGERY.	CAPTURED WHILE ATTEMPTING TO FLEE COUNTRY.	"PRIVATE APPARTMENTS" "PROPER ATTENDANCE"	PLEADED GUILTY. CONDEMNED TO DEATH. REPRIEVED.
3. CHARLES ROWCROFT (1843)	TALES OF THE COLONIES (GYPSEY'S STORY)			POACHED. INVOLVED IN KILLING OF KEEPER.			TRANSPORTED FOR LIFE.
4. JAMES TUCKER (c.1845) (WRITTEN)	RALPH RASHLEIGH	"DECENT PARENTS". "GOOD PLAIN EDUCATION".	BAD COMPANIONS.	FORGERY. BURGLARY. CONSPIRED.	"EVIL FORTUNE". CAUGHT BY THIEF-TAKER.	SCHOOL OF VICE. ORDINARY FATUOUS. ESCAPED, CAUGHT.	"FARCE" CONFEDERATE SUPPLIED HOSTILE EVIDENCE.
5. CHARLES READE (1856)	IT'S NEVER TOO LATE TO MEND (TOM ROBINSON)	"NO BUSINESS OR TRADE" EXPERIENCE ON AMERICAN DIGGINGS.		FORGERY THEFT.	ONE OF POLICE ROBINSON'S FORMER ACCOMPLICE.	MODEL PRISON. PHYSICAL AND MENTAL TORMENTS. HALF-CONVERTED BY EDEN. PRISON REFORMED.	DEFENDED HIMSELF WITH "INGENUITY AND SLEIGHT OF INTELLECT".
6. HENRY KINGSLEY (1859)	GEOFFRY HAMLYN (GEORGE HAWKER)	SON OF "SMALL FARMER" AND THE GYPSEY, HADGE. LITTLE EDUCATION.	"STRANGE" ACTIVITIES. DEVIL.	WITH A RETURNED CONVICT. FORGERY, COINING, ELOPED WITH AND ABANDONED MARY THORNTON.			WITNESSED BY MARY. TRANSPORTED FOR LIFE.
7. CAROLINE LEAKEY (1859)	THE BROAD ARROW	KINDLY FATHER.	SEDUCED.	CHARGED WITH FORGERY, CHILD MURDER.	CAPTURED BY THIEF-TAKER AND CONSTABLES.	MILL BANK. HEAD SHAVED.	CONDEMNED TO DEATH. REPRIEVED.
8. B.F. FARJEON (1866)	GRIF (WELSHER'S STORY)	COMFORTABLE HOME. POORLY EDUCATED.	IDLE.	FALSELY CHARGED WITH BURGLARY.	TREACHERY.	CONVERTED THROUGH MOTHER'S VISIT.	TRANSPORTED FOR LIFE.
9. MARCUS CLARKE (1870-2)	HIS NATURAL LIFE (SERIALISED VERSION)	PROMINENT FAMILY. GOOD EDUCATION TO BE PRESUMED.	DESERTED WIFE. "FOLLY". "SIN".	WRONGFULLY ACCUSED OF MURDER.	THROUGH TREACHERY.	VICTIM OF A "REMORSELESS WHEEL"	MADE IMPASSIONED PLEA TO COURT.

Appendix V

ASSIGNED	PROBATION GANG	NO PERSONAL HARDSHIPS RECORDED	FLOGGED	POOR CLOTHING ACCOMMODATION AND FOOD	HARD LABOUR	IRONS/ROAD GANG	ARBITRARY TREATMENT BY AUTHORITY	ABSCONDED	LIVED WITH ABORIGINES	GAOLED	WITNESSED BRUTALITY	EXPERIENCE AT NORFOLK ISLAND	EXPERIENCE AT MACQUARIE HBR.	EXPERIENCE AT PORT ARTHUR	EXPERIENCE AT OTHER PENAL EST.	BUSHRANGING	PENITENT	IMPENITENT	ADMONITORY	END OF SERVITUDE	SETTLED ON LAND AS EMPLOYEE	SETTLED ON LAND AS PROPRIETOR	OTHER DETAILS
X		X						X								X	X		X	DEATH.			
X										X										PARDONED. RETURNED TO ENGLAND.	X		SERVINTON'S SUFFERINGS WERE CAUSED BY THE SLIGHTS AND INTRIGUES OF THE POWERFUL. MORAL: VIRESCIT VULNERE VIRTUS
X								X			X		X			X				KILLED.			
X		X		X		X	X	X	X	X	X			X			X			PARDONED.	X		TUCKER'S NARRATIVE CONFORMS TO TRADITIONAL COMPONENTS OF LIFE BEFORE TRANSPORTATION AND INCLUDES MANY OF THOSE WHICH WERE INCLUDED IN SUBSEQUENT ACCOUNTS.
X	X																			FREE PARDON AS REWARD FOR HIS INTRODUCTION OF LAW TO DIGGINGS.			ROBINSON'S WANDERINGS ALLOW A PORTRAYAL OF LIFE IN THE BUSH AND ON DIGGINGS. MANY EX-CONVICTS PORTRAYED IN POOR LIGHT. ROBINSON RETURNED TO ENGLAND BRIEFLY, BUT RETURNED TO AUSTRALIA TO LIVE HAPPILY IN THE RESPECTABILITY HE HAD EARNED.
						X		X								X	X			EXECUTED.			
X				X						X	X		X					X	X	DIED.			
X	X											X						X		FREE BY SERVITUDE.	X		WELSHER RELATED TALES OF BUSHRANGING ATTACKS BY NATIVES, LIFE ON DIGGINGS.
			X		X	X	X	X			X		X	X	X					ESCAPED.			DAWES IS SEEN TO BE PURIFIED BY HIS SUFFERINGS. "REDEEMED AND SAVED" BY "A BROTHER'S SYMPATHY".

Appendix V (cont'd)

AUTHOR AND YEAR OF PUBLICATION	SHORT TITLE	EARLY LIFE	INTRODUCTION TO CRIME	PROGRESS IN CRIME	CAPTURE	PRISON LIFE	TRIAL
1874	(REVISED VERSION)	PROMINENT FAMILY. GOOD EDUCATION TO BE PRESUMED.	"IMPETUOUS". "UNGRATEFUL".	WRONGFULLY ACCUSED OF MURDER OR ROBBERY.			
10. ELIZABETH WINSTANLEY (1876)	HER NATURAL LIFE	ORPHAN.	SEDUCED.	ACCUSED OF MURDERING HER CHILD.			TRANSPORTED FOR LIFE.
11. JOHN BOYLE O'REILLY (1880)	MOONDYNE		KILLED A DEER TO FEED POOR.				
12. CARLTON DAWE (1891)	GOLDEN LAKE (JOSEPH MORTON)	PROSPEROUS FATHER. EXCELLENT	DRANK. GAMBLED. EXTRAVAGANT EXCESSES.	FORGERY.			FRIENDS GLOATED OVER HIS MISFORTUNES.
13. MRS. CAMPBELL PRAED (1887)	LONGLEAT OF KOORAL BYN	LABOURER. RADICAL.	KILLED ARISTOCRAT WHO SEDUCED HIS SISTER.				
14. WILLIAM ASTLEY (1898)	"CONVICT HENDY"		POACHED. KEEPER WOUNDED.				PROSECUTOR PUT CASE IN DARKEST ASPECTS.
15. KATHARINE SUSANNAH PRICHARD (1915)	PIONEERS (DAN FARRELL)						
16. MILES FRANKLIN (1928)	UP THE COUNTRY (BOKO POOL)		"SIMPLICITY AND IGNORANCE". PARTICIPATED IN A RIOT.				
17. G.B. LANCASTER (1933)	PAGEANT (ROBERT SNOW)	WEALTHY PARENTAGE. UNIVERSITY EDUCATION.	RIOTOUS LIFE. INDISCRETION.				PARENTS HASTENED HIS DEPARTURE FROM ENGLAND.
18. BRIAN PENTON (1934, 1936)	LANDTAKERS INHERITORS (JOE GURSEY)			TRANSPORTED FOR POLITICAL AGITATION.			
19. ROY CONNOLLY (1940)	SOUTHERN SAGA (MICHAEL MOLLOY)		ROBBED THROUGH HUNGER.				
20. PATRICK WHITE (1957)	VOSS (ALBERT JUDD)			"CIRCUMSTANCES QUITE RIDICULOUS".			

Appendix V 163

ASSIGNED	PROBATION GANG	NO PERSONAL HARDSHIPS RECORDED	FLOGGED	POOR CLOTHING ACCOMMODATION AND FOOD	HARD LABOUR	IRONS/ROAD GANG	ARBITRARY TREATMENT BY AUTHORITY	ABSCONDED	LIVED WITH ABORIGINES	GAOLED	WITNESSED BRUTALITY	EXPERIENCE AT NORFOLK ISLAND	EXPERIENCE AT MACQUARIE HBR.	EXPERIENCE AT PORT ARTHUR	EXPERIENCE AT OTHER PENAL EST.	BUSHRANGING	PENITENT	IMPENITENT	ADMONITORY	END OF SERVITUDE	SETTLED ON LAND AS EMPLOYEE	SETTLED ON LAND AS PROPRIETOR	OTHER DETAILS
			X	X	X	X	X	X		X		X	X	X						DIED WHILE ESCAPING.			SYLVIA SEES HERSELF SAVED BY DAWES FROM "SIN AND DESPAIR", DAWES PRAYS FOR "THE MAN WHO HAD REDEEMED HIM".
X							X	X												DIED WHILE ESCAPING.			
X					X		X	X	X		X									ESCAPED.			MOONDYNE SET OUT TO REFORM ABUSES OF PENAL SYSTEM. DIED HEROIC DEATH.
X					X	X	X	X			X			X		X				ESCAPED.			
							X											X		BY SERVITUDE. PROSPERED UNDER ALIAS.			SUFFERED FROM "TAINT E"
X			X	X			X	X				X		X					X	SHOT WHILE ATTEMPTING TO ESCAPE.			MORAL IS THAT ONLY SCRAGGLE ENJOYED SUCCESS. HAD HENDY SHOT.
									X											GAVE HIMSELF UP TO SAVE DAVEY CAMERON.			FARRELL'S COLONIAL LIFE TOLD IN TERMS OF HIS SERVICE AND NOBILITY.
		X																		BY SERVITUDE		X	PORTRAYED AS USEFUL PIONEER.
X		X					X		X					X		X	X		X	KILLED WHILE BUSHRANGING.			
X			X	X	X		X	X	X					X			X			ESCAPED.	X		
				X	X	X	X													ACTED AS OVERSEER	X		
X			X	X	X	X	X	X							X	X				TICKET OF LEAVE.		X	

Notes

Notes to chapter 1

1. Mircea Eliade, *Myth and Reality* (London: George Allen and Unwin, 1964), p. 157.
2. Lloyd L. Robson, "The Historical Basis of *For the Term of His Natural Life*", *Australian Literary Studies (ALS)* 1 (1963):121.
3. A. G. L. Shaw, "Convicts and Transportation", in *Australian Encyclopedia*, 10 vols. (Sydney: Angus and Robertson, 1958), 3:29.
4. I. D. Muecke, "William Hay and History: A Comment on Aims, Sources and Method", *ALS* 4 (1966):120.
5. Samuel Clemens [Mark Twain], *Following the Equator: A Journey Around the World* (Hartford: American Publishing Company, 1897), p. 251.
6. "Introductory Address", *The Illustrated Australian Magazine* 1 (1850):3.
7. Thomas Dekker, *English Villainies Discovered by Candlelight*, ed. E.D. Pendry (London: Edward Arnold Ltd, 1967), p. 182.
8. Other writers who dealt with this subject included Jonson, Fletcher, Middleton, Rowlands, Harmer and Brome.
9. See William Harrison Ainsworth, *Rookwood: A Romance* (London: George Routledge and Sons, n.d.), p. xxvi, where Ainsworth, after reviewing the kinds of work that have been noted here, claims to have been the first to have written a canting song. For examples of canting songs and ballads see John S. Farmer, *Musa Pedestris: Three Centuries of Canting Songs and Slang Rhymes* (New York: Cooper Square Publishers, 1964). See also David Wright, "The Poet, the Hangman and the Solicitor: An Account of Jack Fireblood", in *The Uncertain Element: An Anthology of Fantastic Conceptions*, ed. Kay Dick (London: Collins, n.d.), pp. 221-29.
10. Jonathan Swift "On the Poor Man's Contentment", in *Sermons and Society: An Anglican Anthology*, ed. Paul A. Welsby (Harmondsworth: Penguin n.d.), p. 159.
11. Daniel Defoe, *A Review of the State of the British Nation*, 15 September 1711, 12 vols. (New York: A.M.S. Press Inc.), 8:75.
12. See Henry Fielding, *An Enquiry into the Causes of the Late Increase in Robbery, Etc. With Some Proposals for Remedying This Growing Evil*, in *Legal Writings of Henry Fielding* (London: Frank Cass and Co., 1967), pp. 23 and following; Patrick Colquhoun, *A Treatise on the Police of the Metropolis Containing a Detail of the Various Crimes AND Misdemeanours by Which Public and Private Property and Security Are at Present injured and endan-

gered and suggesting remedies for their prevention, 6th ed. (London: Joseph Mawman, 1800).
13. William Godwin, *Enquiry Concerning Political Justice and Its Influence on Morals and Happiness,* 2 vols. (Toronto: University of Toronto Press, 1946), 2:324.
14. *British Museum General Catalogue of Printed Books to 1955,* compact ed., 40 vols. (New York: Reader Microprint Corp., 1967), 15:641.
15. John J. Richetti, *Popular Fiction before Richardson: Narrative Patterns 1700-1739* (Oxford: Clarendon Press, 1969), p. 38.
16. George Sherburn, ed., *The Correspondence of Alexander Pope,* 5 vols. (Oxford: Clarendon Press, 1956), 2:350.
17. John Gay, *The Beggar's Opera,* in *Eighteenth Century Plays,* ed. John Hampden (London: Dent, 1958), p. 117.
18. Henry Fielding, *The History of the Life of the late Mr Jonathan Wild* (New York: Frank Cass and Co., 1965), p. 41.
19. Charles Hindley, *Curiosities of Street Literature* (London: Reeves and Turner, 1871), p. 159.
20. John Gay, "Trivia, or the Art of Walking the Streets of London".
21. Henry Mayhew, *London Labour and the London Poor,* 4 vols. (London: Charles Griffin and Co., 1852), 2:206.
22. Hindley, *Curiosities,* p. 160. The patter was cited as an example of the art of "Tragedy Bill".
23. *British Museum Catalogue,* 18:583.
24. George Borrow, *Celebrated Trials, Remarkable Cases: or, Jurisprudence from the Earliest Years to the Year 1825.* 6 vols. (London: Knight and Lacey, 1825), 1:vii.
25. "Camden Pelham", *The Chronicles of Crime and the Newgate Calendar* 6 vols. (London: Thomas Tegg, 1841), 1:vii.
26. For examples of chap-books see Hindley, *Curiosities,* and John Ashton, *Chap-Books of the Eighteenth Century* (London: Reed, 1882).
27. Quoted in David Kunzle, *The Early Comic Strip: Narrative and Picture Stories in the European Broadsheet from c. 1450 to 1825* (Berkeley: University of California Press, 1973), p. 187.
28. Quoted in Dorothy M. George, *Hogarth to Cruikshank: Social Change in Graphic Satire* (London: Allen Lane, Penguin Press, 1967), p. 21.
29. James Boswell, *Life of Johnson,* ed. George Birbeck, 6 vols. (Oxford: Clarendon Press, 1934), 1:34.
30. Howard Miles, ed., *George Crabbe: Tales 1812 and Other Selected Poems* (Cambridge: Cambridge University Press, 1967), p. xxviii.
31. Daniel Defoe, *The Fortunes and Misfortunes of the Famous Moll Flanders etc.* (New York: New American Library), p. vi.
32. George Lillo, *The London Merchant: Or, the History of George Barnwell,* in *Eighteenth Century Plays,* ed. John Hampden (London: Dent, 1958), p. 215. Similar sentiments were expressed by Horace Walpole, Samuel Richardson, Ann Radcliffe and Henry Fielding.
33. Eric Partridge, of course, is noted for his research on language of the underworld. There have been numerous examples of research on the argot of the convicts, particularly by W.S. Ramson, G.W. Turner and R.D. Eagleson.
34. Dekker, "O per Se O", in *English Villainies,* p. 297.
35. Fielding, *Enquiry,* p. 20.
36. Colquhoun, *Police of the Metropolis,* p. 79.
37. Bernard Mandeville, *The Fable of the Bees* (Harmondsworth: Penguin, 1970), p. 48.

38. Henry Mayhew and John Binney, *The Criminal Prisons of London and Scenes of Prison Life*, 2 vols. (London: Frank Cass and Co., 1971), 1:87.
39. Edward Gibbon, *The Decline and Fall of the Roman Empire*, ed. Christopher Dawson, 6 vols. (London: Oxford University Press, 1960), 1:430.
40. William Wilberforce, *A practical view of the prevailing Religious System of professed Christians in the higher and middle classes in this country: Contrasted with real Christianity*, 8th ed. (London: T. Cadell and W. Davies, 1805), p. 133.
41. Daniel Defoe, *The Life of Captain Singleton* (London: Dent, 1950), p. 234.
42. F. W. Head, "The Church of England", in *Encyclopedia of Religion and Ethics*, 13 vols. (Edinburgh: T. and T. Clark, 1967-71), 3:650.
43. James Boswell, "The Execution of Gibson and Payne", *Public Advertiser*, 26 April 1768, in *Eighteenth Century Prose*, ed. J.T. Rose (Harmondsworth: Penguin, 1956), p. 49.
44. Gerald Kennedy, ed., *The Journal of John Wesley* (New York: Capricorn Books, 1963), entry for 26 January 1785.
45. Defoe, *Moll Flanders*, pp. 245-56.
46. Quoted by A.S. Turberville, in *Johnson's England: An Account of the Life and Manners of his Age*, 2 vols. (Oxford: Clarendon Press, 1952), 1:320. For the successes of the Methodists see Kennedy, *Wesley*, entries for 27 May 1739 and 20 March 1779.
47. Edward Gibbon, *Memoirs of My Life*, ed. Georges A. Bonnard (London: Nelson, 1966), p. 3.
48. For examples of this kind of writing see Alban Butler, *The Lives of the Fathers, Martyrs and other Principal Saints compiled from original monuments, and other authentic records* (London: A. Wilson, 1812-13), throughout; and G.A. Williamson, ed., *Foxe's Book of Martyrs* (London: Secker and Warburg), pp. 324, 326, 327 and 329.
49. See Anthony J.C. Kerr, *Schools of Scotland* (Glasgow: William Maclellan, 1962), pp. 17-22 and S.J. Curtis, *History of Education in Great Britain*, 4th ed. (London: University Tutorial Press, 1961), pp. 513-31.
50. John Howard, *The State of the Prisons* (London: Dent, 1929), p. 160.
51. Dekker, *English Villainies*, p. 255.
52. Tobias Smollett, *The Life and Adventures of Sir Launcelot Greaves* (London: Dent, 1973), chapter 20.
53. Howard, *Prisons*, p. 6.
54. Henry B. Wheatley, ed., *The Diary of Samuel Pepys*, 2 vols. (London: Oxford University Press, 1955), 2:731.
55. Colquhoun, *Police*, p. 96.
56. Gillian Avery, *Victorian People* (London: Collins, 1970), p. 240. In 1901 Ambrose Pratt noted that members of Sydney "pushes" had a similar enthusiasm for the police reports in the daily paper, and for the *Annals of Newgate*: " 'Push' Larrikinism in Australia", *Blackwood's Magazine*, February 1901.
57. Jonathan Swift, *Directions to Servants and Miscellaneous Pieces* (London: Dent, 1952), pp. 44-45.
58. Fielding, *Enquiry*, p. 122.
59. *Historical Records of New South Wales* (*HRN.S.W.*), 9 vols. (Sydney: Government Printer, 1892-1901), 1:19. For similar testimony see Colquhoun, *Police*, p. 454; Merril Jensen, ed., *English Historical Documents*, 12 vols. (London: Eyre and Spottiswoode, 1969), 9:482; Ernest Scott, "Transportation", in *The Cambridge History of the British Empire*, ed. Holland J. Rose, A.P. Newton and E.P. Benians, 8 vols. (Cambridge: Cambridge Univer-

sity Press), 2:436; William Edward Hartpole Lecky, *A History of Ireland in the Eighteenth Century*, 5 vols. (London: Longmans, Green and Co., 1892), 5:107.
60. Richard Head and Francis Kirkman, *The English Rogue Described in the Life of Meriton Latroon, a Witty Extravagant: Being a complete history of the most eminent cheats of both sexes* (London: George Routledge and Sons, 1978). Head was responsible for the first part, published in 1665, and Kirkman for the second, in 1671.
61. C. H. Wilkinson, ed., *The King of the Beggars*, by Bampfylde Moore Carew: "The Life and Adventures of Bampfylde Moore Carew, the Noted Devonshire Stroller", and "An Apology of the Life of Bampfylde Moore Carew" reprinted from the edition of 1745 and 1749 respectively (Oxford: Clarendon Press, 1931), "Introduction", p. vi.
62. See James Heath, *Eighteenth Century Penal Theory* (Oxford: Oxford University Press, 1963), p. 117.
63. Godwin, *Enquiry*, 2:390.
64. Samuel Taylor Coleridge, "Conciones ad Populum or Address to the People", in *Lectures 1795 on Politics and Religion*, ed. L. Patton and P. Mann (London: Routledge and Kegan Paul, 1971), p. 68.
65. Thomas Babington Macaulay, *The History of England*, 4 vols. (London: Longman, Green, Longman, Roberts, 1864), 1:308-9.
66. Captain Watkin Tench, *A Narrative of the Expedition to Botany Bay*, in *Sydney's First Four Years*, ed. L.F. Fitzhardinge (Sydney: Angus and Robertson), pp. 12-13.
67. William Godwin, *The Adventures of Caleb Williams or Things as They Are* (New York: Rinehart and Co., 1960), p. viii.

Notes to chapter 2

1. "Prologue By a Gentleman of Leicester on opening the Theatre at Sydney, Botany Bay to be spoken by the celebrated Mr Barrington", in *True Patriots All*, ed. Geoffrey C. Ingleton (Sydney: Angus and Robertson, 1952), p. viii.
2. Lloyd L. Robson, *The Convict Settlers of Australia* (Carlton: Melbourne University Press, 1965), p. 141. I gratefully acknowledge background information gathered from Robson's book and from the works of other historians, including Eris O'Brien, *The Foundation of Australia*, 2nd ed. (Sydney: Angus and Robertson, 1950); Russel Ward, *The Australian Legend* (Sydney: Oxford University Press, 1965); C.M.H. Clark, *A History of Australia*, vol. 1, *From the Earliest Times to the Age of Macquarie* (Carlton: Melbourne University Press, 1962); *A History of Australia*, vol. 2, *New South Wales and Van Diemen's Land 1822-1838* (Carlton: Melbourne University Press, 1968); *A History of Australia*, vol. 3, *The Beginning of An Australian Civilization* (Carlton: Melbourne University Press, 1973); A.G.L. Shaw, *Convicts and the Colonies: A Study of Penal Transportation from Great Britain and Ireland to Australia and other parts of the British Empire* (London: Faber and Faber, 1971); and Frank Crowley, ed., *A New History of Australia* (Melbourne: William Heinemann, 1974). Much data was also found in the *Journal* and *Proceedings* of the Royal Australian Historical Society and in *Proceedings* of the Tasmanian Historical Research Association.

3. Robson, *Convict Settlers*, p. 100. Before the Molesworth Committee, William Ullathorne testified that two-thirds of the population of Norfolk Island engaged in this practice.
4. *Sydney Gazette*, 5 March 1803.
5. Quoted by Henry Mayer, *The Press in Australia* (Melbourne: Lansdowne Press, 1964), p. 10.
6. E. Morris Miller, *Pressmen and Governors: Australian Editors and Writers in Early Tasmania* (Sydney: Sydney University Press, 1968), p. 117.
7. James Tucker, *Ralph Rashleigh: or, the Life of an Exile by Giacomo di Rosenberg*, ed. Colin Roderick (Sydney: Angus and Robertson, 1952), p. 124.
8. Initially about fifteen per cent of expirees returned to England, though in all only about five per cent did so. See Shaw, *Convicts and Colonies*, pp. 142-43.
9. See "Order-in-Council", 6 December 1786, *Historical Records of New South Wales (HRN.S.W.)* 1:451-52; 27 Geo. III, c.2., 1787, *HRN.S.W.* 1: 453-55; Lord Sydney to Lords Commissioners of the Treasury, 18 August 1786, *HRN.S.W.* 1:22, 436-37; Governor Phillip's First Commission, 12 October 1786, *Historical Records of Australia (HRA)*, series IV, 25 vols. (Sydney: Library Committee of Commonwealth Government, 1914-26) 1: 1-2; Governor Phillip's Second Commission, *HRA* 1:2-8; "Instructions to our trusty and well-beloved Arthur Phillip...", *HRA* 1:9-16.
10. "A Concise View of the Present State of Evangelical Religion throughout the World", in *Evangelical Magazine*, transcribed in Bonwick, *Missionary Papers*, Mitchell Library.
11. Rev. Josiah Pratt, "Notes on Eclectic Society", *Missionary Papers 1*, p. 760.
12. Pitt to Wilberforce, 23 September 1786, in *Private Papers of William Wilberforce*, ed. A.M. Wilberforce (London: T. Fisher Unwin, 1897), pp. 16-17.
13. Rev. Henry Venn to Miss Jane C. Venn, n.d., *Missionary Papers* 1, pp. 12-14.
14. Rev. J. Newton to Rev. R. Johnson, 28 November 1789, *Missionary Papers 1*, p. 752.
15. Quoted, Kathleen Raine, *Blake and Tradition*, 2 vols. (Princeton: Princeton University Press, 1968), 1:12.
16. See F. L. Cross, ed., *Oxford Dictionary of the Christian Church* (London: Oxford University Press, 1958), p. 1310. The church was instituted on 7 May 1787; its first chapel was opened on 27 January 1788.
17. See Daniel Southwell to Mrs Southwell, 12 July 1788, *HRN.S.W.* 2:693; Southwell to Rev. W. Butler, 27 July 1790, *HRN.S.W.* 2:715.
18. "Instructions", *HRA* 1:14.
19. *HRA* 1:11.
20. "Lord Sydney to Lords Commissioners of the Treasury", *HRN.S.W.* 1:436 (emphasis mine).
21. Henry Fielding, *The History of the Adventures of Joseph Andrews and his Friend Mr Abraham Adams, Written in the Manner of Cervantes, Author of "Don Quixote"* (New York: Frank Cass and Co., 1965), p. 254.
22. Ingleton, *True Patriots All*, p. 5.
23. David Collins, *An Account of the English Colony in New South Wales: With Remarks on the Dispositions, Customs, Manners Etc. of the Native Inhabitants of that Colony*, 2 vols. (London: T. Caddell and W. Davies, 1798, 1802), 1:179.
24. *HRN.S.W.* 1:38.

25. Richard Johnson, *An Address to the Inhabitants of the Colonies established in New South Wales and Norfolk Island: Written in the Year 1792* (London: Richard Johnson, 1794). Johnson was obviously guided by the Catechism.
26. John Dunmore Lang, *An Historical and Statistical Account of New South Wales From the Founding of the Colony in 1788 to the Present Day*, 4th ed., 2 vols. (London: Sampson, Low, Marston, Low and Searle, 1876), 2: 393.
27. William Pascoe Crook, quoted in a letter from James Grove to his friends, n.d., in John Eldershaw, "Select Letters of James Grove, Convict, Port Phillip and the Derwent, 1803-4, Part II", *Proceedings of the Tasmanian Historical Research Association (PTHRA)* 2 (1959): 34.
28. Crofton T. Croker, ed., *Memoirs of Joseph Holt, General of the Irish Rebels in 1798*, 2 vols. (London: Henry Colburn, 1838), 2:224.
29. Rev. Henry to London Missionary Society, 20 August 1799, *HRN.S.W.* 3:334.
30. Rev. John West, *The History of Tasmania*, ed. A.G.L. Shaw (Sydney: Angus and Robertson, 1971), p. 27.
31. James Lacey to George McCarthy, *HRN.S.W.* 2:479-80. Lacey seems to have been regarded as unctuous by his fellow convicts.
32. Reardon to John Piper, quoted M. Barnard Eldershaw, *The Life and Times of Captain John Piper*, 2nd ed. (Sydney: Ure Smith, 1963), pp. 131-32.
33. *HRN.S.W.* 3:370.
34. M. H. Ellis, *John Macarthur* (Sydney: Angus and Robertson, 1955), p. 406.
35. M. C. I. Levy, *Governor George Arthur: A Colonial Benevolent Despot* (Melbourne: Georgian House), p. 163. This quotation is from a despatch from Arthur to Goderich in 1833, but there is every reason to believe that such were Arthur's sentiments before 1830. The master and servant relationship as here envisaged was simultaneously being discarded in England. See Harold Perkin, *The Origins of Modern English Society* (London: Routledge and Kegan Paul, 1969), pp. 183-84.
36. *Report of the Select Committee on Transportation* [1812], in *Sources of Australian History*, ed. C.M.H. Clark (London: Oxford University Press, 1957), p. 114.
37. Quoted in Levy, *Arthur*, p. 155.
38. Regulation for Penal Settlements, 1 July 1829, *HRA* 15:105.
39. Bernard Smith, *Australian Painting 1788-1960* (Melbourne: Oxford University Press, 1962), pp. 3-4.
40. The early published journals were: Watkin Tench, *A Narrative of the Expedition to Botany Bay* (1789) and *A Complete Account of the Settlement at Port Jackson* (1793); Captain Arthur Phillip, *Voyage . . .* (1789); John White, *Journal of a Voyage . . .* (1790); John Hunter, *An Historical Journal of the Transactions at Port Jackson and Norfolk Island* (1793); David Collins, *An Account . . .* (1798), (1802). In addition, Debrett published *Extracts of Letters from Arthur Phillip . . .* (1791). William Bradley wrote a journal which lay unpublished until 1969; a similar fate befell John Easty's *Memorandum* (1965). Other papers by men like Ralph Clark are still to be published.
41. Collins, *Account* 1:viii.
42. *Account* 1:76.
43. See A.J. Gray, "John Bennet of the *Friendship*", *Journal of the Royal Australian Historical Society (JRAHS)* 6 (1958): 402.
44. James Tuckey, *An Account of a Voyage to Establish a Colony at Port*

Phillip in Bass's Strait on the South Coast of New South Wales in His Majesty's Ship Calcutta in the Years 1802-3-4 (London: Longman, Hurst, Rees and Orme, 1805), pp. 187-88.
45. See Mabel Hookey, ed., *The Chaplain, Being Some further Accounts of the Days of Bobby Knopwood* (Hobart: Fullers Bookshop, 1970).
46. *Edinburgh Review,* 2 (1803), quoted by West, *History,* p. 588.
47. See L. F. Fitzhardinge, "Some First Fleet Reviews", *Historical Studies,* 1 (1944): 85-91.
48. *HRN.S.W.* 2:720.
49. O'Brien, *Foundation,* p. 171.
50. John Ritchie, ed., *Punishment and Profit: The Reports of Commissioner John Bigge on the Colonies of New South Wales and Van Diemen's Land 1822-1823; their origins, nature and significance,* 2 vols. (Melbourne: Heinemann, 1970), 1:184-85.
51. Samuel Taylor Coleridge, "On the Present War", in *The Collected Works of Samuel Taylor Coleridge,* 2 vols., ed., Lewis Patton and Peter Mann (London: Oxford University Press, 1971), 1:14.
52. This poem was included in *Lyrical Ballads* (1795) and in *Remorse* and *Osorio.*
53. Robert Southey, "Botany Bay Eclogues", in *Complete Poems of Robert Southey* (London: Longmans, 1890), pp. 103-8.
54. As early as 1790 there was at least one wronged woman among the convicts. John Nicol of the *Lady Juliana* relates the story of Mary Rose, a "timid, modest girl", seduced by an officer and transported through the evidence of a perjured witness. Her friends' efforts in England secured a pardon for her. John Nicol, *The Life and Adventures of John Nicol, Mariner* (Edinburgh: William Blackwood, 1822), pp. 122-24. The theme would later be taken up in fiction, most notably by Caroline Leakey in *The Broad Arrow.*
55. See for instance, Mrs John Macarthur to Relatives and Friends, 7 March 1791, *HRN.S.W.* 2:500; Arthur Bowes' "Journal", *HRN.S.W.* 1:392.
56. W. E. K. Anderson, ed., *The Journal of Sir Walter Scott* (Oxford: The Clarendon Press, 1972), p. 329.
57. "Distant Correspondents in a Letter to B.F.Esq. at Sydney, New South Wales", in *The Works of Charles and Mary Lamb,* ed. E. V. Lucas (London: Longmans), pp. 104-8. It is through Lamb that we learn that Wordsworth and Coleridge were "hugely taken" with Field's poem "Kangaroo". The problem of the possibility of hereditary taint exercised many minds. See Ken Macnab and Russell Ward, "The Nature and Nurture of the first generation of native-born Australians", *Historical Studies* 10 (1962).
58. Robson, *Convict Settlers,* p. 24.
59. Shaw, "Convicts and Transportation", in *Australian Encyclopedia* 3:31.
60. Clark, *History of Australia* 1, p. 93.
61. John Williams, "Irish Convicts in Van Diemen's Land", *PTHRA* (1972): 118.
62. *Report of the Constabulary Commissioners* (1837), quoted in Henry Mayhew and John Binney, *The Criminal Prisons of London and Scenes of Prison Life,* 2 vols. (London: Frank Cass and Co., 1971), p. 84.
63. Watkin Tench, in *Sydney's First Four Years,* ed. L. F. Fitzhardinge (Sydney: Angus and Robertson, 1962), p. 296.
64. J. A. Semple, *The Life of Major J. A. Semple Lisle* (London: W. Stewart, 1799), p. 6, and *HRN.S.W.* 2:775.
65. Noel McLachlan, ed., *The Memoirs of James Hardy Vaux written by himself* (London: Heinemann, 1964), p. 44. See also pp. 61, 65, 203 and 206.

See, in addition, Averil Fink, "James Hardy Vaux, Convict and Fatalist", *JRAHS* 5 (1962): 321-43.
66. Richard P. Davis, *The Tasmanian Gallows: A Study of Capital Punishment* (Hobart: Cat and Fiddle Press, 1974), p. 15.
67. Sir Walter Scott, *The Heart of Midlothian* (London: Oxford University Press, 1910), p. 32.
68. Quoted, West, *History of Tasmania*, p. 435.
69. M. F. Lloyd Prichard, ed., *The Collected Works of Edward Gibbon Wakefield* (London: Collins, 1968).
70. William Wordsworth, "Preface to *The Borderers*", in *The Prose Works of William Wordsworth*, ed. W. J. B. Owen and J. W. Smyser (Oxford: Oxford University Press, 1974), pp. 77-78.
71. Peter Cunningham, *Two Years in New South Wales*, ed. David S. Macmillan (Sydney: Angus and Robertson, 1966), p. 313.
72. *Report from the Select Committee on Transportation; Together with the Minutes of Evidence Appendix and Index* (London: British Parliamentary Papers, House of Lords, vol. 36), p. 136.
73. Cunningham, *Two Years*, p. 295.
74. See Collins, *Account* 1:239; *Sydney Gazette*, 2 October 1803.
75. Tench described letters he censored. He believed that most letters were sent to solicit gifts. See *Narrative*, p. 12. Cf. instructions issued by Thomas H. Dixon, Superintendent of Convicts, 1 July 1855: "All letters of an improper or evil tendency either to or from the prisoner, or containing *slang* or other objectionable expressions will be suppressed." Boyer Papers, Mitchell Library.
76. For example, convict John Dillingham's scribe included in one letter to the convict's family the false information that Dillingham intended to marry an Aboriginal girl. See Hartley W. Forster, ed., *The Dillingham Convict Letters* (Melbourne: Lansdowne Press, 1970), 4 October 1838, 27 November 1839.
77. Collins, *Account* 2:99-100.
78. "Letter from a female convict", 14 November 1788, published in *Gazetteer*, 29 December 1790, *HRN.S.W.* 2:758.
79. Extracts from "A Letter of a Convict at New South Wales and received a few days since by his Mother in this city", *Ayres Sunday Journal*, 15 July 1792, in Ingleton, *True Patriots*, p. 10.
80. See John Cobley, *The Crimes of the First Fleet Convicts* (Sydney: Angus and Robertson, 1970), pp. xi-xiii; 85. See also White, *Journal*, p. 257.
81. Collins, *Account*, 1:193.
82. John Easty, *Memorandum of Transactions of a Voyage from London to Sydney 1787-1793* (Sydney: Angus and Robertson, 1965), p. 139. (Emphases mine).
83. George Mackaness, ed., *Letters From an Exile at Botany Bay to his Aunt in Dumfries* (Sydney: D. S. Ford, 1945), p. 34.
84. George Mackaness, ed., *Slavery and Famine: Punishments for Sedition...* (Sydney: D. S. Ford, 1947), p. 27.
85. From the Letters of Robert Murray, in H. C. Forster, "'Tyranny, Oppression and Fraud', Port Jackson, N.S.W. 1792-1794", *JRAHS* 2 (1974): 84.
86. John Howard, *The State of the Prisons* (London: Dent, 1929), p. 12.
87. Thomas Paine, *The Rights of Man* (London: Dent, 1958), pp. 27-29.
88. See especially Articles 7, 8, 9.
89. King to Under Secretary Cooke, 20 July 1805, *HRA*, 5:534.
90. See *HRA* 5:538.

91. For examples of pipes see "Anticipation or Birthday Ode", in Ingleton, *True Patriots,* p. 24, and John V. Byrnes, "William Charles Wentworth — and the Continuity of Australian Literature", *Australian Letters* 3 (1963): 10-18.
92. John Grant's letters and papers, MSS. National Library, Canberra, and W.S. Hill-Reid, *John Grant's Journey: A Convict's Story 1803-1811* (London: Heinemann, 1957).
93. *JRAHS* 55 (1969): 43-82.
94. Cunningham, *Two Years,* pp. 214-15. See also pp. 40, 278, 296, 309, 313.
95. West, *History,* p. 425.
96. Tench, *Complete Account,* p. 246.
97. See Patrick Colquhoun, *A Treatise on the Police of the Metropolis,* 6th ed. (London: Joseph Mawman, 1800), p. 107; Vaux, *Memoirs,* p. 148.
98. Edward Gibbon Wakefield, *Punishment of Death,* in *Collected Works,* p. 264, Benjamin Bensley, ed., *Lost and Found; or Light in the Prison: a Narrative; With Original Letters, of a Convict Condemned for forgery* (London: 1859), p. 81.
99. John Philip Gell, *The Penal Settlements in Lectures Delivered before the Church of England Young Men's Society in St Martin's Hall* (London: James Nisbet and Co., 1850), pp. 7-8. Cunningham provides evidence that this odd claim to distinction appeared early. See *Two Years,* p. 296.
100. Bensley, *Lost and Found.*
101. See Eldershaw, "Selected Letters", *PTHRA* 1 (1959): 15.
102. DDX 140/7: Correspondence of Thomas Holden and DDX 505: Correspondence of Richard Taylor and Simon Brown, Lancashire Records Office.
103. The role of the amanuensis (previously adverted to) has to be taken into account here. Judging from Brown's letters, the scribe imposed his own style to such an extent that it is difficult to know how accurately he expressed Brown's feelings. For an excellent example of the art of the amanuensis see the last letter of Samuel Peyton to his mother, 24 June 1788 in Tench, *Narrative,* pp. 62-63. In effect, it is a last dying speech.
104. The most common length of sentence was seven years: nearly half the convicts received it. One quarter of sentences were for life; until 1840 a fourteen-year sentence was common; after that date ten-year sentences were often imposed. See Shaw, *Convicts and the Colonies,* p. 149.
105. West, *History,* p. 343; see also Charles Bateson, *The Convict Ships, 1787-1868* (Sydney: A.H. and A.W. Reed, 1974), p. 261.
106. Nicol, *Life and Adventures,* p. 119.
107. Bathurst to Brisbane, 30 May 1823, *HRA* 11:84.
108. *Sydney Gazette,* 2 October 1803. Seven months previously Lynch had been reprieved on another death sentence. Tracey, known as "The Key of the Works", had led the mutiny on the *Hercules* and escaped punishment by informing on his fellow conspirators.
109. See Smith, *Australian Painting,* p. 20.
110. See John Morgan, *The Life and Adventures of William Buckley,* ed. C. E. Sayers (Melbourne: Heinemann, 1967); Robert Gibbings, *John Graham, Convict 1824* (London: Dent, 1956); Sidney Nolan's paintings "Mr Fraser and the Convict", 1947, and 1957; and Patrick White, *A Fringe of Leaves* (London: Jonathan Cape, 1976).
111. *HRN.S.W.* 2:800-2; James Martin, *Memorandoms,* ed. Charles Blount (Cambridge: Rampant Lions Press, 1937).
112. See Steven J. Watson, *The Reign of George III: 1760-1815* (Oxford: Oxford University Press, 1960), p. 398.

113. West, *History*, p. 363.
114. *HRA*, series III, 2:576.
115. See J. A. Ferguson, "A Bibliography of Literature ascribed to, or relating to George Barrington", *JRAHS* 1 (1930): 51-80.
116. James Hardy Vaux, *Memoirs of the First Thirty-Two Years of the Life of James Hardy Vaux, A Swindler and Pickpocket; now transported, for the second time, and for life, to New South Wales*, ed. Noel McLachlan, *The Memoirs of James Hardy Vaux* (London: Heinemann, 1964).
117. "Advertisement", Vaux, *Memoirs*, p. 1, xxx.
118. Thomas Watling, *Letters from an Exile at Botany Bay*, ed. George Mackaness (Sydney: D. S. Ford, 1945), pp. 7-8.
119. Daniel Dickenson Mann, *The Present Picture of New South Wales; illustrated with four large coloured views from drawings taken on the spot, of Sydney, the seat of Government* (London: John Booth, 1811).
120. Edward Eagar, *Letters to the Rt. Hon. Robert Peel, M.P., Secretary of State for the Home Department, on the advantages of New South Wales and Van Diemen's Land as Penal Settlements* (London: Shacknell and Arrowsmith, 1824).
121. H. M. Green, *A History of Australian Literature, Pure and Applied*, 2 vols. (Sydney: Angus and Robertson, 1961), 1:19.
122. Henry Savery, *The Hermit in Van Diemen's Land*, ed. Cecil Hadgraft (St Lucia: University of Queensland Press, 1964).
123. A. Knapp and W. Baldwin, *The Newgate Calendar: Comprising interesting memoirs of the most notorious characters who have been convicted of outrages on the laws of England*, 4 vols. (London: J. Robbins and Co., 1824), 4:404.

Notes to chapter 3

1. Bernard Smith, *Australian Painting 1788-1960* (Melbourne: Oxford University Press, 1962), pp. 25-56.
2. See C. M. H. Clark, ed. *Select Documents 1788-1850* (Sydney: Angus and Robertson, 1958), pp. 406, 664; A. G. L. Shaw, "Convicts and Transportation", in *Australian Encyclopedia*, 10 vols. (Sydney: Angus and Robertson, 1958), 3:433.
3. Russel Ward, *The Australian Legend* (Sydney: Oxford University Press, 1965), pp. 112-13. For a work which challenges Ward's general thesis, see Ronald Lawson, *Brisbane in the 1890s: A Study of an Australian Urban Society* (St Lucia: University of Queensland Press, 1973), pp. xxi, 317-21.
4. Jesse Lemisch, "Listening to the 'Inarticulate' William Widger's Dream and the Loyalties of American Revolutionary Seamen in British Prisons", *Journal of Social History* 3 (1969): 1-29.
5. Dr Turnbull to the N.S.W. Executive Council, quoted Peter Burroughs, *Britain and Australia* (Oxford: Clarendon Press, 1967), p. 67.
6. John Dunmore Lang, *Reminiscences of My Life and Times Both in Church and State in Australia for Upwards of Fifty Years* (Melbourne: Heinemann, 1972), p. 67.
7. Quoted, Rev. John West, *History of Tasmania*, ed. A. G. L. Shaw (Sydney: Angus and Robertson, 1971), p. 461.
8. Buller to Australian Patriotic Association, quoted, A. C. V. Melbourne, *Early Constitutional Development in Australia* (St Lucia: University of Queensland Press, 1963), p. 227.

9. George Holford, *The Convict's Complaint in 1815 and the Thanks of the Convict in 1825* (Philanthropic Society).
10. Ernest Teagarden, "A Victorian Prison Experiment", *Journal of Social History* 4 (1964): 351-66.
11. Quoted, Philip Collins, *Dickens and Crime*, 2nd ed. (London: Macmillan, 1964), p. 144.
12. Henry Mayhew and John Binney, *The Criminal Prisons of London and Scenes of Prison Life*, 2 vols. (London: Oxford University Press, 1960), 1:127.
13. Roger Therry, *Reminiscences: Thirty Years' Residence in New South Wales and Victoria* (Sydney: Sydney University Press, 1974), p. 354. See also A. G. L. Shaw, *Convicts and the Colonies*, pp. 313-14.
14. "In and out of Jail", *Household Words*, 14 May 1853.
15. Lloyd L. Robson, *The Convict Settlers of Australia* (Carlton: Melbourne University Press, 1965), p. 118.
16. Stanley to Gibbs, *Historical Records of Australia (HRA)* Series 1, 22:516-21.
17. West, *History*, p. 177.
18. Ibid., p. 239.
19. Michael Roe, *Quest for Authority in Eastern Australia 1835-1851* (Carlton: Melbourne University Press, 1965), p. 201.
20. Ibid., p. 149.
21. Quoted, Geoffrey Best, *Mid-Victorian Britain 1851-1875* (London: Weidenfeld and Nicholson, 1971), p. 233.
22. West, *History*, p. 517.
23. See Robson, *Convict Settlers*, p. 91.
24. Shaw, *Convicts and the Colonies*, p. 349.
25. Harry Reynolds, " 'That Hated Stain': The Aftermath of Transportation in Tasmania", *Historical Studies* 14 (1969): 19-31.
26. Peter Bolger, *Hobart Town* (Canberra: Australian National University Press, 1973), p. 111.
27. See J. S. Levi and G. F. J. Bergman, *Australian Genesis: Jewish Convicts and Settlers 1788-1850* (Adelaide: Rigby, 1974), pp. 142-59.
28. R. Nixon Dalkin, *Colonial Era Cemetery of Norfolk Island* (Sydney: Pacific Publications, 1974), pp. 79-80.
29. Anthony Trollope, *Australian and New Zealand*, ed. P. D. Edwards and R. B. Joyce, *Australia* (St Lucia: University of Queensland Press, 1967), p. 152.
30. Robson, *Convict Settlers*, p. 108-9.
31. William Ullathorne, *The Catholic Mission in Australia* (Liverpool: Rockcliffe and Duckworth, 1847).
32. James Murray, *Larrikins: 19th Century Outrage* (Melbourne: Lansdowne Press, 1973). p. 30.
33. Eliza Walker, "Old Sydney in the 'Forties. Recollections of Lower George Street and 'the Rocks' ", *JRAHS* 16 (1930):292-320.
34. "A Picture of Sydney", quoted in *Sydney Morning Herald*, 23 November 1929.
35. See Murray, *Larrikins*, p. 16.
36. See Ward, *Legend*, pp. 75-82.
37. [Alexander Harris], *Settlers and Convicts: or, Recollections of Sixteen Years' Labour in the Australian Backwoods*, ed. C. M. H. Clark (Carlton: Melbourne University Press, 19   ).
38. C. E. W. Bean, *On the Wool Track* (Sydney: Cornstalk Publishing Co., 1925), p. 41.
39. Quoted, Dalkin, *Colonial Cemetery*, p. 70.

40. Bolger, *Hobart Town*, p. 36.
41. David de Giustino, "Reforming the Commonwealth of Thieves: British Phrenologists in Australia", *Victorian Studies* 4 (1972): 447.
42. "Crime in the Bush", *Bulletin*, 1898-99, in Colin Roderick, ed., *Henry Lawson: Autobiographical and Other Writings 1887-1922* (Sydney: Angus and Robertson, 1972), pp. 32-36.
43. Marcus Clarke, "Port Arthur Visited, 1870", in *A Marcus Clarke Reader* ed. Bill Wannan (Melbourne: Lansdowne Press, 1963), pp. 137-48.
44. Trollope, *Australia*, p. 511.
45. Bolger, *Hobart Town*, p. 111.
46. Samuel Clemens [Mark Twain], *Following the Equator* (Hartford: American Publishing Company, 1897), p. 284.
47. *The Life and Adventures of Isaac Solomons, the notorious receiver of Stolen Goods, Better known as Ikey Solomons* (London: Universal Pamphleteer, c.1830).
48. W—, "A Voyage in a Convict Ship", *U.S. Journal* 107 (1837): 193-201.
49. Snowden Dunhill, *The Life of Snowden Dunhill, written by Himself with an Additional account of him Subsequent to the Publication of his Life; the Facts were furnished by a Sea-faring Gentleman who had several interviews with him at Hobart Town in the month of August, 1833* (Howden: W.F. Pratt, 1834).
50. H.W.D., *State of the Convicts in New South Wales, 1835* (Manchester, 1835).
51. "A Copy of a Letter received a few days ago from William Dickson, who was transported to Van Diemen's Land in 1831" (Nottingham: 1833).
52. William Ross, *The Fell Tyrant: or, the Suffering Convict, Showing the horrid and dreadful suffering of the Convict on Norfolk Island* (London: B.J. Ward, 1836).
53. George Loveless, *The Victims of Whiggery: Being a Statement of the Persecutions Experienced by the Dorchester Labourers* (London, 1837).
54. James Mudie, *The Felonry of New South Wales: Being a Faithful Picture of the Real Romance of Life in Botany Bay with Anecdotes of Botany Bay Society and a Plan of Sydney*, ed. Walter Stone (Melbourne: Lansdowne Press, 1964).
55. *Notes d'un condamné politique 1838*, tr. George Mackaness, *Notes of a Convict of 1838* (Sydney: D.S. Ford, 1949).
56. Edward Lilburn, *A Complete Exposure of the Convict System: Its Horrors, Hardships and Severities, Including an Account of the Dreadful Sufferings of the Unhappy Captives. Containing an Extract from a Letter from the Hulks at Woolwich, written by Edward Lilburn* (Lincoln: Thomas Colmer, 1841).
57. *Life of John Knatchbull. Written by Himself. 23rd January – 13th February 1844*, in Darlinghurst Gaol in ed. Colin Roderick *John Knatchbull from Quarterdeck to Gallows* (Sydney: Angus and Robertson, 1963).
58. *The Recollections of James Connor, a Returned Convict: Containing an Account of his Sufferings in, and Ultimate Escape from, New South Wales* (Cupar-Fife: G.S. Tullis, 1845).
59. *The Case of Mr W.H. Barber, containing Copies of all the documents recently submitted to the Right Hon. Sir George Grey, Bart., Secretary of State for the Home Department* (London: Effingham Wilson, 1849). Barber was transported in 1844. He received a free pardon in 1848.
60. Rev. Richard Cobbold, *The History of Margaret Catchpole, A Suffolk Girl* (London: Simms and McIntyre, 1852).

61. John Mitchell, *Jail Journal: or, Five Years in British Prisons* (New York: "Citizen", 1854).
62. Rev. Colin Browning, *The Convict Ship*, 6th ed. (London: Thomas Nisbet and Co., 1856).
63. Anon. (review), "The Life and Adventures of John Leonard, a Prisoner in V.D. Land. (MSS)", *Australian Magazine* 2 (1859): 97-110.
64. *The Horrors of Transportation as related by Joseph Platt* (London: printed for the author, 1862).
65. J. F. Mortlock, *Experiences of a Convict Transported for Twenty-one Years*, ed. G. A. Wilkes (Sydney: Sydney University Press, 1966).
66. George Levine, "Can you forgive him? Trollope's *Can You Forgive Her* and the Myth of Realism", *Victorian Studies* 2 (1974): 6-7.
67. Anon., *Songs, Duets, Glees, Chorusses etc. in the New Musical Extravaganza "Yclept Giovanni in Botany, or the Libertine Transported"* (London, c.1822).
68. E. Morris Miller, "Australia's First Two Novels: Origins and Backgrounds", *Proceedings of the Tasmanian Historical Research Association (PTHRA)* 6 (1957): 37-65. I have not had access to the novel and I therefore rely upon Dr Miller's extensive synopsis and notes. In the same paper Miller mentions a novel by Thomas Gaspey, *The History of George Godfrey written by Himself*, in which there is "some imaginary bushranging in New South Wales".
69. E. Morris Miller, *Pressmen and Governors* (Sydney: Sydney University Press, 1968), pp. 58-59.
70. John Howison, "One False Step" in *Tales of the Colonies*, 2 vols. (London: Henry Colburn and Richard Bentley, 1830).
71. W. T. Moncrieff, *Van Diemen's Land! An Operatic Drama in Three Acts* (London: Thomas Richardson, 1831).
72. David Burn, *The Bushrangers*, ed. W. and J. E. Heiner (Melbourne: Currency Press, 1971).
73. Henry Savery, *Quintus Servinton: A Tale founded upon Incidents of Real Occurrence*, ed. Cecil Hadgraft (Brisbane: Jacaranda Press, 1962).
74. [Charles Rowcroft], *Tales of the Colonies: or, The Adventures of an Emigrant* (London: Saunders and Oatley, 1843).
75. James Tucker, *Ralph Rosleigh*, ed. Colin Roderick (Sydney: Angus and Robertson, 1952), pp. 129-29. This work bore the manuscript title *Ralph Rashleigh or, the Life.of an Exile* by Giacomo di Rosenberg. The original text was not published until 1952.
76. Charles Rowcroft, *The Bushranger of Van Diemen's Land* (New York: Harper and Brothers, 1846).
77. G. P. R. James, *The Convict: A Tale*, 3 vols. (London: Smith, Elder and Co., 1847).
78. Alexander Harris, *The Emigrant Family: or, The Story of an Australian Settler*, ed. W. S. Ramson (Canberra: Australian National University Press, 1967).
79. Mrs Francis Vidal, *Tales for the Bush* (London: Francis and John Rivington, 1852).
80. John George Lang, "Three Celebrities", in *Botany Bay, or True Tales of Early Australia* (Hobart: T. Walch and Sons, n.d.), p. 38.
81. Ernest A. Baker, *History in Fiction: A Guide to the Best Historical Romances, Sagas, Novels and Tales*, 2 vols. (London, n.d.) 2:195.
82. Robert Lowe, *Sydney Morning Herald*, 11 June 1849.
83. Henry Kingsley, *The Recollections of Geoffry Hamlyn* (London: Collins, n.d.), p. 481.

84. Oliné Keese [Caroline Leakey], *The Broad Arrow: Being Passages from the History of Maida Gwynnham, "Lifer"* (Hobart: J. Walch and Sons, 1900).
85. B. L. Farjeon, *Grif: A Story of Colonial Life* (Dunedin: W. Hay, 1866).

Notes to chapter 4

Sources of display quotations:

Oscar Wilde, A Letter to Robert Ross, September 1896, in *De Profundis* (London: Methuen, 1969), p. 12.
Benedetto Croce, *Aesthetic: A Science of Expression and General Linguistics* (London: Peter Owen–Vision Press, 1967), p. 28.
Norman Mailer, *The Armies of the Night: History as a Novel* (London: Hodder and Stoughton, 1968), p. 255.

1. Herman Melville, *Billy Budd, Sailor: (An Inside Narrative)* ed. Harrison Hayford and Merton M. Sealts (Chicago: University of Chicago Press, 1962).
2. Thomas Bastard, *The Autobiography of Cockney Tom* (Adelaide: McLory and Masterman, 1881). Bastard spent only a short time in Horsemonger Lane Gaol. He subsequently migrated to Australia, where, he claims, not the least of his contributions was the introduction of Turkish baths. The latter part of his brief memoir describes his struggle against the "demon drink".
3. Martin Cash, *A Personal Narrative of his Exploits in the Bush and his Experiences at Port Arthur and Norfolk Island* (Hobart: J. Walch and Sons, 1954).
4. A. G. Stephens, *The Red Pagan* (Sydney: Bulletin Publishing Co., 1904), p. 153.
5. Like many such titles, this term does not convey the achievements of some works of writers like Ainsworth, Dickens, Bulwer, Lytton and Thackeray. *It's Never Too Late to Mend* (1856) by Charles Reade, and *Uncle Tom's Cabin: or Life Among the Lowly* (1852) by Harriet Beecher Stowe are other treatments of crime and punishment.
6. Victor Hugo, *Les Misérables*, 4 vols. (Paris: Nelson, Editeurs, 1959), 4:455.
7. See his press conference, 10 April 1975 in *Times* Literary Supplement, 23 May 1975.
8. *His Natural Life* (London, 1874). *For the Term of His Natural Life* (London, 1855). The former is Clarke's revision of *His Natural Life*, first published in serial form, in the *Australian Journal*, November 1870–June 1872. The 1885 edition bore the title by which the novel is usually known. The original (serialized) version has been reprinted, edited by Stephen Murray-Smith (Ringwood: Penguin), 1970.
9. Sir Charles Gavan Duffy, *My Life in Two Hemispheres* 2 vols. (London: T. Fisher Unwin, 1898), 2:313.
10. See "A Melbourne Alsatia", in *A Colonial City. High and Low Life: Selected Journalism of Marcus Clarke*, ed. L. T. Hergenhan (St Lucia: University of Queensland Press, 1972), pp. 127-28.
11. See Brian Elliott, *Marcus Clarke* (Oxford: Oxford University Press, 1958), p. 65.
12. "Port Arthur Revisited", *Argus*, 1873, in Wannan, p. 141.
13. "A Night at the Immigrants' Home", *Australasian*, 12 June 1869, in Hergenhan, *Colonial City*, p. 139.
14. Joan Poole, ed., *Old Tales of a New Country* (Sydney: Sydney University Press, 1972).

15. Murray P. Braidwood and Alfred J. Cope, eds., *The "Parramatta" Times*, 2 April–25 May 1886.
16. *Journal*, MS., p. 62.
17. See for example L. T. Hergenhan, "The Redemptive Theme in *His Natural Life*", *Australian Literary Studies* (*ALS*) 2 (1965).
18. See Joan E. Poole, "Marcus Clarke: Christianity is Dead", *ALS* 10 (1973); 128–42.
19. See Elliott, *Marcus Clarke*, p. 163.
20. Elizabeth Winstanley, "Her Natural Life. A Tale of 1830", *Bow Bells* 25 (1876) 629-30.
21. John Boyle O'Reilly, *Moondyne: A Story of Life in West Australia* (Melbourne: George Robertson, 1880).
22. William Hay, *The Escape of the notorious Sir William Heans (and the Mystery of Mr Daunt)* (Carlton: Melbourne University Press, 1955).
23. Earle F. Hooper, "William Hay: A Memoir", *Southerly* 6 (1946): 136.
24. Patrick White, *Voss* (Ringwood: Penguin, 1974), p. 345.
25. Patrick White, *A Fringe of Leaves* (London: Jonathan Cape, 1976), p. 245.
26. Ibid., p. 367.
27. Ibid., p. 405.
28. Hal Porter, *The Tilted Cross* (Adelaide: Rigby, 1971).
29. Thomas Keneally, *Bring Larks and Heroes* (Melbourne: Sun Books, 1968), p. 230. The passage from Chesterton is:

   > "Suppose I am God", said the voice, "and suppose I made the world in idleness. Suppose the stars, that you think eternal are only the idiot fireworks of an everlasting schoolboy. Suppose the sun and the moon, to which you sing alternately, are only the two eyes of one vast and sneering giant, opened alternately in a never-ending wink. Suppose the trees, in my eyes, are as foolish as enormous toad-stools. Suppose Socrates and Charlemagne are to me only beasts, made funnier by walking on their hind legs. Suppose I am God, and having made things, laugh at them."

   G. K. Chesterton, *The Napoleon of Notting Hill* (London: John Lane, 1904), pp. 196-97. This passage was written almost twenty years before Chesterton's conversion to Catholicism.

Notes to appendix I

1. William Baldwin, *How Jack Cade Traitorously Rebelling Against His King Was For His Treasons and Cruell Doings Wurtheley Punyshed*, In *Mirror for Magistrates*, pp. 171-82.
2. "Sarah Malcolmson, The Ordinary's Account", in Anon., *Tyburn Calendar* 2:35-42.
3. "William Ray, for the Murder of His Wife", in *Tyburn Calendar* 2:48-50.
4. "Trial and Execution of John Austin, Convicted at the Old Bailey on Saturday, Nov. 1st, 1783, of a Cruel Highway Robbery on John Spicer, a Poor Man", in Hindley, *Curiosities of Street Literature*, p. 173.
5. "Execution of Six Unfortunate Malefactors at Tyburn, Yesterday Morning, August 30, 1783", in Hindley, *Curiosities*, p. 172.
6. "The Trial, Confession, and Execution of John Swan and Elizabeth Jeffreys Who Were Found Guilty at Chelmsford Assizes for the Murder of Mr Joseph

Jeffreys, at Walshamstow, in Essex, on the 3rd of July, 1775", in Hindley, *Curiosities*, p. 171.
7. "Life, Trial and Execution of William Nevison, the Highwayman, at York Gaol", in Hindley, *Curiosities*, p. 169.
8. "John Donellan Esq; For Murder", in A. Knapp and W. Baldwin, *The Criminal Chronology: or, The New Newgate Calendar* ... (London, 1811) 2: 307–327.
9. "Minutes of the Trial of John Donellan, Esquire, for the Murder if Sir Theodosius Boughton, Baronet, at Warwick Assizes, Held March 30, 1781, *Gentleman's Magazine,* April 1781, pp. 156–58.
10. "Samuel Denmore Hayward, For Burglary", in Borrow, *Celebrated Trials* 6: 452–56.
11. "A Brief Relation of the Adventures of M. Bamfield Moore Carew, for More Than Forty Years Past the King of the Beggars", in Ashton, *Chap-book of the Eighteenth Century,* pp. 423–26.
12. "The Bloody Tragedy of a Dreadful Warning to Disobedient Children ... ", in Ashton, *Chap-books,* p. 439.
13. "The Life and Adventures of Dick Turpin", in Hindley, *History of the Catnach Press,* pp. 214–19.
14. "The Life, Trial, Character, Confession, Behaviour, and Execution of James Ward, Aged 25, Who Was Hung [sic] in Front of the Gaol, for the Wilful Murder He Committed on the Body of His Own Wife, to Which is Added a Copy of Affectionate Verses Which He Composed in the Condemned Cell the Night Before His Execution", Hindley, *History,* pp. 273–80.

Notes to appendix II

1. Richard Head, *Meriton Latroon.*
2. Daniel Defoe, *Colonel Jacque.*
3. Daniel Defoe, *Moll Flanders.*
4. John Gay, *The Beggar's Opera.*
5. George Lillo, *The London Merchant.*
6. Henry Fielding, *Jonathan Wild.*
7. William Hogarth, *The "Idle Prentice".*
8. Oliver Goldsmith, "Serious Reflections on the Life and Death of the Late Mr. T- C-, by the Ordinary of Newgate" in A. Friedman (ed.) *Works* 3:46–48.
9. Oliver Goldsmith, "The Citizen of the World", Letter CXIX", in *Works* 2: 458–65.

Notes to appendix III

1. "A Convict's Letter" (James Lacey), 19 August 1792, *HRN.S.W.*, ii, 479–80.
2. "Extracts from a Letter of a Convict at New South Wales", *Ayre's Sunday London Gazette,* 15 July 1792, Ingleton, p. 10.
3. "A Letter From the Reverend Fysshe Palmer to Doctor John Disney", 13 June 1795, Ingleton, p. 18.
4. George Barrington, *A Voyage to Botany Bay* (T.R. Gordon, 1799) and *A Sequel to Barrington's Voyage* (London, 1801).

5. James Martin, *Memorandoms*, ed. Blount (London, 1937).
6. J.G. Semple, *The Life of Major J. G. Semple Lisle* (London, 1799).
7. Benjamin, Bensley, *Lost and Found: or, Light in the Pirson; a Narrative* (London, 1889).
8. John Grant, Letters, Papers, *Journals*, MSS., National Library (Canberra).
9. John Slater, *A Description of Sydney, Parramatta, Newcastle, etc., Settlements in New South Wales, with Some Account of the Manners and Employment of the Convicts* (Bridlesmith-Gate, 1819).
10. Noel McLachlan, ed., *The Memoirs of James Hardy Vaux, Written by Himself* (London, 1964).
11. Thomas Wells, *Michael Howe, The Last and Worst of the Bushrangers of Van Diemen's Land* (1818), in Curr and Edward, *An Account of the Colony of Van Diemen's Land* (London, 1824), pp. 177–207.
12. "The Unhappy Transport: or, The Sufferings of William Dale . . . ", Mitchell Library.
13. *Confessions of a Gentleman Convict* (London, 1822).
14. James Mackenzie, *The Life and Adventure of James Mackenzie* (Glasgow, 1825).
15. - Mellish, *A Convict's Recollections of New South Wales, Written by Himself* (London, 1825), Mitchell Library, copy defective.
16. James Revell, *The Unhappy Transport* (London, 1824), Mitchell Library.
17. John Jackson, *A Remarkable Narrative* (London, 1825), Mitchell Library.
18. H. Augustus, *The Convict* (London, c. 1830).
19. *Memoir*, MS., Mitchell Library.
20. "The London Convict Maid", Mitchell Library.

Notes to appendix IV

1. *The Life and Adventures of Isaac Solomons, the Notorious Receiver of Stolen Goods, Better Known as Ikey Solomons* (London: Universal Pamphleteer, c. 1830).
2. *A Copy of a Letter received a few days ago, from William Dickson, who was transported to Van Diemen's Land in the year 1831, from the town of Nottingham, written to John Elson, of York Street* (Nottingham, 1833).
3. *The Life of Snowden Dunhill, written by himself with an additional account of him subsequent to the Publication of his life, the facts of which were furnished by a Sea-faring Gentleman, who had several interviews with him at Hobart Town in the month of August, 1833* (Howden, 1834).
4. *State of the Convicts in New South Wales, 1835* (Manchester, 1835).
5. *The Fell Tyrant: or, The Suffering Convict, Showing the horrid and dreadful suffering of the convict on Norfolk Island* (London, 1836).
6. *Particulars of the awful execution of nine unfortunate convicts, who were executed at Van Diemen's Land on Saturday July the second 1836, for rebelling against their masters, through the heavy punishment inflicted on them written by a convict to his friend at Castle Connington dated Copper Valley, July 3rd 1836* (Leicester, 1837).
7. "A Voyage in a Convict Ship", *U.S. Journal* no. 107 (1837), pp. 193–201.
8. *A Narrative of the Sufferings of Jas. Loveless, Jas. Brine and Thomas and John Standfields* (London, 1838).
9. *The Felony of New South Wales: Being a Faithful Picture of the Real*

Romance of Life in Botany Bay with Anecdotes of Botany Bay Society and a Plan of Sydney (Melbourne, 1837).
10. *Notes d'un Condamné Politique 1838*, translated by G. Mackaness (Sydney, 1949).
11. *A Warning Voice from a Penitent Convict: The Life, Hardships and Dreadful Sufferings of Charles Adolphus King Who was Tried at Liverpool Assizes for Returning from Transportation With an Affecting Speech he made* (1840, n.ed. London, 1956).
12. *A Letter from Mr John Frost, to his Wife, from Port Arthur in Van Diemen's Land, His Place of Settlement* (Manchester, 1840).
13. *A Complete Exposure of the Convict System: its Horrors, Hardships and Severities, Including an Account of the Dreadful Sufferings of the Unhappy Captives. Containing an Extract from a Letter from the Hulks at Woolwick* (London, 1841).
14. *A Narrative of a Visit to the Australian Colonies* (London, 1843).
15. *Life of John Knatchbull Written by Himself 23rd January—13th February 1844 in Darlinghurst Gaol* in *John Knatchbull from Quarter Deck to Gallows*, ed. Colin Roderick (Sydney, 1963).
16. *The Recollections of James Connor, a Returned Convict: Containing an Account of His Sufferings in, and Ultimate Escape from, New South Wales* (Cupar-Fife, 1845).
17. *Notes of an Exile to Van Diemen's Land, Comprising Incidents of the Canadian Rebellion of 1835* (New York, 1846).
18. *A Narrative of a Journey to and from New South Wales, Including a Seven Years' Residence in that Country* (Chapel-en-le-Frith, 1846).
19. *Adventures of a Guardsman* (London, 1848).
20. *The Case of Mr W. H. Barber Containing Copies of all the Documents Recently Submitted to the Right Hon. Sir George Grey, Bart. Secretary of State for the Home Department* (London, 1849).
21. *Life of John Broxup, Late Convict, at Van Diemen's Land* (Wetherby, 1850).
22. *Horrors of Transportation as Related by M.A. Smith, in a Letter to Her Parents in this Town* (1851).
23. *London Labour and the London Poor* (London, 1851).
24. *The Life and Adventures of William Buckley* (1852, n.ed. London, 1967).
25. *MSS. Reminiscences* (FM 4/2278, Mitchell Library), pp. 329 ff.
26. *The History of Margaret Catchpole, a Suffolk Girl* (London, 1845).
27. *The Convict Ship* (London, 1856).
28. *Life Among the Convicts* (London, 1863).
29. *The Horrors of Convict Life: Two Lectures by John Frost* (London, 1856).
30. *The Life and Adventures of John Leonard, a Prisoner in Van Diemen's Land. Australian Magazine*, ii (1859): 97–110.
31. *The Horrors of Transportation as Related by Joseph Platt* (London, 1862).
32. *Experiences of a Convict Transported for Twenty-one Years* (1864–65, n.ed. Sydney, 1966).

Notes to appendix V

1. *One False Step* in *Tales of the Colonies* (London, 1830).
2. *Quintus Servinton* (1830, n.ed., Brisbane, 1962).
3. *Tales of the Colonies: or, The Adventures of an Emigrant* (London, 1843).

4. *Ralph Rashleigh* (Original ed., Sydney, 1952).
5. *It Is Never Too Late to Mend* (1856, n.ed. London, 1908).
6. *The Recollections of Geoffry Hamlyn* (1859, n.ed. London, n.d.).
7. *The Broad Arrow* (1859, n.ed. Hobart, 1900).
8. *Grif* (Dunedin, 1866).
9. *His Natural Life* (1870-72, n.ed. Stephen Murray-Smith, ed., Ringwood, 1970). *For The Term of His Natural Life* (1874, n.ed. Adelaide, 1974).
10. *Her Natural Life, Bow Bells* (London, 1876).
11. *Moondyne: A Story of Life in Australia* (Melbourne, 1880).
12. *The Golden Lake: or, The Marvellous History of a Journey Through the Great Lone Land of Australia* (Melbourne: 1891).
13. *Longleat of Kooralbyn: or, Policy and Passion* (London, 1887).
14. "The Evolution of Convict Hendy" in *Tales of the Isle of Death* (Melbourne, 1898).
15. *The Pioneers* (1915, n.ed. Adelaide, 1963).
16. *Up the Country: A Tale of the Early Australian Squattocracy* (1928, n.ed. Sydney, 1951).
17. *Pageant* (Sydney, 1933).
18. *Land Takers: The Story of an Epoch* (1934, n.ed. Sydney, 1963); *Inheritors: A Novel* (Sydney, 1936).
19. *Southern Saga* (1940, n.ed. Sydney, 1946).
20. *Voss* (1957; n.ed. Ringwood, 1974).

Bibliography

There seems to be an obvious value in drawing up a complete bibliography of works relating to the transportation era in Australia. The following select list of books and sources (extending to the early 1970s) is a contribution to that task.

Manuscripts and books are generally arranged in order of publication. This arrangement is designed to assist in a study of the development of perceptions about the convicts and transportation. Where it is appropriate to indicate when a work was written, rather than when it was published, the entry is accompanied by an asterisk (*).

The texts are arranged to correspond with the chapters of the book, with subdivisions as appropriate to each period under discussion.

Chapter 1 The Background

Newspapers and magazines

1. 1704–13. *Review of the State of the British Nation.* 12 vols. New York: A.M.S. Press Inc., 1965.
2. 1711–14. *Spectator.* Edited by D.F. Bond. 5 vols. Oxford: Clarendon Press, 1965.
3. 1731–. *Gentleman's Magazine.*
4. 1749–50, '52. *Rambler.* Edited by W.J. Bate and Albrecht B. Strauss. New Haven: Yale University Press, 1969.
5. 1785–. *Times.*

Virtuous and Vicious Lives: Treatments and Commentaries

6. c.1450–1550. Zall, P. M. ed. *A Hundred Merry Tales and other English Jestbooks of the Fifteenth and Sixteenth Centuries.* Lincoln, Nebraska: University of Nebraska Press, 1963.
7. Skelton, John. 1517*. *The Tunnyng of Elynour Rummyng.* In *John Skelton: Poems,* edited by Robert Kinsman. Oxford: Clarendon Press, 1969.
8. Baldwin, William. 1559. *The Mirror for Magistrates.* Edited by Lily B. Campbell. New York: Barnes and Noble, 1960.
9. Foxe, John. 1563. *Actes and Monuments.* In *Foxe's Book of Martyrs,* edited by C. A. Williamson. London: Secker and Warburg, 1965.
10. Greene, Robert. 1592. *The third and last part of CONY-CATCHING with the new devised Knavish Art of fool-taking the like cozenages and villainies never before discovered.* In *Three Elizabethen Pamphlets,* edited by G. R. Hibbard. London: 1951.
11. Dekker, Thomas. 1606. *English Villainies Discovered by Lantern and Candlelight.* Edited by E. D. Pendry. London: Edward Arnold Ltd, 1967.
12. Evelyn, John, 1620–1706*. *Diary,* in *The Diary of John Evelyn.* Edited by E. S. Beer. London: Oxford University Press, 1959.
13. Pepys, Samuel. 1660–69*. *The Diary.* Edited by Henry B. Wheatley. London: Oxford University Press, 1955.
14. Head, Richard, and Kirkman, Francis. 1665–71. *The English Rogue Described in The Life of Meriton Latroon, a Witty Extravagant: Being a complete history of the most eminent cheats of both sexes.* London: George Routledge and Sons, 1928.
15. Ward, Ned. 1698–1700. *The London Spy.* Edited by K. Fenwick. London: Folios Society, 1955.
16. Mandeville, Bernard. 1714. *The Fable of the Bees.* Harmondsworth: Penguin, 1970.
17. Ward, Ned. 1715. *A Vade Mecum for Maltworms: Or, a Guide to Good Fellows.* London: T. Bickerston.
18. LeSage, Alain-René. 1715–47. *Histoire de Gil Blas De Santillane.* Paris: Editions Garnier Frères, 1955.
19. Smith, Alexander. 1719. *History of the Lives and Robberies of the most noted Highway-men, Foot-pads, House-breakers,*

       Shop lifts and Cheats of both Sexes in and about London and Westminster. London: Navarre Society, 1926.
20. Defoe, Daniel. 1720. *The Life of Captain Singleton*. London: Dent, 1951.
21. ———. 1722. *A Journal of the Plague Year*. London: Dent, 1961.
22. ———. 1722. *The History and Remarkable Life of the Truly Honourable Col. Jacque, commonly called Col. Jack*. London: Oxford University Press, 1965.
23. ———. 1722. *The Fortunes and Misfortunes of the Famous Moll Flanders, Etc*. New York: New American Library, 1964.
24. Gay, John. 1728. *The Beggar's Opera*. In *Eighteenth-Century Plays* edited by John Hampden. London: Dent, 1958.
25. Lillo, George. 1731. *The London Merchant: Or, The History of George Barnwell*. In *Eighteenth - Century Plays*, edited by John Hampden. London: Dent, 1958.
26. Swift, Jonathan. 1733-42. *Directions to Servants and Miscellaneous Pieces*. London: Dent, 1952.
27. Johnson, Charles. 1734. *Great Lives and Adventures of the Most Famous Highwaymen*. London: Navarre Society, 1926.
28. Fielding, Henry. 1742. *The History of the Adventures of Joseph Andrews and his Friend Mr Abraham Adams. Written in the Manner of Cervantes, Author of "Don Quixote"*. New York: Frank Cass and Co., 1967.
29. ———. 1743. *The History of the Life of the late Mr Jonathan Wild*. New York: Frank Cass and Co., 1965.
30. Carew, Bampfylde Moore. 1745-49. *The King of the Beggars*. Edited by C. H. Wilkinson. Oxford: Clarendon Press, 1931.
31. Fielding, Henry. 1749. *The History of Tom Jones, a Foundling*. New York: Barnes and Noble Inc., 1967.
32. ———. 1751. *An Enquiry into the Causes of the Late Increase of Robbery, etc. With some Proposals for Remedying This Growing Evil*. London: Frank Cass and Co., 1967.
33. ———. 1752. *Amelia*. New York: Barnes and Noble Inc., 1967.
34. Richardson, Samuel. 1753. *The History of Sir Charles Grandison*. London: Oxford University Press, 1972.
35. Smollett, Tobias. 1753. *The Adventures of Ferdinand Count Fathom*. London: Oxford University Press, 1971.

36. Rousseau, Jean-Jacques. 1755. *On the Origin of Inequality.* Chicago: Encyclopedia Britannica Inc., 1952.
37. Butler, Alban. 1756-59. *The Lives of the Fathers, Martyrs and other Principal Saints.* London: A. Wilson, 1812-13.
38. Rousseau, Jean-Jacques. 1762. *Emile.* Translated by Barbara Foxley. London: Dent, 1969.
39. Smollett, Tobias. 1764. *The Life and Adventures of Sir Launcelot Greaves.* London: Dent, 1973.
40. Walpole, Horace. 1764. *The Castle of Otranto: A Gothic Story.* London: Oxford University Press, 1964.
41. Goldsmith, Oliver. 1766. *The Vicar of Wakefield.* Cambridge: Cambridge University Press, 1966.
42. ————. 1768. "Some Reflections on the Life and Death of Mr T-C-, by the Ordinary of Newgate". *Weekly Magazine,* 17th December, 1768. In *Collected Works of Oliver Goldsmith,* edited by A. Friedman. 4 vols. Oxford: Clarendon Press, 1966.
43. Anon. 1768. *The Tyburn Chronicles: or, Villainy displayed in all its branches. Containing an authentic account of the lives, adventures, tryals, executions and last dying speeches of the most notorious malefactors . . . who have suffered . . . in England, Scotland and Ireland, from the year 1700, to the present time.* 4 vols. London: J. Cooke.
44. Anon. 1768. *The Tyburn Calendar: or, Malefactors' Bloody Register.* 2 vols. Manchester: G. Swindells.
45. Howard, John. 1777. *The State of the Prisons.* London: Dent, 1929.
46. Reeve, Clara. 1778. *The Old English Baron: A Gothic Story.* London: Oxford University Press, 1967.
47. Boswell, James. 1791. *Life of Johnson.* Edited by George Birkbeck Hill. 6 vols. Oxford: Clarendon Press, 1934.
48. Godwin, William. 1793. *Enquiry Concerning Political Justice and its Influence on Morals and Happiness.* Toronto: University of Toronto Press, 1946.
49. Radcliffe, Ann. 1794. *The Mysteries of Udolpho: A Romance interspersed with some pieces of Poetry.* London: Oxford University Press, 1966.
50. Godwin, William. 1794. *The Adventures of Caleb Williams: or, Things as they are.* New York: Rinehart and Co., 1960.
51. Coleridge, S. T. 1795. *Lectures 1795 on Politics and Religion.*

Edited by L. Patton and P. Mann. London: Routledge and Kegan Paul, 1971.
52. Colquhoun, Patrick. 1795. *A Treatise on the Police of the Metropolis containing a detail of the various crimes and misdemeanors by which public and private property and security are at present injured and endangered: and suggesting remedies for their prevention.* 6th ed. London: Joseph Mawman, 1800.
53. Wilberforce, William. 1797. *A practical view of the prevailing Religious System of professed Christians in the higher and middle classes in this country. Contrasted with real Christianity.* 8th ed. London: T. Cadell and W. Davies, 1805.
54. Eden, Sir Frederick Morton. 1797. *The State of the Poor.* 3 vols. London: Frank Cass and Co., 1966.
55. Medland, W. M. and Woebly, Charles. 1803. *A Collection of Remarkable and Interesting Criminal Trials, Actions at Law and other Legal Decisions.* 2 vols. London: John Badcock.
56. Student of the Joiner Temple, A. *The Criminal Recorder: or, Biographical Sketches of Notorious Public Characters.* 4 vols. London: Albion Press.
57. Knapp, Andrew, and Baldwin, William. 1811. *Criminal Chronology: or, The New Newgate Calendar, being interesting memoirs of notorious characters who have been convicted of outrages on the laws of England during the seventeenth century: and brought down to the present time, chronologically arranged.* 4 vols. London: Nuttall, Fisher and Dixon.
58. ―――. 1824. *The Newgate Calendar: Comprising interesting memoirs of the most notorious characters who have been convicted of outrages on the laws of England.* 4 vols. London: J. Robbins and Co.
59. Borrow, George. 1825. *Celebrated Trials, Remarkable Cases:* or *Criminal Jurisprudence: From the earliest records to the year 1825.* 6 vols. London: Knight and Lacey.
60. "Pelham, Camden". 1841. *The Chronicles of Crime and the Newgate Calendar.* 6 vols. London: Thomas Tegg.
61. Johnson, Captain Charles. 1842. *Lives and exploits of English Highwaymen, pirates and robbers; drawn from the most authentic sources, revised and continued to the present time by C. Whitehead Esq.* Embellished with sixteen spirited drawings. London: H. G. Bohu.

62. Hindley, Charles. 1871. *Curiosities of Street Literature.* London: Reeves and Turner, 1871.
63. Ashton, John. 1882. *Chap-books of the Eighteenth Century.* London: Albion Press.
64. Marks, Alfred. 1890. *Tyburn Tree. Its History and Annals.* London: Brown and Langham.
65. Atlay, J. B. 1899. *Famous Trials of the Century.* London: Grant Richards.
66. Gordon, Charles. 1902. *The Old Bailey and Newgate.* London: T. Fisher Unwin.
67. Rayner, T. L., and Crook, G. T., eds. 1926. *The Complete Newgate Calendar.* 5 vols. London: Navarre Society.
68. Farmer, John S. 1964. *Musa Pedestris: Three Centuries of Canting Songs and Slang Rhymes (1536-1896).* New York: Cooper Square Publishers, 1964.

Chapter 2   1788–1829:
The Beginnings of Convict Literature in Australia

Manuscripts

69. 1756–93, 1829–40. Old Bailey's Session's Records 1756-93 and Transportation Accounts, 1829-40. ML, FM4/2282-3.
70. 1796–98. Papers in the National Archives of Mexico concerning the American vessel *Otter* and certain convicts who escaped on her. ML, B1622–B1627.
71. 1797–1811. Margaret Catchpole Papers. 1797-1811. ML, MSS 51.
72. c.1797–1812. Vaucluse House: transcripts of old letters etc., re Vaucluse. ML, B1365–B1366.
73. 1799–1825. Letters written by Michael Hayes. ML, A3586.
74. 1801–4. Margarot's Journal (parts only), section 8. ML, 1374.
75. 1803–11. John Grant Letters. Papers, Journal. MSS. National Library, Canberra.
76. 1803–43. Conduct Registers of Male Convicts arriving in the period of the Assignment System. (Selected volumes.) TA, CON.31.
77. 1803–43. Conduct Registers of Female Convicts arriving in the period of the Assignment System. (Selected volumes.) TA, CON.40.

78. 1804–39. Alphabetical Registers of Male Convicts. TA, CON.23.
79. 1806–12. Miscellaneous Memorials to the Governor concerning Judicial Matters. 1154, State Archives of New South Wales.
80. 1812–16. Thomas Holden Correspondence. DDX. 140/7. Lancashire Records Office.
81. 1815(?)*. Mitchell, James. "Norfolk Island 1804 till 1809". ML, MSS, 27 II.
82. 1822–25. List of Absconding Convicts and Assigned Servants. 4/4525, State Archives of New South Wales.
83. 1825–35. Deposition Books. 4/4673–4/4676, State Archives of New South Wales.
84. 1827–31. Indents of Male Convicts. TA, CON.14.
85. 1829–33. (Macquarie Harbour) Commandant's Letter Book. TA, CON.85.
86. c.1830. Papers re New South Wales 1799–1830+ . . . anonymous MS. labelled "A Convict Narrative". ML, MSS. 681/1–2.

Published Government Papers

87. 1762–1811. *Historical Records of New South Wales.* Sydney: Government Printer, 1892–1901.
88. 1776–95. Bonwick Transcripts. Missionary Papers I. ML, BT49.
89. 1786–1827. *Historical Records of Australia.* Series 4, vol. 1. Sydney: Library Committee of Commonwealth Government, 1922.
90. 1788–1848. *Historical Records of Australia.* Series 1. 26 vols. Sydney: Library Committee of Commonwealth Parliament, 1914–26.
91. 1803–30. *Historical Records of Australia.* Series 3, vols. 1–3, 5–6. Sydney: Library Committee of Commonwealth Government, 1921.
92. 1816–30. *British Parliamentary Papers Colonies. Australia. 3. Sessions 1816–30.* Shannon: Irish University Press, 1968–70.
93. 1822–35. *British Parliamentary Papers Colonies. Australia. 1. Sessions 1822–35.* Shannon: Irish University Press, 1968–70.
94. 1822. *British Parliamentary Papers Colonies. Australia. Report of the Commission of Inquiry into the state of the Colony of New South Wales* (448). Shannon: Irish University Press, 1968–70.

95. 1823. *British Parliamentary Papers Colonies. Australia.* (532). Shannon: Irish University Press, 1968–70.
96. 1826. *British Parliamentary Papers Colonies. Australia.* (277). Shannon: Irish University Press, 1968–70.

Newspapers and Magazines

97. 1803–42. *Sydney Gazette and New South Wales Advertiser.*
98. 1816–17. *Hobart Town Gazette* 1, 2. Hobart: Platypus Publications, 1965.

Eyewitness Accounts

99. Bradley, William. 1786–92*. *A Voyage to New South Wales.* Sydney: Ure Smith, 1969.
100. Easty, John. 1787–93*. *Memorandum of the Transactions of a Voyage from England to Botany Bay 1787–1793.* Sydney: Angus and Robertson, 1965.
101. Anon., ed. 1789. *The Voyage of Governor Phillip to Botany Bay with contributions by other Officers of the First Fleet and observations on affairs of the time by Lord Auckland.* Edited by J. J. Auchmuty. Sydney: Angus and Robertson, 1970.
102. Tench, Watkin. 1789. *A Narrative of the Expedition to Botany Bay.*
    ———. 1793. *A Complete Account of the Settlement at Port Jackson.* Edited by L. F. Fitzhardinge. *Sydney's First Four Years.* Sydney: Angus and Robertson, 1962.
103. White, John. 1790. *Journal of a Voyage to New South Wales.* Edited by Alec Chisholm. Sydney: Angus and Robertson, 1962.
104. Phillip, Arthur. 1791. *Extracts of Letters from Arthur Phillip Esq., Governor of New South Wales to Lord Sydney: To which is annexed a description of Norfolk Island by Philip Gidley King Esq.* London: J. Debbrett.
105. Hunter, John. 1793. *An Historical Journal of the Transactions at Porth Jackson and Norfolk Island (. . .) compiled from the official papers.* London: John Stockdale.
106. Johnson, Rev. Richard. 1794. *An Address to the Inhabitants of the Colonies established in New South Wales and Norfolk Island. Written in the year 1792.* London: Richard Johnson.

107. Collins, David. 1798, 1802. *An Account of the English Colony in New South Wales: With remarks on the dispositions, customs, manners, etc. of the Native Inhabitants of the Country.* 2 vols. London: T. Caddell and W. Davies.
108. Tuckey, J.H. 1805. *An Account of a Voyage to establish a Colony at Port Phillip in Bass's Strait on the South coast of New South Wales in his Majesty's Ship* Calcutta *in the years 1802–3–4.* London: Longman, Hurst, Rees and Orme.
109. Anon. 1806. *New South Wales Pocket Almanac and Colonial Remembrancer.* Sydney: Public Library of New South Wales, 1966.
110. Mann, Daniel Dickenson. 1811. *The Present Picture of New South Wales: Illustrated with four large coloured views from drawings taken on the spot, of Sydney, the seat of Government.* London: John Booth.
111. Evans, George William. 1822. *A Geographical, Historical and Topographical Description of Van Diemen's Land.* Adelaide: Heinemann, 1972.
112. Nicol, John. 1822. *The Life and Adventures of John Nicol, Mariner.* Edinburgh: William Blackwood.
113. Curr, Edward. 1824. *An Account of the Colony of Van Dieman's Land: Principally Designed for the Use of Emigrants.* Hobart: Platypus Publications, 1967.
114. Cunningham, Peter. 1827. *Two Years in New South Wales.* Sydney: Angus and Robertson, 1966.
115. Wakefield, Edward Gibbon. 1829. *A Letter from Sydney: The Punishment of Death in the Metropolis.* In *The Collected Works of Edward Gibbon Wakefield,* edited by M. F. Lloyd Prichard. London: Collins, 1968.

Accounts of the Convict Experience

116. Barrington, George (?). 1791. *The Genuine Life and Times of George Barrington from his birth in June, 1755 to the time of his conviction at the Old Bailey in September 1790.* London: Robert Barker.
117. Martin, James. 1791(?)* *Memorandoms.* Edited by Charles Blount. Cambridge: Rampant Lions Press, 1937.
118. Thompson, George. 1794. *Slavery and Famine: Punishments for Sedition With Preliminary Remarks by George Dyer, B.A.* London: J. Ridgway.

119. Watling, Thomas. 1794. *Letters from an Exile at Botany Bay to his Aunt in Dumfries.* Edited by George Mackaness. Sydney: D. S. Ford, 1945.
120. Southey, Robert. 1795. "Botany Bay Eclogues". In *Complete Poems.* London: Longmans, 1890.
121. Barrington, George (?). 1799. *A Voyage to Botany Bay together with his life and trial and sequel to his voyage.* New York: Brummell Press, 1969.
122. Semple, J. G. 1799. *The Life of Major J. G. Semple Lisle.* London: W. Stewart.
123. Barrington, George (?). 1801. *A Sequel to Barrington's Voyage.* New York: Brummell Press, 1969.
124. ———. 1801. *Barrington's Voyage to Botany Bay in New South Wales with a description of the country, and its productions. Written by himself.* London: J. Letbe.
125. Grove, James. 1802–4*. *Letters from Port Phillip and the Derwent.* In *Lost and Found or Light in the Prison* edited by B. Bensley. London: 1859. And "Select Letters of James Grove, Convict Port Philip and the Derwent", edited by John Earnshaw. *PTHRA* 8, i, ii (1959).
126. Barrington, George (?). 1803. *The Life and Trials of George Barrington, Officer of the Peace at Parramatta. Author of the Voyage to, and History of, New South Wales.* London: W. Flint.
127. Robinson, Michael Massey. 1810–21*. *Odes.* In *Odes of Michael Massey Robinson, first Poet Laureate of Australia 1754–1826,* edited by George Mackaness. Sydney: George Mackaness, 1946.
128. Anon. 1815. *Confessions of a Gentleman Convict, written during a residence at Botany Bay, whither for his extraordinary robberies on the highway, he was sentenced to be transported for life (. . .), written by himself.* London: J. Bailey.
129. Wells, Thomas. 1818. *Michael Howe, The Last and Worst of the Bushrangers of Van Diemen's Land.* Hobart: Platypus Publications, 1966.
130. Slater, John. 1819. *A Description of Sydney, Parramatta, Newcastle, etc., Settlements in New South Wales, with some account of the manners and employment of the convicts in a letter from John Slater to his wife.* Bridlesmith Gate.
131. Vaux, James Hardy. 1819. *Memoirs of the First Thirty-Two*

Years of The Life of James Hardy Vaux, a Swindler and Pickpocket; now transported, for the second time, and for life, to New South Wales. N.ed., The Memoirs of James Hardy Vaux, edited by Noel McLachlan. London: Heinemann, 1964.

132. Dale, William. c.1820. *The Unhappy Transport: or, The Sufferings of William Dale*. London (broadsheet).
133. Anon. 1822. *Songs, Duets, Glees, Chorusses, etc., in the New Musical Extravaganza "Yclept Giovanni in Botany, or the Libertine Transported"*. London.
134. Eagar, Edward. 1824. *Letters to the Rt Hon. Robert Peel, M.P., Secretary of State for the Home Department, on the advantages of New South Wales and Van Diemen's Land as Penal settlements*. London: Shacknell and Arrowsmith.
135. Revell, James. 1824. *The Unhappy Transport, Giving a Sorrowful Account of His Fourteen Years' Transportation to Botany Bay in New South Wales, in August 1810 and his return to London*. York (broadsheet).
136. By Himself. 1824. *Confessions of a Gentleman Convict written during a Residence in Botany Bay; Whither, for his extraordinary robberies on the highway, he was sentenced to be transported for life*. Rev. ed. London: J. Bailey.
137. Holford, George. 1825. *The Convict's Complaint in 1815 and the Thanks of the Convict in 1825*. London: Philanthropic Society.
138. Jackson, John. 1825. *A Remarkable Narrative: or, The Punishment of Transportation Explained*. London (broadsheet).
139. MacKenzie, James. 1825. *The Life and Adventures of James MacKenzie, A Native of Glasgow*. Glasgow: John Muir.
140. Mellish, —. 1825. *An Account of the Treatment of Convicts, and How They Are Disposed of in New South Wales*. London.
141. Savery, Henry. *The Hermit in Van Diemen's Land, from the Colonial Times*. Edited by Cecil Hadgraft. St Lucia: University of Queensland Press, 1964.

Chapter 3 1830–68:
The End of Transportation; The Beginning of Fiction

Manuscripts

142. 1830–33. Commandant's Daily Diary. 4/5644 State Archives of New South Wales.
143. 1831–39. Annotated Printed Indents. X633-42. State Archives of New South Wales.
144. 1832. Muster-Master's Letterbook. TA, CON.9.
145. 1833. Judge's Notebooks. Burton, J. Criminal Sessions. 2/2405. State Archives of New South Wales.
146. 1833–36. Berrima Bench Books. 4/5667. State Archives of New South Wales.
147. 1833–36. Register of Convict's Punishments, Patrick's Plains. 7/3714. State Archives of New South Wales.
148. 1834. Gunton, Henry, Lieut. Diary of a voyage of the *Susan*, convict ship, in charge of troops, 21 February–11 July 1834. ML, A2892.
149. 1834–43. Port Arthur, Tasmania. Extracts recording offences and punishments of convicts. ML, MSS.51.
150. 1836–39. Black Book. 7/3714. State Archives of New South Wales.
151. 1837–43. Returns of convict's applications for wives and families to be brought to N.S.W. at Government expense. 4/4492. State Archives of New South Wales.
152. 1840–59. Richard Taylor and Simon Brown correspondence. DDX.505. Lancashire Records Office.
153. 1842. Indents of Female Convicts. TA, CON.15.
154. 1844. Alphabetical Register of Convicts secondarily transported from New South Wales to Norfolk Island and remaining there. TA, CON.26.1.
155. 1844–45. Assistant Comptroller-General's Letterbook. TA, CON.8.
156. 1844–45. Register of Free Pardons issued to Political Prisoners transported from Canada. TA, CON.60.
157. 1844–45. Register of Charges laid and sentences imposed on Prisoners under Probation. TA, CON.97.
158. 1844–52. Indents of Male Convicts Arriving from Norfolk Island. TA, CON.17.

159. c.1845– . Diary of John Ward. MS. 3275, National Library, Canberra.
160. 1849–57. Judges' and Chairmens' Reports on Criminal Cases in the Supreme Court and Court of Quarter Sessions. TA, CON.4.
161. 1849–60. Convicts from *Hashemy* – Assignment and History. 4/4526. State Archives of New South Wales.
162. 1849–67. Convict Classification Board. Copies of letters sent, 4/4517-8. State Archives of New South Wales.
163. 1851. Journal of the Religious Instructor on Board the Convict Ship *Blenheim*. (4) TA, CON.76.
164. 1851–56. Donochue, Mary, Mrs [alias Murphy]. Conduct sheet of Mary Donochue. ML, DOC.923.
165. 1854. Fyans, Foster, Capt. Reminiscences. 1810–c.1854(?) ML, FM 4/2278.
166. 1856. Boyer, Griffith, A. L. S. To his mother and father from Convict Establishment, Fremantle 21st November. ML, DOC.1110.
167. 1860–71. Returns of Convicts' Deaths and Casualties. TA, CON. 64.
168. 1868–69. Conduct Registers, Port Arthur. TA, CON.94.

Published Government Papers

169. 1838. *Report from the Select Committee on Transportation; together with the minutes of evidence, appendix and index.* British Parliamentary Papers, House of Lords, 1838, vol. 36.
170. Molesworth, Sir William. *Report from the Select Committee of the House of Commons on Transportation; together with a letter from the Archbishop of Dublin on the same subject, and notes by Sir William Molesworth, Bart., Chairman of the Committee.* London: Henry Hooper.
171. 1858. *Regulations for the Penal Settlement at Port Arthur.*

Newspapers and Magazines

172. 1831– . *Sydney Morning Herald.*
173. 1832. *The Village Magazine or Wath Repository.*
174. 1833. *Gentleman's Magazine.*
175. 1833–34. *Hobart Town Magazine.*
176. 1838. *Colonist.*

177. 1838, 1850–52, 1859. *Australian Magazine.*
178. 1840. *Colonial Magazine.*
179. 1841. *London Saturday Journal.*
180. 1844. *Atlas.*
181. 1850–51. *Illustrated Australian Magazine.*
182. 1863–66. *Blackwood's Magazine.*

Eyewitness Accounts

183. Sturt, Charles. 1833. *Two Expeditions into the interior of Southern Australia during the years 1828, 1829, 1830 and 1831: with observations on the soil, climate and general resources of the Colony of New South Wales.* 2 vols. London: Smith, Elder and Co.
184. Howison, John. 1834. *European Colonies in Various Parts of the World viewed in their Social, Moral and Physical Condition.* 2 vols. London: Richard Bentley.
185. Watt, William. 1834. *Party Politics exposed, in a letter to the Right Honorable The Secretary of State for the Colonies; containing comments on convict discipline in New South Wales.* Sydney: Sydney Gazette Office.
186. Melville, Henry. 1836. *The History of Van Diemen's Land from the Year 1824 to 1835 inclusive: During the Administration of Lieut.-Governor George Arthur.* Sydney: Horwitz-Grahame, 1965.
187. Ullathorne, William. 1837. *The Catholic Mission in Australia.* Liverpool: Rockcliffe and Duckworth, 1837.
188. Dixon, John. 1839. *The Conditions and Capabilities of Van Diemen's Land, as a place of emigration, being the practical experience of nearly ten years' residence in the Colony.* London: Smith, Elder and Co.
189. Franklin, Sir John. 1840–43. *Narrative of Some Passages in the History of Van Diemen's Land During the Last Three Years of Sir John Franklin's Administration.* Hobart: Platypus Publications, 1967.
190. Burn, David. 1842. *An Excursion to Port Arthur in 1842.* Melbourne: H. A. Evans and Son, 1972.
191. Backhouse, James. 1843. *A Narrative of a Visit to the Australian Colonies.* London: Hamilton Adams and Co.
192. de Strezelecki, P. E. 1845. *Physical Description of New South Wales and Van Diemen's Land. Accompanied by a Geo-*

logical Map, Sections and Diagrams, and Figures of the Organic Remains. London: Longman, Brown, Green and Longmans.
193. Braim, Thomas Henry. 1846. *A History of N.S.W. from its Settlement to the Close of the Year 1844.* London: Bentley.
194. Harris, Alexander. 1847. *Settlers and Convicts: or, Recollections of Sixteen Years' Labour in the Australian Backwoods.* Edited by C.M.H. Clark. Carlton: Melbourne University Press, 1954.
195. Westgarth, William. 1848. *Victoria, Late Australia Felix: or, Port Phillip District of New South Wales: being an historical and descriptive account.* Edinburgh: Oliver and Boyd.
196. Gates, William. 1850. *Recollections of Life in Van Diemen's Land.* Lockport.
197. West, John, Rev. 1852. *The History of Tasmania.* Edited by A.G.L. Shaw. Sydney: Angus and Robertson, 1971.
198. Henning, Rachel. 1853–82*. *Letters.* N.ed. *The Letters of Rachel Henning.* Edited by David Adams. Ringwood: Penguin, 1969.
199. Brown, Henry. 1862. *Victoria As I Found It.* London: Longmans, Green and Co.
200. Therry, R. 1863. *Reminiscences of Thirty Years' Residence in New South Wales and Victoria.* Sydney: Sydney University Press, 1974.

Factual Accounts of Convicts' Lives

201. Anon. 1830. *The Life and Adventures of Isaac Solomons, the Notorious Receiver of Stolen Goods, Better Known as Ikey Solomons.* London: Universal Pamphleteer.
202. Anon. c.1830. *The London Convict Maid.* London (broadsheet).
203. Dillingham, John. 1831–39*. *Letters.* Edited by W. Hartley Forster. Melbourne: 1970.
204. Anon. 1832. "The Convict". *The Village Magazine or Wath Repository* 2, xx, xxiii, xxiv (1832).
205. Anon. 1833. "A Tale of Blood". *Hobart Town Magazine* 1, iii (1833).
206. Dickson, William. 1833. *A Copy of a Letter received a few days ago, from William Dickson, who was transported to Van Dieman's Land, in the year 1831, from the town of*

Nottingham, written to John Elson, of York Street, Nottingham (broadsheet).

207. Dunhill, Snowden. 1834. *The Life of Snowden Dunhill, written by Himself with an Additional account of him Subsequent to the Publication of his life, the Facts of which were furnished by a Sea-faring Gentleman, who had several interviews with him at Hobart Town in the month of August, 1833.* Howden: W. F. Pratt.

208. Watt, William. 1834. *Secondary Punishments discussed: with some comments on convict discipline in New South Wales and the present state of the Government.* Sydney: Sydney Gazette Office.

209. H. W. D. 1835. *State of the Convicts in New South Wales, 1835.* Manchester (broadsheet).

210. Anon. 1836. *Particulars of the Awful Execution of Nine Unfortunate Convicts . . . Executed in Van Diemen's Land, on Saturday July the Second, 1836.* Leicester.

211. Ross, William. 1836. *The Fell Tyrant: or, The Suffering Convict.* London: B. J. Ward.

212. Mudie, James. 1837. *The Felonry of New South Wales: Being a Faithful Picture of the Real Romance of Life in Botany Bay with Anecdotes of Botany Bay Society and a Plan of Sydney.* Edited by Walter Stone. Melbourne: Lansdowne Press, 1964.

213. Thompson, William. 1837. *Particulars of the awful execution of nine unfortunate convicts, who were executed at Van Dieman's Land, on Saturday July the second 1836, for rebelling against their masters, through the heavy punishment inflicted on them. Written by a convict to his friends, at Castle Connington.* Leicester.

214. W.— . 1837. "A Voyage In A Convict Ship". *U.S. Journal* no. 107 (October, 1837).

215. Loveless, George. 1838. *The Victims of Whiggery: Being a Statement of the Persecutions Experienced by the Dorchester Labourers.* London.

216. Anon. 1838. *A Narrative of the Sufferings and Adventures of Certain of the Convicts who piratically seized the* Frederick *at Macquarie Harbour in Van Diemen's Land, as related by one of the pirates whilst under sentence of death at Hobart Town.* Friendly Contributions.

217. Anon. 1838. "Extracts from a Reporter's Notes (no. II): A Death Bed Relation". *Australian Magazine* ii (1838).
218. Anon. 1838. "Recollections of a Late Undertaker, Parts I and II". *Australian Magazine* ii (1838).
219. Croker, T., ed. 1838. *Memoirs of Joseph Holt, General of the Irish Rebels, in 1798*. 2 vols. London: Henry Colburn.
220. Loveless, Jas. and Brine, Jas. 1838. *A Narrative of the Sufferings of Jas. Loveless, Jas. Brine and Thomas and John Standfields, Four of the Dorchester Labourers Displaying the Horrors of Transportation*. London: Cleave, Hetherington and Watson.
221. Ullathorne, William. 1838. *The Horrors of Transportation Briefly Unfolded*. Dublin: R. Coyne.
222. Frost, John. 1840. *A Letter from Mr John Frost to his Wife, from Port Arthur in Van Diemen's Land*. Manchester: A. Heywood.
223. ———. 1840. *The Life of John Frost, Esq*. 7th ed. London: Thomas White and John Cleave.
224. King, Charles Adolphus. 1840. *A Warning Voice from a Penitent Convict: The Life, Hardships and Dreadful Sufferings of Charles Adolphus King Who Was Tried at Liverpool Assizes for Returning from Transportation: With an Affecting Speech he made to the Judge, imploring him to hang him, instead of sending him to Norfolk Island, and the manner of treating run-away convicts. With a copy of Verses*. London: Birts.
225. Anon. 1841. "The Horrors of Transportation". *London Saturday Journal*, 15 May, 1841.
226. Lilburn, Edward. c.1841. *A Complete Exposure of the Convict System: Its Horrors, Hardships and Severities, Including an Account of the Dreadful Sufferings of the Unhappy Captives. Containing an Extract from a Letter from the Hulks at Woolwich*. Lincoln: Thomas Colmer.
227. Knatchbull, John. 1844*. *Life of John Knatchbull. Written by Himself. 23rd January–13th February 1844, in Darlinghurst Gaol*. Edited by Colin Roderick. *John Knatchbull from Quarterdeck to Gallows*. Sydney: Angus and Robertson, 1963.
228. Connor, James. 1845. *The Recollections of James Connor, A Returned Convict: Containing an Account of his Sufferings in,*

and *Ultimate Escape from, New South Wales.* Transcribed by Yle. Cupar–Fife: G. S. Tullis.

229. Ducharmé, Leon. 1845. *Journal of a Political Exile.* Translated by G. Mackaness. Sydney: D. S. Ford, 1944.

230. Lingard, Joseph. 1846. *A Narrative of a Journey to and from New South Wales, Including a Seven Years' Residence, in that Country.* Chapel-en-le-Frith.

231. Easy, Henry. c.1846. *Horrors of Transportation: or, The danger of keeping bad company, or being careless in the choice of companions.* Bristol.

232. M'Combie, Thomas. 1846. "Australian Sketches No. VII — Distinguished Convicts". London: Simmons and Ward.

233. Miller, Linus, W. 1846. *Notes of an Exile to Van Diemen's Land.* Fredonia, New York: W. McKinstry and Co.

234. Cozens, Charles. 1847. *Adventures of a Guardsman.* London.

235. Cockney, S. L. c.1848. *The Life of S. Cockney, a returned convict, containing a faithful account of his dreadful sufferings in Hobart Town.* Manchester.

236. Barber, W. H. 1849. *The Case of Mr W. H. Barber, containing copies of all the documents recently submitted to the Right Hon. Sir George Grey, Bart., Secretary of State for the Home Department.* London: Effingham Wilson.

237. Broxup, John. 1850. *Life of John Broxup, Late Convict at Van Diemen's Land.* Leeds: J. Cook.

238. Gell, John Philip. 1850. *The Penal Settlements: Lectures delivered before the Church of England Young Men's Society in St Martin's Hall.* London: James Nisbet and Co.

239. Smith, M. A. 1851. *Horrors of Transportation as related by M. A. Smith in a letter to her parents in this town.*

240. Cobbold, Richard. 1852. *The History of Margaret Catchpole, A Suffolk Girl.* London: Simms and McIntyre.

241. Morgan, John. 1852. *The Life and Adventures of William Buckley.* Edited by C. E. Sayers. Melbourne: Heinemann, 1967.

242. Mitchell, John. 1854. *Jail Journal: or, Five Years in British Prisons.* New York: "Citizen".

243. Bonwick, James. 1856. *The Bushrangers: Illustrating the early days of Van Diemen's Land.* Hobart: Cat and Fiddle Press, 1967.

244. Browning, Rev. Colin Arrott. 1856. *The Convict Ship.* 6th ed. London: Thomas Nisbet and Co.

245. Frost, John. 1858(?). *The Horrors of Convict Life*. Hobart: Sullivan's Cove, 1973.
246. Anon. (review) 1859. "The Life and Adventures of John Leonard, A Prisoner in V.D. Land (MSS.)." *Australian Magazine* 1, 2 (1859).
247. Bensley, Benjamin. 1859. *Lost and Found; or, Light in the Prison*. London.
248. Platt, Joseph. 1862. *The Horrors of Transportation as related by Joseph Platt, who was transported for fourteen years, with an account of the hardships he endured and his return to England*. London: Printed for Author.
249. Gibson, Charles B. 1863. *Life Among Convicts*. London: Hurst and Blackett.
250. Mortlock, J. F. 1864–65. *Experiences of a Convict*. Edited by G. A. Wilkes. Sydney: Sydney University Press, 1961.
251. Prieur, François-Xavieur. 1869. *Notes of a Convict of 1838*. Translated by G. Mackaness. Sydney: D. S. Ford, 1949.
252. Anon. *Eight Years Penal Servitude and What Lead to It.** London: n.d.

Fictional Accounts of Convicts' Lives

253. Burn, David. 1829–35. *The Bushrangers*. Edited by W. and J. E. Heiner. Melbourne: Currency Press, 1971.
254. Anon. 1830. *Alfred Dudley: or, The Australian Settlers*. London: Smith, Elder and Co.
255. Howison, John. 1830. *Tales of the Colonies*. 2 vols. London: Henry Colburn and Richard Bentley.
256. Moncrieff, W. T. 1830. *Van Diemen's Land! An Operatic Drama in Three Acts*. London: Thomas Richardson.
257. Savery, Henry. 1830–31. *Quintus Servinton: A Tale, Founded upon Incidents of Real Occurrence*. Brisbane: Jacaranda, 1962.
258. K*. 1834. "The Three Letters: An Incident from the Life of a Scoundrel." *Hobart Town Magazine* 2, xiii (1834).
259. Rowcroft, Charles. 1843. *Tales of the Colonies: or, The Adventures of an Emigrant*. London: Saunders and Otley.
260. Tucker, James. 1844–45*. *Jemmy Green in Australia*. See no. 447.
261. ———. 1845*. *Ralph Rashleigh*. See no. 444.
262. M'Combie, Thomas. 1845. *Arabin: or, The Adventures of a*

Colonist in New South Wales: With an Essay on the Aborigines of Australia. London: Summons and Ward.
263. Rowcroft, Charles. 1846. *The Bushranger of Van Diemen's Land.* New York: Harper and Brothers.
264. James, G. P. R. 1847. *The Convict: A Tale.* 3 vols. London: Smith, Elder and Co.
265. Harris, Alexander. 1849. *The Emigrant Family: or, The Story of an Australian Settler.* Canberra: Australian National University Press, 1967.
266. Vidal, Mrs Francis. 1852. *Tales For The Bush.* London: Francis and John Rivington.
267. Lang, John. 1853. *Too Clever by Half: or, The Harroways.* Melbourne: E. W. Cole, n.d.
268. ————. 1854. *Too Much Alike: or, The Three Calendars.* London: Ward Lock.
269. Lang, John. 1855. *The Forger's Wife: or, Emily Orford.* London: Ward Lock.
270. Reade, Charles. 1856. *It Is Never Too Late To Mend: A Matter-of-Fact Romance.* London: Cassell, 1908.
271. Gerstäcker, Friedrich. 1857. *The Two Convicts.* London: G. Routledge and Co.
272. Keese, Oliné [Leakey, Caroline]. 1859. *The Broad Arrow: Being Passages from the History of Maida Gwynnham, "Lifer".* Hobart: J. Walch and Sons, 1900.
273. Kingsley, Henry. 1859. *The Recollections of Geoffry Hamlyn.* London: Collins, n.d.
274. Lang, John. 1859. *Botany Bay: or, True Stories of the Early Days of Australia.* Hobart: T. Walch and Sons, n.d.
275. Anon. 1860. *Wolfingham: or, The Convict Settler of Jervis Bay.* London: Rivingtons.
276. Winstanley, Elizabeth. 1864. *Twenty Straws.* London: John Dick.
277. Farjeon, B. L. 1866. *Grif: A Story of Colonial Life.* Dunedin: W. Hay.
278. De Boos, Charles. 1867. *Fifty Years Ago: An Australian Tale.* Sydney: Gordon and Gotch, 1867.

Overseas Treatments of Crime and Punishment

279. Scott, Sir Walter. 1818. *The Heart of Midlothian.* London: Oxford University Press, 1910.

280. Hugo, Victor. 1828. *Le Dernier Jour d'un Condamné*. In *Oeuvres Romanesques Complètes*. Paris: Jean-Jacques Pauvert, 1962.
281. Lytton, Bulwer. 1829. *Paul Clifford*. London: Richard Edward King, n.d.
282. ———. 1831. *Eugene Aram*. London: Collins, n.d.
283. Austin, John. 1832. *The Province of Jurisprudence Determined and the Uses of the Study of Jurisprudence*. London: Weidenfeld and Nicholson, 1971.
284. Balzac, Honoré. 1835. *de Le Père Goriot*. Paris: Editions Garnier Frères, 1960.
285. Dickens, Charles. 1837. *Sketches by Boz: Illustrative of Everyday Life and Everyday People*. London: Oxford University Press, 1957.
286. ———. 1838. *The Adventures of Oliver Twist*. London: Oxford University Press, 1961.
287. Thackeray, William Makepeace. 1839–40. *Catherine: A Story*. New York: A.M.S. Press, 1968.
288. Dana, Richard Henry. *Two Years Before The Mast: A Personal Narrative*. New York: New American Library, 1964.
289. Ainsworth, William Harrison. 1840. *Rookwood: A Romance*. London: George Routledge and Sons, n.d.
290. ———. 1840. *The Tower of London*. London: Dent, 1935.
291. ———. 1841. *Old Saint Paul's: A Tale of the Plague and the Fire*. London: Dent, n.d.
292. Dickens, Charles. 1841. *Barnaby Rudge: A Tale of the Riots of "Eighty"*. London: Oxford University Press, 1961.
293. Thackeray, William Makepeace. 1843–44. *The Memoirs of Barry Lyndon Esq.: Written by Himself*. New York: A.M.S. Press, 1968.
294. Dickens, Charles. 1849–50. *The Personal History of David Copperfield*. London: Oxford University Press, 1960.
295. ———. 1850. *Household Words*. In *The Uncollected Writings of Charles Dickens*, edited by Harry Stone. London: Longmans, 1969.
296. Mayhew, Henry. 1852. *London Labour and the London Poor*. 4 vols. London: Charles Griffin and Co.
297. Stowe, Harriet Beecher. 1852. *Uncle Tom's Cabin: or, Life Among The Lowly*. Cambridge, Massachusetts: Harvard University Press, 1962.

298. Dostoyevsky, Fyodor. 1860. *The House of the Dead*. Translated by H. Sutherland. London: Edward Dent, 1910.
299. Dickens, Charles. 1861. *Great Expectations*. London: Oxford University Press, 1960.
300. Hugo, Victor. *Les Misérables*. 4 vols. Paris: Nelson, Editeurs, 1959.
301. Mayhew, Henry and Binny, John. 1862. *The Criminal Prisons of London and Scenes of Prison Life*. 2 vols. London: Frank Cass and Co., 1971.

Chapter 4   After 1968: Transportation in Retrospect

Newspapers and Magazines

302. 1870. *Paglesham Oyster*.
303. 1876. *Bow Bells*.
304. 1880– . *Bulletin*.
305. 1882–84. *Standard* (Warrnambool).
306. 1888–94. *Bookworm*.
307. *Sydney Morning Herald*.

Eyewitness Accounts

308. Trollope, Anthony. 1873. *Australia and New Zealand*. Edited by P. D. Edwards and R. B. Joyce. N.ed. *Australia*. St Lucia: University of Queensland Press, 1967.
309. MacDermott, Marshall. 1874. *A Brief Sketch of the Long and Varied Career of Marshall MacDermott, Esq., J.P. of Adelaide, South Australia: Written solely for private distribution amongst relatives and special friends*. Adelaide: William Kyffin Thomas.
310. Lang, John Dunmore. 1875. *An Historical and Statistical Account of New South Wales From the Founding of the Colony in 1788 to the Present Day*. 4th ed. London: Sampson, Low, Marston, Low and Searle, 1876.
311. ————. 1878. *Reminiscences of My Life and Times, Both in Church and State in Australia for Upwards of Fifty Years*. Melbourne: Heinemann, 1972.
312. Cornish, Henry. 1880. *Under the Southern Cross*. Madras: Mail

313. Tolmer, Alex. 1882. *Reminiscences of an Adventurous Career at Home and at the Antipodes.* London: Sampson, Low, Marston, Searle and Rivington.
314. Twopenny, Richard. 1883. *Town Life in Australia.* London: Elliot Stock.
315. Westgarth, William. 1883. *Personal Recollections of Early Melbourne and Victoria.* Melbourne: George Robertson and Co.
316. Froude, James Anthony. 1886. *Oceania or England and Her Colonies.* London: Longmans Green and Co.
317. Garran, Andrew, ed. 1888. *Picturesque Atlas of Australia.* 2 vols. Sydney: Ure Smith, 1974.
318. Lawson, Henry. 1888–1922*. *Short Stories and Sketches.* In *Short Stories and Sketches 1888–1922,* edited by Colin Roderick. Sydney: Angus and Robertson, 1972.
319. Martin, A. Patchett. 1889. *Australia and The Empire.* Edinburgh: David Douglas.
320. Boswell, Annabella. 1890. *Journal.* N.ed. *The Journal of Annabella Boswell.* Edited by Herman Morton. Sydney: Angus and Robertson, 1965.
321. Braddon, Sir Edward. 1891–92. *Australasia: A Vindication. Proceedings of the Royal Colonial Institute* 23 (1891–92): 50–89.
322. Fenton, James. 1891. *Bush Life in Tasmania Fifty Years Ago.* London: Hazell Watson and Viney.
323. Parkes, Sir Henry. 1892. *Fifty Years in the Making of Australian History.* London: Longmans Green and Co.
324. Clemens, Samuel [Twain, Mark]. 1897. *Following The Equator: A Journey Around the World.* Hartford: American Publishing Co.
325. Davitt, Michael. 1898. *Life and Progress in Australasia.* London: Methuen and Co.
326. Duffy, Sir Charles Gavan. 1898. *My Life in Two Hemispheres.* London: T. Fisher Unwin.
327. Sadlier, John. 1913. *Recollections of a Victorian Police Officer.* Melbourne: G. Robertson and Co.
328. Hamilton, J.C. 1914. *Pioneering Days in Western Victoria.* Melbourne: G. Robertson and Co.

Books Dealing with The Convict Experience

329. Clarke, Marcus. 1870–72. *His Natural Life*. *Australian Journal*, November 1870–June 1872.
330. Dunderdale, George. 1870. *The Book of The Bush*. Ringwood: Penguin Colonial Facsimile, 1973.
331. Cash, Martin. 1870. *A Personal Narrative of his Exploits in the Bush and his Experiences at Port Arthur and Norfolk Island*. Hobart: J. Walch and Sons, 1954.
332. Clarke, Marcus. 1871. *Old Tales of a Young Country*. Sydney: Sydney University Press, 1972.
333. ———. 1874. *His Natural Life*. Melbourne: G. Robertson.
334. Winstanley, Elizabeth. 1876. *Her Natural Life: A Tale of 1830*. Bow Bells 2, 5, nos. 629–30 (1876).
335. Browne, Thomas Alexander [Boldrewood, Rolf]. 1878. *The Squatter's Dream: A Story of Australian Life*. London: MacMillan and Co., 1890.
336. O'Reilly, John Boyle. 1880. *Moondyne: A Story of Life in West Australia*. Melbourne: George Robertson.
337. Bastard, Thomas. 1881. *The Autobiography of Cockney Tom*. Adelaide: McLory and Masterman.
338. Browne, Thomas Alexander [Boldrewood, Rolf]. 1881–88. *Robbery Under Arms: A Story of Life and Adventure in the Bush and in the Goldfields of Australia*. London: Oxford University Press, 1961.
339. O'Reilly, John Boyle. 1882. *Songs, Legends and Ballads*. Boston: Pilot Publishing Co.
340. Clarke, Marcus. 1885. *For The Term of His Natural Life*. London: Bentley. (First ed. with this title.) N.ed. Adelaide: Rigby, 1974.
341. Farjeon, B. L. 1886. *The Golden Land: or, Links from Shore to Shore*. London: Ward Lock.
342. Melville, Herman. 1886–91*, 1924. *Billy Budd, Sailor. (An Inside Narrative)*. Chicago: University of Chicago Press, 1962.
343. Praed, R. C. 1887. *Longleat of Kooralbyn: or, Policy and Passion: A Novel of Australian Life*. London: Richard Bentley and Son.
344. Dawe, W. Carlton. 1871. *The Golden Lake: or, The Marvellous History of a Journey Through the Great Lone Land of Australia*. Melbourne: E. A. Petherick.

345. Browne, Thomas Alexander [Boldrewood, Rolf]. 1891. *A Colnial Reformer*. London: MacMillan and Co.
346. Hogan, James Francis. 1891. *The Convict King: The Life and Adventures of Jorgen Jorgenson*. Hobart: J. Walch and Sons, 1967.
347. White, Charles. 1891–93. *Early Australian History*. Part 4. *History of Australian Bushranging*. Hawthorn: Lloyd O'Neil, 1970.
348. Adams, Francis. 1891. *Australian Life*. London: Chapman and Hall.
349. Astley, William [Warung, Price]. 1892. *Tales of The Convict System*. Sydney: Bulletin Newspaper Co.
350. Nisbet, Hume. 1892. *The Bushranger's Sweetheart: An Australian Romance*. London: F. V. White and Co.
351. Jeffrey, Mark. 1893. *A Burglar's Life: or, The Stirring Adventures of the Great English Burglar Mark Jeffrey; A Thrilling History of the Dark Days of Convictism in Australia*. Hobart: J. Walch and Sons, 1969.
352. Praed, R. C. 1893. *Outlaw and Lawmaker*. London: Richard Bentley and Sons.
353. Astley, William [Warung, Price]. 1894. *Tales of the Early Days*. London: G. Robertson and Co.
354. Gibb, Eric. 1895. *Thrilling Incidents of the Convict System in Australia Compiled from authentic sources, from information contained in official documents and other records*. London: Hammond and Green.
355. Suffolk, Owen. c.1895. *Days of Crime and Years of Suffering*. Melbourne.
356. Hornung, Ernest. 1896. *The Rogue's March: A Romance*. London: Cassell.
357. Becke, Louis and Jeffrey, Walter. 1896. *A First Fleet Family*. London: Unwin and Co.
358. Paterson, A. B. 1896. *The Old Bush Songs Composed and Sung in the Bushranging, Digging and Overlanding Days*. Sydney: Angus and Robertson, 1906.
359. Roberts, Morley. 1897. *The Adventure of the Broad Arrow: An Australian Romance*. London: Hutchinson.
360. Astley, William [Warung, Price]. 1897. *Tales of the Old Regime and the Bullet of the Fated Ten*. London: G. Routledge and Sons.

361. Clarke, Marcus. 1897. *Australian Tales of the Bush*. Biography by Hamilton MacKinnon. Melbourne: George Robertson and Co.
362. Astley, William [Warung, Price]. 1898. *Tales of the Isle of Death*. London: G. Robertson and Co.
363. Boxall, George. 1899. *The Story of the Australian Bushrangers*. Ringwood: Penguin, 1974.
364. Derrincourt, William. 1899. *Old Convict Days*. Ringwood: Penguin Colonial Facsimile, 1975.
365. Nisbet, Hume. 1899. *Seven Romances*. London: Hunt and Blackett.
366. Bradshaw, Jack. c.1900. *Twenty Years' Experience of Prison Life*. Bathurst.
367. Stephens, A. G., ed. 1880–1901. *The Bulletin Reciter: A Collection of Verses for Recitation from "The Bulletin"*. Sydney: New South Wales Bookstall Co.
368. Stephens, James Brunton. 1902. *The Poetical Works*. Sydney: Angus and Robertson.

The Twentieth Century

Biographies, Histories and Commentaries

369. Barton, G. B. 1924. *The True Story of Margaret Catchpole*. Sydney.
370. Stephensen, P. G. 1936. *The Foundations of Culture in Australia*. Croydon: W. J. Miles.
371. O'Brien, Eris. 1937. *The Foundation of Australia*. 2nd ed. Sydney: Angus and Robertson, 1950.
372. Smith, Coultman. 1941. *Shadow over Tasmania: The Whole Story of the Convicts*. Hobart: J. Walch and Sons, 1967.
373. Clune, Frank. 1948. *Wild Colonial Boys*. Sydney: Angus and Robertson.
374. Ingleton, Geoffrey, C. 1952. *True Patriots All: or, News from Early Australia as told in a Collection of Broadsides*. Sydney: Angus and Robertson.
375. Mackaness, George. 1953. *Blue Bloods of Botany Bay: A Book of Australian Historical Tales*. Sydney: Collins.
376. Clune, Frank, and Stephensen, P. R. 1954. *The Viking of Van Diemen's Land*. Sydney: Angus and Robertson.

377. Ward, Russel. 1954. *Felons and Folk Songs*. Melbourne: Commonwealth Literary Fund.
378. Clune, Frank. 1955. *Martin Cash*. Sydney: Angus and Robertson.
379. Gibbings, Robert. 1956. *John Graham, Convict, 1824*. London: Dent.
380. Hill-Reid, W. S. 1957. *John Grant's Journey*. London: Heinemann.
381. Barry, John Vincent. 1958. *Alexander Maconochie of Norfolk Island: A Study of a Pioneer in Penal Reform*. Melbourne: Oxford University Press.
382. Pearl, Cyril. 1958. *Wild Men of Sydney*. Sydney: Angus and Robertson.
383. Phillips, A. A. 1958. *The Australian Tradition: Studies in a Colonial Culture*. Carlton: Melbourne University Press, 1958.
384. Ward, Russel. 1958. *The Australian Legend*. Sydney: Oxford University Press, 1965.
385. Bateson, Charles. 1959. *The Convict Ships 1787–1868*. Sydney: A. H. and A. W. Reed, 1974.
386. Durack, Mary. 1959. *Kings in Grass Castles*. London: Constable.
387. Hasluck, Alexandra. 1959. *Unwilling Emigrants: A Study of the Convict Period in Western Australia*. Melbourne: Oxford University Press.
388. Wright, Judith. 1959. *The Generations of Men*. Melbourne: Oxford University Press, 1960.
389. Green, H. M. 1961. *A History of Australian Literature: Pure and Applied*. 2 vols. Sydney: Angus and Robertson, 1971.
390. Clark, C. M. H. 1962. *A History of Australia*. Vol. 1. *From the Earliest Times to the Age of Macquarie*. Carlton: Melbourne University Press.
391. Roderick, Colin, ed. 1963. *John Knatchbull: From Quarterdeck to Gallows*. Sydney: Angus and Robertson, 1963.
392. Barry, John Vincent. 1964. *The Life and Death of John Price*. Carlton: Melbourne University Press.
393. Bateson, Charles. 1966. *Patrick Logan: Tyrant of Brisbane Town*. Sydney: Ure Smith.
394. Robson, L. L. 1965. *The Convict Settlers of Australia*. Carlton: Melbourne University Press, 1970.
395. Shaw, A. G. L. 1966. *Convicts and the Colonies: A Study of Penal Transportation from Great Britain and Ireland to Australia and other parts of the British Empire*. London: Faber and Faber, 1971.

396. Robson, L. L. 1967. *A Convict*. Melbourne: Oxford University Press.
397. Clark, C. M. H. 1968. *A History of Australia*. Vol. 2. *New South Wales and Van Diemen's Land 1822–1838*. Carlton: Melbourne University Press.
398. Conlon, Anne. 1969. " 'Mine Is a Sad Yet True Story': Convict Narratives 1818–1850". *JRAHS* 55 (1969): 43–72.
399. Cobley, John. 1970. *The Crimes of the First Fleet Convicts*. Sydney: Angus and Robertson.
400. McQueen, Humphrey. 1970. *A New Britannia: An Argument concerning the Social Origins of Australian Radicalism and Socialism*. 2nd ed. Ringwood: Penguin, 1975.
401. Ritchie, John. 1970. *Punishment and Profit: The Reports of Commissioner John Bigge on the Colonies of New South Wales and Van Diemen's Land, 1822–1823; Their Origins, Nature and Significance*. 2 vols. Melbourne: Heinemann.
402. Moore, T. Inglis. 1971. *Social Patterns in Australian Literature*. Sydney: Angus and Robertson.
403. Hergenhan, L. T., ed. 1972. *A Colonial City; High and Low Life: Selected Journalism of Marcus Clarke*. St Lucia: University of Queensland Press.
404. Bolger, Peter. 1973. *Hobart Town*. Canberra: Australian National University Press.
405. Clark, C. M. H. 1973. *A History of Australia*. Vol. 3. *The Beginning of an Australian Civilization 1824–1851*. Carlton: Melbourne University Press.
406. Lawson, Ronald. 1973. *Brisbane in the 1890s*. St Lucia: University of Queensland Press.
407. Plomley, N. J. B. 1973. *An Immigrant of 1824*. Hobart: Tasmanian Historical Research Association.
408. Weidenhofer, Margaret. 1973. *The Convict Years: Transportation and the Penal System*. Melbourne: Lansdowne Press.
409. Butler, J. Marjorie. 1974. *Convict by Choice*. Melbourne: Hill of Content.
410. Crowley, Frank, ed. 1974. *A New History of Australia*. Melbourne: William Heinemann.
411. Dalkin, R. Nixon. 1974. *Colonial Era Cemetery of Norfolk Island*. Sydney: Pacific Publications.
412. Inglis, K. S. 1974. *The Australian Colonists: An Exploration of Social History 1788–1870*. Carlton: Melbourne University Press.

413. Levi, J. S., and Bergman, G. F. J. 1974. *Australian Genesis: Jewish Convicts and Settlers 1788—1850*. Adelaide: Rigby.

Fiction Based on the Convict Experience

414. Hay, William. 1901. *Stifled Laughter*. London: L. Macqueen.
415. ———. 1907. *Herridge of Reality Swamp*. London: Allen and Unwin.
416. ———. 1912. *Captain Quadring*. London: Allen and Unwin.
417. Bridges, Roy. 1914. *The Fugitive*. London: Hodder and Stoughton.
418. Prichard, Katharine Susannah. 1915. *The Pioneers*. Adelaide: Rigby, 1963.
419. Abbott, J. H. M. 1919. *The Governor's Man*. Melbourne: The Bookstall Co.
420. Hay, William. 1919. *The Escape of the Notorious Sir William Heans (and the Mystery of Mr Daunt)*. Carlton: Melbourne University Press, 1955.
421. Allnutt, A. 1921. *Two Convicts: A Romance with a Moral*. London: Drane.
422. Abbott, J. H. M. 1922. *Ensign Calder*. Sydney: N.S.W. Bookstall Co. Ltd.
423. ———. 1923. *Castle Vane: A Romance of Bushranging on the Upper Hunter in the Olden Days*. Sydney: Angus and Robertson.
424. Devaney, James. 1927. *The Currency Lass: A Tale of the Convict Days*. Sydney: Cornstalk Publishing Co.
425. Franklin, Miles [Brent of Bin Bin]. 1928. *Up The Country: A Tale of the Early Australian Squattocracy*. Sydney: Angus and Robertson, 1951.
426. Eldershaw, M. Barnard. 1929. *A House is Built*. Sydney: Australian Publishing Co., 1961.
427. Franklin, Miles [Brent of Bin Bin]. 1930. *Ten Creeks Run: A Tale of the Horse and Cattle Stations of the Murrumbidgee*. Sydney: Angus and Robertson, 1952.
428. Bridges, Roy. 1930. *Negrohead*. London: Hutchinson.
429. Franklin, Miles. 1931. See no. 459 below.
430. Bridges, Roy. 1931. *Trinity*. London: Hutchinson.
431. ———. 1932. *Cloud*. London: Hutchinson.
432. Lancaster, G. B. 1933. *Pageant: A Novel of Tasmania*. Sydney: Endeavour Press.

433. Penton, Brian. 1934. *Land Takers: The Story of an Epoch.* Sydney: Angus and Robertson, 1963.
434. Franklin, Miles. 1936. *All that Swagger.* Sydney: Angus and Robertson, 1948.
435. Penton, Brian. 1936. *Inheritors: A Novel.* Sydney: Angus and Robertson.
436. Franklin, Miles, and Cusack, Dymphna. 1939. *Pioneers on Parade.* Sydney: Angus and Robertson.
437. Connolly, Roy. 1940. *Southern Saga.* Sydney: Dymock's, 1946.
438. Dark, Eleanor. 1941. *The Timeless Land.* Sydney: Angus and Robertson.
439. ———. 1948. *Storm of Time.* Sydney: Collins, 1970.
440. Timms, E. V. 1948. *Forever to Remain.* Sydney: Angus and Robertson.
441. ———. 1949. *The Pathway of the Sun.* Sydney: Angus and Robertson, 1971.
442. Bridges, Roy. 1950. *The League of the Lord.* Sydney: Australian Publishing Co.
443. Timms, E. V. 1950. *The Beckoning Shore.* Sydney: Angus and Robertson.
444. Tucker, James. 1952, c.1845*. *Ralph Rashleigh.* Edited by Colin Roderick. Sydney: Angus and Robertson.
445. Dark, Eleanor. 1954. *No Barriers.* Sydney: Collins, 1963.
446. Roderick, Colin. 1955. *The Lady and the Lawyer.* Sydney: Angus and Robertson.
447. Tucker, James. 1955, 1844–45*. *Jemmy Green in Australia.* Edited by Colin Roderick. Sydney: Angus and Robertson.
448. White, Patrick. 1957. *Voss.* Ringwood: Penguin, 1974.
449. Porter, Hal. 1961. *The Tilted Cross.* Adelaide: Rigby, 1971.
450. Hunter, Wilkes. 1965. *Convict Girl.* Sydney: Horwitz Publications Inc.
451. Keneally, Thomas. 1967. *Bring Larks and Heroes.* Melbourne: Sun Books, 1968.
452. Clarke, Marcus. 1970, 1870–72*. *His Natural Life.* Edited by Stephen Murray-Smith. Ringwood: Penguin.
453. Buzo, Alexander. 1973. *Macquarie.* Sydney: Currency Press.
454. Mills, J. S., ed. 1973. *William Thornley: The Adventures of an Emigrant in Van Diemen's Land.* Adelaide: Rigby.
455. Andrews, B. G., ed. 1975. *Tales of the Convict System: Selected Stories of Price Warung.* St Lucia: University of Queensland Press.

456. White, Patrick. 1976. *A Fringe of Leaves*. London: Jonathan Cape.

Related Works

457. Pratt, Ambrose. 1902. *The Great "Push" Experiment*. London: Grant Richards.
458. Furphy, Joseph [Collins, Tom]. 1903. *Such Is Life: Being certain extracts from the Diary of Tom Collins*. Sydney: Angus and Robertson, 1966.
459. Franklin, Miles [Brent of Bin Bin]. 1931. *Back to Bool Bool: A Ramiparous Novel with several prominent characters and a hantle of others disposed as the atolls of Oceania's Archipelagos*. Edinburgh: Blackwood.
460. Furphy, Joseph [Collins, Tom]. 1948. *The Buln-Buln and the Brolga*. Adelaide: Rigby, 1971.
461. Stewart, Douglas, and Keesing, Nancy. 1957. *Old Bush Songs and Rhymes of Colonial Times*. Sydney: Angus and Robertson.
462. Anderson, Hugh, ed. 1962. *Colonial Ballads*. Melbourne: F. W. Cheshire.
463. Manifold, J. S. 1964. *Who Wrote The Ballads: Notes on Australian Folksong*. Sydney: Australasian Book Society.
464. Ward, Russel, ed. 1971. *The Penguin Book of Australian Ballads* Ringwood: Penguin, 1971.
465. Lahey, John. 1972. *Great Australian Folksongs*. Melbourne: Hill of Content.
466. Meredith, John, and Anderson, Hugh, eds. 1973. *Folksongs of Australia and the Men and Women Who Sang Them*. Sydney: Ure Smith.

Index

Numbers in italics refer to citations in the bibliography; numbers in parentheses refer to appendixes; other numbers refer to pages in the text. Thus:

Connolly, Roy, *Southern Saga*, *437*; (5:19); 130

Southern Saga is item 437 in the bibliography, it is dealt with as item 19 in Appendix 5, and it is referred to on page 130 of the text.

Abbott, J.H.M., *Castle Vane*, *423*; *Governor's Man*, *419*
Aborigines, 1, 36, 71-72
Adams, Francis, *Australian Life*, *348*
Ainsworth, William, *Old St Paul's*, *291*; *Tower of London*, *290*; 7, 30, 79, 164, 177
Alfred Dudley, 108
Allnutt, A., *Two Convicts*, *421*
amanuensis, 58, 103, 172
Anderson, Hugh (ed.), *Colonial Ballads*, *462*
Andrews, B.A., *Tales of the Convict System Selected Stories of Price Warung*, *455*
Annual Register, 12
Anon., *Alfred Dudley*, *254*
Anon., *A Tale of Blood*, *205*
Anon., *Botany Bay*, 108, 176
Anon., *Confessions of a Gentleman Convict*, *128*
Anon., *Extracts from a Reporter's Notes*, *217*
Anon., *Giovanni in Botany*, *133*; 108, 176
Anon., *Horrors of Transportation*, *225*
Anon., *Life and Adventures of John Leonard*, *246*; (4:30)
Anon., *London Convict Maid*, *202*

Anon., *Narrative of Sufferings and Adventures*, *216*
Anon., *Particulars of the Awful Execution of Nine Unfortunate Convicts*, *210*; (4:6)
Anon., *Recollections of a Late Undertaker*, *218*
Anon., *Wolfingham*, *275*
Arthur, George, 24, 40, 44, 77, 85
Ashton, John, *Chap books of the Eighteenth Century*, *63*; 165, 179
Astley, William, *Tales of the Convict System*, *349*; *Tales of the Old Regime*, *360*; *Tales of the Early Days*, *353*; *Tales of the Isle of Death*, *362*; (5:14); 130, 133
Auchmuty, James J. (ed.), *Voyage of Governor Phillip*, *101*
Awdeley, John, *Fraternitye of Vacabones*, 6, 16

Backhouse, James, *Narrative of a Visit*, *191*; (4:14)
Baldwin, William, *A Mirror for Magistrates*, 6, 55-56, 178
Banks, Joseph, 45
ballads, 76
Barber, W.H., *The Case of W.H. Barber*, *236*; (4:20); 104, 175
Barrington, George, 116, 121, 123,

Index

124, 126; (3:4); 31, 54, 68, 73, 167, 179
Barry, John V., 246; *Alexander Maconochie, 381; John Price, 392*
Barton, G.B., *True Story of Margaret Catchpole,* 369
Bastard, Thomas, *Autobiography of Cockney Tom, 337:* 127, 177
Bateson, Charles, *Convict Ships, 385; Patrick Logan,* 393
Bean, C.E.W., *On the Wool Track,* 95, 174
Becke, Louis (ed.), *Old Convict Days,* 364
Becke, Louis, and Walter, Jeffrey, *A First Fleet Family,* 357
Bedford, William, 42
Bennett, John, 47
Bensley, Benjamin, *Lost and Found, 247;* (3:7); 172
Bentham, Jeremy, *Pantopicon, 49; Introduction to the Principles of Morals,* 9, 27
Bigge, John, 35, 49
biography, 4
Bligh, William, 36, 48
Boldrewood, Rolf (Thomas Alexander Browne), *Robbery Under Arms, 338; Squatter's Dream, 335; Colonial Reformer,* 345
Bolger, Peter, *Hobart Town, 404:* 174, 175
Bonwick, James, *The Bushrangers, 243; William Buckley,* 102, 107, 168
Borrow, George, *Celebrated Trials, 59;* (1:10); *Romany Rye,* 1, 12, 165
Boswell, Annabella, *Journal,* 320
Boswell, James, *Life of Johnson,* 47, 14, 19, 165, 166
Bowes, Arthur, 47, 170
Boxall, George, *The Story of the Australian Bushrangers,* 363
Boyle, Charles, 62
Bradley, William, 169
Braim, Thomas Henry, *A History of New South Wales,* 193
"Brent of Bin Bin" (Miles Franklin), *Back to Bool Bool, 459; Ten Creeks Run, 427; Up the Country,* 425; (5:16)
Bridges, Roy, *Fugitive, 417; League of the Lord,* 442
broadsheets, 10-11, 78
Brown, Henry, *Victoria as I Found it,* 199

Brown, Simon, 66-68, 172
Brown, Tom, *Cheats of London,* 8
Browne, Thomas Alexander. *See* Boldrewood, Rolf
Browning, Colin, *The Convict Ship,* 244; (4:27); 105, 176
Broxup, John, *Life,* 237; (4:21)
Bryant, William, 36
Buckley, Willilam, 172
Burn, David, *The Bushrangers, 253; Excursion to Porth Arthur, 190;* 111, 176
Burroughs, Peter, *Britain and Australia 1831—1855,* 173
Butler, Alban, *Lives of the Fathers,* 37, 166
Butler, J. Marjorie, *Convict by Choice,* 409
Buzo, Alexander, *Macquarie,* 453
Byrnes, John V., "Andrew Thompson", "William Charles Wentworth", 172

Campbell, Lily (ed.), *The Mirror for Magistrates,* 6
Campbell, Robert, 34
cant, 16
Carew, Bampfylde Moore, *King of the Beggars, 30;* 13, 16, 26-27, 28, 167, 179
Cash, Martin, *A Personal Narrative, 331:* 127-29, 177
Catchpole, Margaret, 104, 175
Catnach Press, 11
Causes Célèbres, 12
chap-books, 12, 74, 78
Chesterton, G.K., 178
Clark, C.M.H., *History of Australia I, 390; History of Australia II, 397;* (ed.) *Select Documents in Australian History,* 167, 169, 170, 173, 174
Clark, Ralph, 33, 48, 169
Clarke, Marcus, "Port Arthur Visited 1870", *For the Term of His Natural Life, 329,* (5:9), *Old Tales of a Young Country, 332,* 2-3, 35, 96, 131-36, 175, 177
Clune, Frank, *Wild Colonial Boys,* 373
Cobbold, Richard, *History of Margaret Catchpole,* 240; (4:26); 175
Cobley, John, *Crimes of the First*

Fleet Convicts, 399; 171
Cockney, S.L., *Life of S. Cockney,* 235
Coleridge, Samuel Taylor, "Conciones ad Populum", 27, 49, 167, 170
colonial press, 34-35
Collins, David, *Account of the English Colony I, Account of the English Colony II, 107;* 43, 47, 48, 57, 58, 65, 168, 169, 171
Collins, Philip, *Dickens and Crime,* 174
Colquhoun, Patrick, *Police of the Metropolis, 52;* 8, 9, 17, 172
Conlon, Anne, "Convict Narratives 1818—1850", *398;* 63
Connolly, Roy, *Southern Saga, 437;* (5:19); 130
Connor, James, *Recollections, 228,* (4:16), 103, 175
Conolly, Phillip, 42
convicts: absconding, 71-72; background, 2; in the bush, 94-96; expirees, 35; flogging of, 69-70; Irish, 53, 170; outlook, 52-71
"Convict Narrative, A", MSS, 189
Copland, William, *Hyeway to the Spytel House,* 6
Cowper, William, 42
Cozens, Charles, *Adventures of a Guardsman, 234;* (4:19)
Croce, Benedetto, *Aesthetic as Science of Expression,* 177
Croker, T. Crofton (ed.), *Memoirs of Joseph Holt, 219;* 43, 101-2, 169
Crook, William Pascoe, 169
Crowley, Frank (ed.), *A New History of Australia, 410;* 167
Cunningham, Peter, *Two Years in New South Wales, 114;* 56, 63-64, 171, 172
Curr, Edward, *An Account of the Colony of Van Diemen's Land,* 113
Curtis, S.J., *History of Education in Great Britain,* 166

Dale, William, *The Unhappy Transport, 132*
Daley, James, 46
Dalkin, R. Nixon, *Colonial Era Cemetery of Norfolk Island,* 411
Dark, Eleanor, *No Barriers, 445;* *Storm of Time, 439; Timeless Land,* 438
Darling, Ralph, 35, 45, 61, 77
Darwin, Erasmus, "Visit of Hope to Sydney Cove", 39
Davies, John, 91
Davies, John George, 91
Davis, Richard P., *The Tasmanian Gallows,* 171
Dawe, W. Carlton, *The Golden Lake, 344;* (5:12)
De Boos, Charles, *Fifty Years Ago,* 278
Defoe, Daniel, *Captain Singleton, 20; Colonel Jacque, 22;* (2:2); *Moll Flanders, 23;* (2:3); *Review 1,* 8, 15, 19, 25-26, 164, 165, 166, 179
Dekker, Thomas, *English Villainies, 11;* 6, 7, 16-17, 22
Devaney, James, *The Currency Lass,* 424
Dickens, Charles, *Barnaby Rudge, 292; Boz, 285; David Copperfield, 294; Great Expectations, 299; Household Words, 295; Oliver Twist, 286;* 74, 79, 81, 83, 84, 174, 177
Dickson, W., broadsheet, *206;* (4:2); 99, 175
Dillingham, John, Letters, 171
Disciplina Clericalis, 5
Dixon, John, *Conditions and Capabilities of Van Diemen's Land,* 188
documents: effects on relating experience, 2, 3
Ducharmé, Leon, *Journal of a Political Exile,* 229
Duffy, Sir Charles Gavan, *My Life in Two Hemispheres, 326;* 177
Dunderdale, George, *Book of the Bush,* 330
Dunhill, Snowden, *Life, 207;* (4:3); 99, 175
Durack, Mary, *Kings in Grass Castles,* 386

Eagar, Edward, *Letters to Rt. Hon. Robert Peel, 134,* 75
Eagleson, R.D., "Convict Jargon and Euphemism", 165
Eardley-Wilmot, John, 87
Easty, John, *Memorandum, 100,* 59, 171
Eclectic Society, 37
Eden, Frederick Morton, *The State of the Poor,* 54
Eldershaw, John, "Select Letters of

James Grove", 169, 172
Eldershaw, M. Barnard, *A House is Built*, 426; *Life and Times of Captain John Piper*, 169
Eliade, Mircea, *Myth and Reality*, 1-2, 164
Elliott, Brian, *Marcus Clarke*, 177, 178
Ellis, M.H., *John Macarthur*, 169
emancipists, 35
Evangelical Magazine, 36
engravings, 13
Evelyn, John, 45

Farjeon, B.L., *Grif*, 277; (5:8); 122-23, 177
Fenton, James, *Bush Life in Tasmania*, 322
Ferguson, J.A., "Bibliography of Literature ascribed to George Barrington", 173
Field, Barron, 73, 108, 170
Fielding, Henry, *Enquiry*, 32; *Jonathon Wild*, 29; (2:6); *Joseph Andrews*, 28; 8, 13, 17, 23-24, 27, 39, 164, 168, 179
Fink, Averil, "James Hardy Vaux", 171
First Fleet, 46, 57
Fitzgerald, Charles, 136-37
Fitzhardinge, L.F., "A Convict's Letters from New South Wales, 1792", "Some First Fleet Reviews", 167, 170
Forster, H.C., "Tyranny Oppression and Fraud", 171
Foxe, John, *Actes and Monuments*, 9
Franklin, John, 86
Franklin, Miles, *All That Swagger*, 434. See also "Brent of Bin Bin"
Franklin, Miles, and Dymphna Cusack, *Pioneers on Parade*, 436
Frederick (ship), 198
Frost, John, "A Letter from . . . ", 222; (4:12); *The Life of John Frost*, 223
Frost, John, *Horrors of Convict Life*, 245; (4:29)
Froude, Anthony, *Oceana*, 316
Fulton, Henry, 42
Furphy, Joseph, *The Buln Buln and the Brolga*, 460; *Such is Life*, 458
Fyans, Foster, "Reminiscences", 165; (4:25); 46

Gay, John, *Beggar's Opera*, 24; (2:4); "Trivia", 10, 15, 18, 165, 179
Gates, William, *Recollections of Life in Van Diemen's Land*, 196
Gell, John Philip, *The Penal Settlements*, 238; 172
Gentleman's Magazine, 3
George, M. Dorothy, *Hogarth to Cruickshank*, 165
Gerstäcker, Friedrich, *The Two Convicts*, 271
Gibb, Eric, *Thrilling Incidents of the Convict System*, 354
Gibbings, Robert, *John Graham Convict*, 379
Gibbon, Edward, *Decline and Fall of the Roman Empire*, *Memoirs of My Life*, 19, 21, 166
Gibson, Charles, *Life Among Convicts*, 249; (4:28); 106
Giovanni in Botany, 108, 176
Giustino, David de, "Reforming the Commonwealth of Thieves", 175
Godwin, William, *Enquiry*, 48; *Caleb Williams*, 50; 8, 9, 27, 28-30, 165, 167
goldrushes, 88-89, 93
Goldsmith, Oliver, *Vicar of Wakefield*, 41; 179
Gordon, Charles, *The Old Bailey and Newgate*, 66
Gordon, Lord George, 28
Gould, Nat, 93
Graham, John, 172
Grant, John, Letters, Journal and Papers, 75; (3:8); 31, 60-63, 172
Gray, A.J., "John Bennett of the *Friendship*", "John Irving", 169
Green, H.M., *History of Australian Literature*, 389; 74, 173
Greene, Graham, 135
Greene, Robert, *The Third and Last Part of Cony Catching*, 6
Grimstone, Mary Leman, *Woman's Love*, 108
Grove, James, Letters, 125; (3:7); 65-66, 169

H.W.D., *State of Convicts in New South Wales*, 209
Hamilton, J.C., *Pioneering Days in Western Victoria*, 328

Harris, Alexander, *The Emigrant Family,* 265; *Settlers and Convicts, 194;* 94, 118-20, 174, 176
Hashemy (ship), 88
Hasluck, Alexandra, *Unwilling Immigrants, 387*
"hatters", 95
Hay, William, *Sir William Heans, 420;* 3, 137-42, 178
Hayes, Henry Browne, 60-61
Hazlitt, William, "The Drama No. 111", 52
Head, Richard, *Meriton Latroon, 14;* (2:1); 7, 16, 17, 25, 28, 55, 73, 167, 179
Heath, James, *Eighteenth Century Penal Theory,* 167
Henning, Rachel, *Letters, 198*
Hergenhan, L., *Colonial City, 403;* 177, 178
Hibbard, G.R. (ed.), *Three Elizabethan Pamphlets,* 6
Hill-Reid, W.S., *John Grant's Journey, 380;* 172
Hindley, Charles, *Curiosities of Street Literature, 62; History of the Catnach Press,* 165, 178, 179
Historical Records of Australia, 189
Historical Records of New South Wales, 189
Hogan, James Francis, *The Convict King,* 346; 127
Hogarth, William, *Harlot's Progress, Rake's Progress, Industry and Idleness;* (2:7); 13, 22, 24, 165, 179
Holden, Thomas, 66, 172
Holford, George, *The Convict's Complaint,* 137; 82-83, 174
Holt, Joseph. *See* Croker, T. Crofton
Hookey, Mabel (ed.), *The Chaplain,* 170
Hooper, F. Earle, "William Hay: A Memoir", 178
Hornung, E.W., *The Rogue's March, 356*
Howard, John, *State of the Prisons, 45,* 9, 22, 23, 60, 166, 171
Howe, George, 34, 71
Howe, Michael, 36, 74
Howison, John, *One False Step, 255;* (5:1); 109-10, 176
Hugo, Victor, *Dernier Jour d'un Condamné, 280; Les Misérables, 300;* 79, 177
Hunter, John, 61; *An Historical Journal of the Transactions at Port Jackson, 105;* 41, 169

industry, 38-44
Ingleton, Geoffrey, C. (ed.), *True Patriots All, 374;* 167, 168, 172
Inglis, K.S., *Australian Colonists, 412*
Irish Rebellion, 36
Irving, John, 35

Jackson, John, *A Remarkable Narrative, 138*
James, R., *The Convict, 264;* 118, 176
Jeffrey, Mark, *A Burglar's Life, 351;* 127
Jeffreys, Judge, 28
Johns, Joseph Bolitho, 97, 137
Johnson, Richard, *Address, 106;* 37, 41-42, 168, 169
Johnson, Samuel, *Rambler,* 4; 14, 19, 20, 24
Jorgenson, Jorgen. *See* Hogan, James Francis
journals, First Fleet, 46-47

K*, "The Three Letters", 258
"Keese, Oline" (Caroline Leakey), *The Broad Arrow, 272;* (5:7); 122, 170, 177
Kenealy, Thomas, *Bring Larks and Heroes, 451;* 144-45, 178
Kerr, Anthony, *Schools of Scotland,* 166
King, Charles Adolphus, *A Warning Voice from the Penitent, 224;* (4:11)
King, Philip Gidley, 35, 43, 62
Kingsley, Henry, *Geoffry Hamlyn, 273;* (5:6); 121-22, 176
Knapp and Baldwin (ed.), *Newgate Calendar,* 57
Knatchbull, John, *Life, 227;* (4:15), 102-3, 175
Knopwood, Robert, 42, 47, 65, 170
Kunzle, David, *The Early Comic Strip Narrative,* 165

Lacey, James, 44, 169
Lahey, John, (ed.), *Great Australian Folk Songs,* 465
Lamb, Charles, "Christ's Hospital Five and Thirty Years Ago", "Distant Correspondents", 2, 52, 170
Lancaster, G.B. (Edith Joan Lyttleton), *Pageant, 432;* (5:17)
Lang, John Dunmore, *Historical and Statistical Account of New South Wales, 310; Reminiscences of My Life and Times, 311;* 19, 34, 42, 81, 82, 87, 169, 173

Lang, John, 228, *Botany Bay, 274; The Forger's Wife, 269; Too Clever by Half, 267;* 120-21, 176
Larra, James, 34
Lawson, Henry, *318;* 96, 175
Lawson, Ronald, *Brisbane in the 1890s, 406;* 173
Leakey, Caroline. *See* Keese, Oliné
Lecky, William Edward, *History of Ireland,* 41, 167
Lemisch, Jesse, "Listening to the Inarticulate", 173
Leonard, John, 106, 176
LeSage, Alain-René, *Gil Blas, 18*
Levi, J.S., and G.F.J. Bergman, *Australian Genesis, 413;* 174
Levy, M.C.I., *Governor George Arthur,* 169
Levy, Samuel, 91
Lilburn, Edward, *A Complete Exposure, 226;* (4:13); 102, 175
Lillo, George, *London Merchant, 25;* (2:5); 15, 165
Lingard, Joseph, *Narrative of a Journey, 230;* (4:18)
Lord, Simeon, 34
Lorrain, Paul, 9-10
Loveless, George, *Victims of Whiggery, 215;* (4:8); 100, 175
Lowe, Robert, 176
Lyttleton, Edith. *See* Lancaster, G.B.
Lytton, Edward Bulwer, *Eugene Aram, 282; Paul Clifford, 281;* 30, 79, 177

M'Combie, Thomas, *Arabin,* 262
Macarthur, John, 31, 32, 44
Macarthur, James, 85
Macaulay, Thomas Babington, *History of England,* 28, 167
Mackaness, George, *Blue Bloods of Botany Bay,* 375
Mackenzie, James, *Life and Adventures, 139;* (3:14)
Macquarie, Lachlan, 35, 40, 42
McQueen, Humphrey, *A New Britannia,* 400
Mailer, Norman, *Armies of the Night,* 124, 177
Malcolmson, Sarah, 178
Mandeville, Bernard, *Fable of the Bees, 16;* 18, 165
Manifold, J.S., *Who Wrote the Ballads,* 463

Mann, Daniel, *The Present Picture of New South Wales, 110;* 75, 173
Margarot, Maurice, 49, 60-61, 102
Marsden, Samuel, 37, 42, 70, 102
Martin, James, *Memorandoms, 117;* (3:5); 172
Mayer, Henry, *The Press in Australia,* 168
Mayhew, Henry, 129, *London Labour and the London Poor, 296;* (4:23); 21, 165
Mayhew, Henry, and John Binny, *Criminal Prisons,* 18, 166, 170, 174
Melbourne, A.C.V., *Early Constitutional Development in Australia,* 173
Mellish, —, *A Convict's Recollections, 140;* (3:15)
Melville, Henry, *History of Van Diemen's Land,* 186
Melville, Herman, *Billy Budd, 342;* 125-27, 177
Miles, Howard (ed.), *George Crabbe Tales 1812,* 14, 165
Miller, E. Morris, "Australia's First Two Novels", *Pressmen and Governors,* 35, 108, 168, 176
Miller, Linus, *Notes of an Exile, 233;* (4:17)
Mitchell, John, *Jail Journal, 242;* 105, 176
Molesworth, Sir William, *Report from the Select Committee on Transportation, 170;* 85-87, 95
Moncrieff, W.T. *Van Diemen's Land!, 256;* 78, 110-11, 176
More, Thomas, 9
Morgan, John, *Life and Adventures of William Buckley, 241;* (4:24); 172
Mortlock, John, *Experiences of a Convict, 250;* (4:32); 106-7, 176
Mudie, James, *Felonry of New South Wales, 212;* (4:9); 94, 100, 175
Muecke, I.D., "William Hay and History", 164
Muir, Thomas, 49, 60
Murray, James, *Larrikins 19th Century Outrage,* 174
Murray, Robert, 59
Murray-Smith, Stephen (ed.), *His Natural Life, 452;* 182
mutiny, 46, 48, 58, 68-69, 172
Mynshul, Geoffrey, *Certain Characters and Essays of Prison and Prisoners,* 7

Newgate Calendar, 12, 23, 173
Newgate School, 130
Newton, John, 36-37, 42, 168
Nicol, John, *Life and Adventures and John Nicol, 112;* 69, 170, 172
Nisbet, Hume, 258, *The Black Drop, 365* (in *Seven Romances*)
Nolan, Sidney, 172

O'Brien, Eris, *Foundation of Australia, 371;* 167, 170
O'Reilly, John Boyle, *Moondyne, 336;* (5:11); "The Monster Diamond", *339;* 137, 178
oral tradition, 4, 63-65, 77
ordinary, 9, 20

Paine, Thomas, *Rights of Man,* 60, 171
Palmer, Thomas Fysshe, 49, 59, 60
Pantisocracy, 49-50
Parkes, Sir Henry, *Fifty Years in the Making of Australian History, 323*
Partridge, Eric, *Dictionary of the Underworld,* 165
Paterson, A.B., 225; (ed.) *Old Bush Songs, 358*
"Pelham, Camden", *Chronicles of Crime, 60;* 12, 165
Penton, Brian, *Inheritors, 435; Landtakers, 433;* (5:18); 182
Pepys, Samuel, 23, 45, 166
Phillip, Arthur, 33-34, 38, 39-40, 41, 168, 169
Phillips, A.A., *The Australian Tradition, 383*
"pipes", 108, 172
Platt, Joseph, *Horrors of Transportation, 248;* (4:31); 106, 176
Plomley, N.J.B., *An Immigrant of 1824, 407*
Poole, Joan E., "Marcus Clarke: Christianity is Dead", 177, 178
Porter, Hal, *The Tilted Cross, 449;* 144, 178
Praed, R.C., *Longleat of Kooralbyn, 343;* (5:13); *Outlaw and Lawmaker, 352*
Pratt, Ambrose, "'Push' Larrikinism in Australia"; *The Great "Push" Experiment, 457;* 93, 166
Prichard, Katharine Susannah, *The Pioneers, 418;* (5:15)
Prieur, Francis-Xavier, *Notes of a Political Prisoner 1838, 251;* (4:10); 100-101, 175
"pushes", 93

Radcliffe, Ann, *Mysteries of Udolpho,* 49
Raine, Kathleen, *Blake and Tradition,* 168
Ramson, W.S., *Australian English* (ed.); *English Transported* (ed.); *The Emigrant Family,* 165
Reade, Charles, *It's Never Too Late to Mend, 270;* (5:5); 83, 84, 177
Reardon, Bartholomew, 44
reformation of heart, 19-20, 43-44, 133-36, 140
Reibey, Mary, 34
Revell, James, *The Unhappy Transport, 135;* (3:16)
Review of the State of the British Nation, 1
Reynolds, H. *"That Hated Stain",* 174
Reynolds, John, *The Triumphs of God's Revenge,* 7
Richetti, John, *Popular Fiction Before Richardson,* 165
Ritchie, John, *Punishment and Profit, 401,* 170
Roberts, Morley, *The Adventure of the Broad Arrow, 359*
Robinson, Michael Massey, *Odes, 127;* 60-61
Robson, L.L., *Convict Settlers of Australia, 394;* "Historical Basis of *For the Term of His Natural Life",* 2, 3, 33, 164, 167, 168, 170, 174
Roderick, Colin, *The Lady and the Lawyer, 446;* (ed.) *Life of John Knatchbull,* 227; (ed.) *Ralph Rashleigh, 261;* 168, 175, 176
Roe, Michael, *Quest for Authority,* 174
Ross, W.; *Fell Tyrant, 211;* 99-100
Rousseau, Jean-Jacques, 38-39
Rowcroft, Charles, *Tales of the Colonies, 259;* (5:3); *The Bushranger of Van Diemen's Land, 263;* 113-15, 117-18, 176
Rowlandson, Thomas, 10

Savery, Henry, *Quintus Servinton, 257;* (5:2); *The Hermit in Van Diemen's Land, 141;* 75-76, 111-13, 173, 176
Scott, Sir Walter, *Heart of Midlothian, 279;* 52, 55, 170, 171
Second Fleet, 47

Select Committee on Criminal Laws, 49
Select Committee on Finance and Police Establishments (1798), 48
Select Committee on Transportation (1812), 44, 49
Select Committee on the State of the Gaols (1819), 49
Semple, J.A., *The Life of Major J.A. Semple Lisle, 122*; (3:6); 54, 170
Seven Dials Press, 11, 71
Shaw, A.G.L., *Convicts and the Colonies, 395*; 164, 167, 168, 170, 172, 173, 174
Skelton, John, 6
Slater, John, *A Description of Sydney, 130*; (3:9)
Smith, Alexander, *Lives of Highwaymen*, 11-12
Smith, Bernard, *Australian Painting 1788—1960*, 169, 172, 173
Smith, Coultman, *Shadow Over Tasmania, 372*
Smith, M.A., *Horrors of Transportation, 239*; (4:22)
Smollett, Tobias, *Sir Lancelot Greaves, 39*; 22-23, 166
Solomons, Isaac, Life and Adventures of 201; (4:1), 98, 175
Sorell, William, 40
Southey, Robert, *Botany Bay Eclogues, 120*; 50-52, 170
Southwell, Daniel, 48, 168
squatters, 81-82
Stephens, A.G., *The Red Pagan*, 129, 177
Stephens, James Brunton, "Convict Once", in *Poetical Works, 368*
Stewart, Douglas, and Nancy Keesing, (eds.), *Old Bush Songs and Rhymes of Colonial Times, 461*
Stone, Louis, 93
Stowe, Harriet Beecher, *Uncle Tom's Cabin, 297*; 177
Strezelecki, P.E. de, *Physical Description of New South Wales, 192*
"Student of the Joiner Temple, A", *Criminal Recorder,* 56
Sturt, Charles, *Two Expeditions, 183*; 94
Suffolk, Owen, *Days of Crime, 355*
Swedenborg, Emanuel, 37-38
Swift, Jonathan, *Directions to Servants,* 8, 23, 164, 166
Sydney Gazette, 34, 172

Taylor, Richard, 66-67, 172
Teagarden, Ernest, "A Victorian Prison Experiment", 83, 174
Tench, Watkin, 28, 40, 47, 57, 167, 169, 170, 171, 172
Terrific Register, 12
Thackeray, W.M., *Catherine, 287*; 177
Therry, Joseph, 42, 46
Therry, Roger, *Reminiscences, 200*; 84, 90, 174
Thompson, Andrew, 34
Thompson, George, *Slavery and Famine, 118*; 59
Thompson, William, *Particulars of the Awful Execution,* 210
Times, 5; 34
Timms, E., *The Pathway of the Sun,* 441
Tolmer, Alexander, *Reminiscences, 313*
transportation: to America, 24-27
Trollope, Anthony, *Australia, 308*; 91, 96, 98, 174, 175
Tucker, James, *Ralph Rashleigh, 261*; (5:4); 6, 27, 28, 35, 115-17, 168, 176
Tuckey, J.H., *Account of a Voyage, 108;* 169
Turner, G.W., 165
Twain, Mark [Samuel Clemens], *Following the Equator, 324*; 3, 97, 164, 175
Tyburn Chronicle, 12

Ullathorne, William, *Catholic Mission in Australia, 187*; 85, 92-94, 168, 174; *The Horrors of Transportation Briefly Unfoled,* 221

Vaux, James Hardy, *Memoirs, 131*; (3:10); 6, 16, 27, 28, 54, 73-74, 77, 170, 172, 173
Vidal, Francis, *Tales for the Bush, 266*; 120, 176

W____, "A Voyage in a Convict Ship", 214; (4:7); 98-99, 175
Walker, Gilbert, 6
Wainewright, Thomas Griffiths, 144
Wakefield, Edward Gibbon, *A Letter from Sydney: The Punishment of Death in the Metropolis, 115*; 55-56, 171, 172
Walker, Eliza, "Old Sydney in the 'Forties", 174
Walpole, Horace, *The Castle of Otranto,* 40

Ward, Ned, *The London Spy*, 7
Ward, Russel, *Australian Legend*, 377;
  (ed.), *Penguin Book of Australian Ballads*,
  464; 80, 167, 170, 173
Warung, Price. *See* Astley, William
Watling, Thomas, *Letters from an Exile*,
  119; 59, 60, 74-75, 173
Watt, William, *Party Politics Exposed*, 185
Weidenhofer, Margaret, *Convict Years*,
  408
Wells, Thomas, *Michael Howe*, *129;*
  (3:11); 74
Wentworth, William Charles, 34, 95
Wesley, John, 20, 166
West, John, *History of Tasmania*, *197;* 89,
  169, 171, 172, 173, 177
Westgarth, William, *Victoria, Late Australia Felix*, 195
Westwood, William, 133

White, John, *Journal of a Voyage*, *103;* 48,
  169
White, Patrick, *Voss*, *448;* (5:20); *Fringe
  of Leaves*, 142-44, 172, 178, 182
Wilberforce, A.M. (ed.), *Private Papers of
  William Wilberforce*, 168
Wilberforce, William, *Practical View . . .
  of Professed Christianity*, 19, 36, 37, 166
Wilde, Oscar, *De Profundis*, 124, 177
Wilkes, G.A. (ed.), *Experiences of a Convict*, *250;* 176
Winstanley, Elizabeth, *Her Natural Life*,
  334; (5:10); 136, 178
Wordsworth, William, Preface to *The
  Borderers*, 56, 170, 171
Wright, Judith, *Generations of Men*, 388
Wright, Thomas, 56
Wright, Thomas Soulsby, 91

Zall, P.M. (ed.), *C. Merry Tales*, 6, 5